JUSTIN

ABE MORRIS

ISBN# 978-1-932636-54-3 Trade Paper

Library of Congress Control Number: 200930378

The contents of this book comprise the author's story of his ongoing battle for custody for his son and he is solely responsible for the information it contains based on his own memories, witness accounts, correspondence and court documents. While the events are true, some of the names have been changed.

Cover Design: Antelope Design
Justice image based on artwork by Edwin Abbey
Photo of Justin Abraham Morris

www.pronghornpress.org

I wish to dedicate this book to all of my immediate family.

Thanks to my parents the Reverend Abraham J. Morris, Sr. and Christine Morris for providing for me and for all the years of support and encouragement. I want to thank my sisters Patricia Morris, Janice Corbin and Rosalyn Hairston. I want to thank my younger brothers David Morris and Reuben Morris. You guys have been the best family members that a person could have asked for.

Last but not least, I am very grateful for my only son Justin Abraham Morris. Justin is the spark in my daily life that reminds me to keep on going and to never ever give up.

I thank God for you all.

Other Books by Abe Morris

My Cowboy Hat Still Fits

The Beginning

On June 24, 1996 I became a homeowner for the first time in my life. I felt that things were falling into place and I was finally ready to settle down. It was major sense of accomplishment because just six years earlier I'd only had about $200 in my checking account. I'd had no money in savings and was, for the most part, broke. The creditors were constantly calling and hounding me and emotionally, I was at a very low stage in my life.

And my girlfriend of six years had left me and moved to Alaska.

In April 1991 I'd started working for Marketing & Management Corporation of America, specializng in insurance and annuity products. I enjoyed a very successful career with them and I was on a roll. In 1995, I had purchased a brand new Saturn and was still able to keep my pickup truck since it was already paid for. By the time I was ready to purchase my home, I'd managed to save about $16,000 and never had less than $1,500 in my checking account.

I had two roadworthy vehicles. My Nissan truck was silver and my Saturn was gold—two of the most precious metals known to man and personally meaningful. I wasn't living beyond my means and simply wrote a check to pay for whatever bill was due at the time. I was happy and living very well and comfortably. I occasionally dated, but by no means was I lonesome. For the most part I was content.

It didn't cost me anything to move into my new house because I gathered up several of my friends, and they brought their vehicles and trailers. I thought, what a way to spend my birthday, moving into my first nice home.

My new home had an evaporative cooler, a fish pond, a separate pen for the dogs and a one car garage. It had a carpeted basement, two bathrooms, three bedrooms, a dishwasher and a washer and dryer. No one lived behind me. There was a horse pasture with a large tree out in the middle. When I bought the home the previous owners said, "Bald eagles visit that tree out back in the winter." I really didn't believe them, but sure enough, when the weather cooled off, the eagles showed up and stayed for the entire season.

The yard was very nice and had beautiful roses and flowers. Needless to say, I was very grateful and felt like I had died and gone to heaven. The first night I spent in my home, I went downstairs and gazed out at the backyard and almost cried. I couldn't believe all of this was happening to me. I had lived in a rented house for nine years that was an icehouse in the winter and an oven in the summer. Now, I would be comfortable year-round.

The only thing that was missing was a soulmate. I figured it was high time I filled that void in my life.

On the Bull Riders Only Tour, I'd gotten to be pretty good friends with Skip Ross, a medical doctor and trainer from Cheyenne, Wyoming. He had it all, including a beautiful home and a very attractive girlfriend. Skip was single. One summer he had been involved in a motorcycle accident. Skip told me, "As I was lying in bed I knew that there was something missing in my life, so I said a prayer to God and asked him for someone special to come into my life." At that very moment the telephone rang and a woman named Sonya was calling to check and see how he was doing. Skip and Sonya later were married and he felt that she had been the answer to his prayers.

Though I was a churchgoer, my father having been a pastor in the Baptist Church, I was reluctant to follow Skip's lead. But after a few months in my home alone, I thought if a big strong macho guy like Skip can pray for a mate, then what's stopping me from doing the same thing? I finally broke down and prayed that before the year was over, I'd meet someone I could spend the rest of my life with.

I diligently kept my eyes wide open. Before I knew it, I was heading home to my mom's house in New Jersey for the holidays. By the time the final three days of the year rolled around I very clearly remember sitting in Mom's house and thinking to myself, *I guess I'm not going to meet anyone this year, and therefore my prayer won't be answered.*

On Sunday, December 28, 1996 I attended the morning worship service at Morning Star Baptist Church in Woodstown, New Jersey. After the service, as I was leaving, someone tapped me on the shoulder. When I turned around, a very attractive woman in a red dress said, "Hi Abe."

She could tell from my reaction that I didn't have a clue who she was.

"Don't tell me that you don't know who I am."

Suddenly, I thought to myself, *Who the heck is this?* My next thought surely was, *Memory, oh memory, please don't fail me now.* My memory kicked in gear and I said, "Lorena! Wow, you sure are looking good."

We had graduated together in 1974 from Woodstown High School. I told her several more times how great she looked.

Finally, she said to me with big blush, "Oh, Abe stop it."

I said, "No."

Right away we started asking each other questions. "Where are you living now? How long are you going to be home for Christmas?"

Lorena asked, "So did you bring your family with you?"

I said, "What family? The only family I have is two dogs and I left them in Colorado." So I grabbed her left hand looking for a wedding ring and asked, "Did you bring your family with you?"

I was glad to hear her say, "No I'm single. I'm leaving to go back to Chicago on Wednesday morning."

So, I asked her if she'd like to go out to dinner before she left. She readily accepted.

About that time Mom walked up and teasing her I said, "Aw, Mom you just had to walk up when I was about to ask Lorena to marry me."

We were both staying with our respective mothers during the holiday vacation. We exchanged phone numbers and decided to go out on a date that Tuesday evening.

When I got home from church, Mom told my sisters what I'd said about the marriage proposal and suddenly I was the talk of the house.

Rosalyn said, "Hey Skaber, I heard you have a big date." Then she wanted to know who it was and if she was a sister, because I'd dated quite a few white women in the past.

When they found out that Lorena was an African-American woman, they all started shouting, dancing and jumping around the kitchen like they were still in church. I told them to knock it off, and to stop acting so loud and silly. In my own little way, I felt pretty good but tried not to show it. I even said to myself (when no one else could hear) the jingle made popular by Eddie Murphy in *The Nutty Professor*. "Got me a date. Pick her up at eight. Just can't wait. Can't be late."

Later, I remembered a few months earlier when I had prayed to meet someone I could settle down with for the rest of my life. I felt that this chance meeting was the answer to my prayer. I was meant to be with this woman, and she was the chosen one for me.

I didn't sleep very well the night before our date. There was something in the air.

I picked up Lorena at her mom's house in Elmer. I made

sure I wasn't late for our first date. We went to a Chinese restaurant in Pennsville and had the best time. We talked the entire time. I found out just how many things we had in common including the fact that we both were involved in very successful financial services careers.

We laughed our heads off at each other's stories and carried on like two little kids. I'm sure that some of the other diners around us wondered what kind of drugs we were on. We ignored everyone else in the restaurant.

I had my insurance license which allowed me to sell life insurance as well as fixed annuity products. Lorena had her life insurance license and also had her Series 7 securities license which allowed her to sell stocks, bonds, mutual funds and variable annuity products.

In 1994, I had finished third in the nation in sales with my company, and in 1995 I'd finished seventh. The 1995 win had earned me a trip to Mexico, paid for by Mike McVicar who was our regional manager.

After dinner, we stopped at my brother David's home in Salem because he was having a Morris family get-together. Most of the time Lorena and I completely ignored everyone else and paid attention only to each other. The family was watching a couple of my VHS tapes of my rides and wrecks during my rodeo career.

Lorena said, "Gosh Abe, I don't know if I could have been married to you while you were still riding bulls."

My response was, "Well I don't ride them now, so would you consider it?"

Her reply was, "Yes," without the slightest bit of hesitation.

My heart skipped a beat. I asked again, "Seriously?"

"Yes, seriously."

After a wonderful and very memorable evening we said, "goodbye" to everyone and headed back to Elmer. We sat in the car and talked for awhile. We had our first kiss. I knew that I had been smitten and bitten by the big one and had fallen in love. During our conversation I formally asked Lorena to marry me.

Her response was, "You're kidding aren't you? You don't even know me."

I said, "No, I'm serious. I'm asking you to marry me."

We talked for awhile and then we went inside the house. We exchanged mailing addresses and phone numbers and vowed to keep in touch. On a pink sticky note I wrote the words, *I am asking you to marry me* and dated it December 30, 1996.

I told Lorena that I wasn't going to put any pressure on her, and that I'd give her a whole year to give me an answer.

She said, "Okay."

We both got in a big hug and kiss and said our goodbyes, and I left the house on a magic carpet. I was on cloud nine and I knew that I'd been swept off my feet.

Knowing that Lorena was flying back to Chicago the next morning, I asked her to call me at my mom's house when she got home. Lorena called me back and we had a good conversation.

When I returned to Fort Collins Lorena kept in touch via the telephone. This was before the internet and e-mails.

My company MMCA was going to have their winter convention in Denver the last weekend in January. I thought this would be an opportune time to get together and so I asked Lorena to come out for the occasion. I figured it would be a good way to introduce her to my company, and a good way for us to see if our relationship was going to work or not.

Since I'd finished seventh in the nation the previous year, I was awarded a free room for the convention courtesy of MMCA. By that time Lorena and I had spent a lot of time talking on the phone and getting to know each other.

The convention commenced on a Thursday evening with the "Top of the Line" reception for the top sales people of the previous year. Lorena wouldn't be able to come to Colorado until Friday evening. I was scheduled to give a short speech at the convention on Friday afternoon, but was able to switch with another person because I had to go to the airport to pick her up. I refused to tell anyone at the event what I was up to and kept everything a big secret.

On our way to the motel, I asked Lorena when I introduced her to my friends and company workers if I should refer to her as an old high school friend or my girlfriend.

She said, "Oh, 'girlfriend' will be just fine."

Everyone was surprised when I walked into the Friday evening reception with Lorena at my side. They had no idea that I had a girlfriend. Until Lorena arrived, I guess I hadn't known that for sure, either.

We had a great time during the whole weekend. My company workers were all very receptive to Lorena and many people went out of their way to get introduced to her.

Karen Ketcham, my dear friend, was extremely proud of me and said, "Lorena has more class than any other woman that I've seen you with."

Jennifer Dizmang-Smith remarked on how lucky I was to have discovered a single black woman who was so successful, attractive and had so much on the ball.

On Saturday night, we had a huge company sponsored dinner. It really made me feel extra special when my name was called. We had been seated in the VIP section before the other company sales people were allowed into the room. I'm sure this made a grand impression on Lorena, because it meant I was someone special.

The next day Lorena wanted to see my new home before catching her flight back to Chicago. After a brief tour of my house, we grabbed a quick bite to eat and then headed for the airport.

When we were at my house I tried to imagine what it would be like if this woman were to indeed become my wife. I relished the thought and put that image into my memory bank, where I'd think about it many times in the coming months.

We continued to keep in touch on the phone. Lorena invited me to come to Chicago to visit her. Actually, she lived in Streamwood which was a suburb. I decided to fly there on February 14th for Valentine's Day.

Before I left, I'd mailed her a special card which was postmarked from Loveland, Colorado. I also took a second card with me. I bought some roses and took those on the flight with me. I kept them in a vase with water so they would survive the trip. Of course this was pre-9/11, when airport security wasn't as tight as it is now. The flight attendants were very aware of my flowers and kept asking me who the lucky lady was.

I had previously told Lorena that I couldn't wait to give her a big sloppy wet kiss. She was extremely glad to see me and surprised that I'd bring her flowers all the way from Colorado.

We had a good visit, and really got serious talking about the possibility of spending the rest of our lives together. During that visit, we went to the PRCA Rodeo in Rock Island, Illinois. I felt a little weird being at a rodeo, sitting in the grandstands and being incognito. I didn't bring along my cowboy hat for that visit.

When it was time for me to go home I really was sad to leave and was sure that Lorena was the woman for me.

We had a mandatory MMCA meeting in Fort Collins and Karen Ketcham picked me up at the airport in Denver. I was dog tired but instead of sleeping on the way to our meeting, I talked the entire time about Lorena. I was in love, and I guess I wanted the whole world to know it.

Lorena and I continued to spend long hours on the telephone. Once, we had a conversation that lasted for seven and a half hours.

She got a little lonesome again and asked me if I would come out to visit. So in April I went back to Chicago again. There was another PRCA rodeo at the Rosemont Horizon. This time I took my hat and introduced Lorena to a few of the cowboys that I knew.

I also surprised Lorena with an engagement ring. It was kind of neat the way I gave it to her. Lorena had a wooden jewelry box on her dresser and I took the ring out that she always wore and replaced it with the diamond engagement ring.

When she reached in the box for her ring she asked, "Is this my ring? Is this my engagement ring?"

I said, "Yes it is." Then I formally placed it on her finger, knelt down and asked her to marry me. Lorena readily accepted. I couldn't wait to tell my family that we were now officially engaged.

I had decided that if Lorena was the woman that God had chosen for me, I wasn't going to do anything to mess it up. One night in a Fort Collins bar, I ran into a woman I'd previously had sex with. I told her I was now engaged, but she still insisted that I give her a ride home. She was very drunk so I agreed. I kept reminding her that I was engaged and refused to cheat on my fiancée. Even though I knew Lorena would never find out, I was determined to be faithful.

In the car, that tall blonde woman did everything that she could think of to get me to take her back to my house rather than to hers. I wouldn't give in to her advances, and finally she cursed me out and called me every name in the book, saying she'd never been turned down for sex by a man in her life.

My resolution held, though it wasn't always easy. Another time, I had a business sales appointment with a beautiful woman named Nicole whom I had met at the Pulse health club. She was a young college student and asked me to hang out with her and her friends. I knew I'd give in and have sex with her in a heartbeat, if I was in the right situation. Again, I wanted to be true to Lorena and reluctantly told Nicole that I couldn't because I was engaged.

I went back to Chicago again the end of June with plans to return on the evening of July 3, because I wanted to go to the Greeley Independence Stampede and Rodeo for the championship round on July 4. I also figured I could scare up some more prospects for my MMCA sales.

Lorena and I had had several conversations about where we would live. I told her early on that there was no way that I could relocate to the Chicago area. A big part of the reason was because I was heavily involved in my financial services career, and 98% of my clients were in the Colorado-Wyoming region.

Lorena had told her mother when she was home for the Christmas holidays that she was going to move back to New

Jersey sometime in 1997. Lorena and I had several heart to heart discussions over the telephone and decided she would move to Fort Collins.

At the time she was working for a bank in Chicago. She had applied for a promotion in early 1996 and was turned down. Lorena threatened her boss with a discrimination lawsuit against the corporation and they agreed to her terms and a very lucrative severance package. But, the sad thing is that with or without the severance package, Lorena had already been planning to leave. Her deceitful bluff had worked and she got paid handsomely.

This should have been a red flag to me, but at the time I thought very little of it. But a few years later, I would personally find out that Lorena was all about the money and getting paid, regardless of what she had to do to achieve her goals.

In July, Lorena put her townhouse on the market. At first she got a little discouraged because she didn't have any good prospects or interest. Finally, after about six weeks, a young woman stopped by to see the place. She decided to buy and Lorena closed on her townhouse sale in late August.

Lorena lied to one of her friends across the street, saying she was moving back to New Jersey. I knew about the little white lie and didn't really think much of it at the time. Just one more indication of the kind of person she was, yet these events had not started to stack up for me. I was in love.

Lorena came to visit me in Fort Collins in August. While she was there she had a few job interviews including TIARRA in Denver. Although Lorena had been in the financial services field for several years, she'd never heard of TIARRA. I introduced her to the company because a recruiter had tried to get me to interview with them in October 1993.

Next, Mom came out to visit me. She hadn't seen my new home yet. I dropped Lorena off at the airport, and walked around the corner and picked up Mom who had just flown in from New Jersey. It was perfect timing.

In late August, I purchased a one-way ticket to Chicago so I could help Lorena with the packing and the drive back to

Colorado. I was held up at Denver International Airport by a United Airlines security agent right before I boarded my plane.

The woman asked, "When did you purchase this ticket?"

I said, "Just a few days ago."

She took some keys and locked her drawer and said, "I need you to come with me."

When I asked the reason she said, "I really can't divulge that information. I need you to come with me."

I was asked to go down the hall to a private room and my carry-on luggage was thoroughly searched. I felt it was because I was the only African-American man on the flight. It really irritated me watching the lady unpack my bag and handle my underwear and other items like I was some kind of criminal. The woman never would tell me the reason why I was pulled out of the line.

Lorena had hired a moving company to transport most of her things to Fort Collins. We drove her car and it was loaded with all of her plants. She was overly concerned about her plants, and we watered them often because it was so hot.

At a rest stop, I took one of her large plants out of the car and was in the process of watering it when an old man hit me in the hip with his car while backing up. I didn't even see the car, but I sure felt it. I was extremely lucky that he didn't knock me down and run over me. My thoughts afterward were that surely none of those plants were worth risking my life over.

We arrived in Fort Collins on a Saturday evening. The next morning we found out that Princess Diana had been killed in a horrific car accident.

Thus, we began our life together. Lorena decided to take some time off because she had worked pretty hard for a few years in Chicago. Her seventeen thousand dollar severance package would sustain her for a few months. I cut back a little on my sales appointments so we could spend more time together. Also, I didn't want Lorena to get the impression that once I got her to Colorado I was going to abandon her.

Looking back, I'd say we got along okay, but I can see now that we should've gotten along a lot better. Time and time again those red flags popped up and I refused to change course.

Lorena seemed to love to argue. I didn't like the conflict. During that time I also learned that Lorena had a very short fuse. She'd get upset at some of the most trivial things. It was another one of those red flags, but again I chose to ignore it.

For Thanksgiving, Lorena flew back to New Jersey to spend some time with her family. I opted to stay in Colorado and went to dinner in Wellington with some of my rodeo friends.

Together we celebrated Christmas with Mike Bond and his family. It was a tradition with me. Lorena didn't approve of it, though.

She told me, "Now that we are together, it doesn't mean you have to continue your old traditional holiday habits."

Lorena got into an argument with me on Christmas Day. We went to dinner, and she pretended to be in a good mood. We returned from dinner and didn't say much to each other. In fact, we didn't even open up our presents to each other until the day after Christmas. It certainly wasn't a memorable way to spend our first Christmas together.

On one occasion we argued and Lorena told me that I was going to sleep in the guest room that night. She closed the door to the bedroom and went to bed. When it was time for me to go to bed, I entered the master bedroom and went to sleep. My name was on the mortgage, and there was no way I was going to allow her to put me out of my own bedroom.

Before she moved in we had agreed that Lorena would split the mortgage payment with me but during another argument she stormed up the stairs and told me that I was going to have to pay the mortgage all by myself in the future. Yet when the next payment was due, she anted up.

We never discussed these outbursts, never addressed what

was causing the problems or how we felt about the arguments. Her mood would improve and we would just go on as if nothing had happened, as if the things she said to me had never come out of her mouth. This seemed to be fine with her. Frankly, I didn't know what else to do.

During one of my trips to New Jersey, Lorena had asked me to talk to Rev. Benjamin Mike from the Morning Star Baptist Church in Woodstown. I asked him if he would be willing to marry us. He said yes, but only with the condition that we went through pre-marital counseling with our minister in Colorado.

Then I asked Rev. David A. Williams from the Abyssinian Christian Church I attended at home if he would be willing to conduct the structured classes for us. The classes lasted about two months. We had to read a book and do homework assignments pertaining to our relationship and pending marriage.

During the course of the counseling sessions Lorena and I had a few arguments. It really bothered her that I had dated several white women. I certainly couldn't go back and change the past and I could see it had been a mistake to share that with her. This confused me. She would want information, and then when I gave it to her, she would save it up to use later against me. Of course I can see this now. At the time I was in it, I couldn't understand it or see the pattern that was starting to develop.

Lorena turned down the offer from TIARRA and accepted a job working for U.S. Bank instead. She went to their Minneapolis headquarters for a few days to do some training. When she returned she was assigned to work out of three different offices on a rotating basis. One office was in Fort Collins, another was in Greeley and the third office was in Boulder.

On February 7, 1998, my father, the Reverend Abraham J. Morris, Sr., suffered a stroke and passed away. My sister Janice called me at about 3:00 a.m. on a Saturday morning and told me.

I took it very hard. I usually played challenge court racquetball on Saturday mornings. I really wasn't up to playing after I received the news. I wanted to stay home and drown myself in my sorrow, but instead I opted to tough it out and go.

I got into my car and turned on the radio. *The Men in Black* by Will Smith was the first song that I heard. At the words, "...here come the men in black," I pictured the pallbearers. It was hard for me to listen to that song for years afterward without fogging up.

That night Lorena and I were renting a movie to take home. A woman saw me and asked if my father was going to perform our marriage ceremony. I could've told her no because he had just died that morning. But instead I just said, "No."

After we left the store Lorena said she was glad that I didn't say anything because then the woman would have really felt bad.

My cousin Jimmy Lee Walker called to see how I was doing. As soon as I recognized his voice, I broke down and started sobbing over the telephone. Lorena had purchased a round trip airline ticket from Chicago to Denver that she hadn't used. I was able to transfer it to my name. So she paid my fare to attend my father's funeral. I was very grateful for her support.

In Woodstown I took a walk. At the Morning Star Baptist church there was a funeral going on. I knew the next day my dad would be lying in the front of that church. The thought to me was overwhelming. His funeral and burial were going to be on Friday the 13th.

As that other funeral procession left the church, I went and sat on the front stairs and cried my head off. I heard cars drive by in front of me, but I refused to look up. After awhile, I got up to go inside the church so I could blow my nose and wipe away my tears. I ran into a woman from the church. She was the wife of one of the deacons. She recognized me and I burst out crying. She gave me big hug, just as if she were my mom. Although I felt a little awkward, I didn't resist. I was thankful for her concern.

The morning of the funeral, my sister Patricia and I went

to the church to see if Dad's body was already there. Unbeknownst to me, my family had decided on *Nearer My God to Thee* for the funeral. It was a song that Dad had been the lead singer for while in the Morning Star Male Chorus.

When we walked into the church, someone was doing a test of the music setup. I immediately found the first seat and doubled over crying. Seeing this, Patricia ran to the back of the church and got them to turn off the song. Everyone else in my family knew it was going to be played.

My cousin Willie Ed Walker came into the church. He was also all broken up and in tears. Willie Ed apologized and said he wouldn't be coming to the funeral because he couldn't handle it. My brothers Reuben and David seemed to manage a lot better than I did.

When it was time for us to go to the funeral Mom and I sat on the couch because we were having a hard time leaving the house.

Mom emotionally cried out, "I just don't want to go."

I said in tears, "Mom, I don't want to go either."

Uncle James Pope came over and helped her get composed so we could walk outside and get into that black limousine. It wasn't a ride that I looked forward to taking.

I took the death of my father very hard. I was a grown man. I figured I could handle it okay, but I broke down on several occasions and cried like a little baby. I chose not to be a pallbearer because I thought I might collapse or something. There was no disrespect intended, it was just my personal decision. I taped the viewing, funeral and the burial at Mom's request with my VHS camera but to this day I have yet to sit down and watch it.

My brother David played the piano at Dad's viewing, but opted not to play at his funeral. David didn't think he could do it. I didn't blame him at all. We were most concerned about our sister Rosalyn, because she had always been Dad's pet. We all thought that Roz would fall apart at the funeral and send the rest of us spiraling downward. But Roz did very well throughout all of the services.

We had a final viewing with the immediate family only. All of a sudden, Patricia fainted and fell out and onto the floor with a loud boom. I almost fell and my stomach muscles really tightened up, but I held onto the side of the casket. There were lipstick marks on Dad's face where the girls had kissed him. And so I kissed him on the forehead and said my last goodbye.

After I came home to Colorado, it still took me a few weeks to recover. I broke down and cried. Lorena came over and gave me a big hug. Hap Kellogg from California called me and I cried. He prayed for me over the telephone.

I was still doing my financial services and sales and was working from home on commission. I was also being recruited by some guys in Greeley, Colorado, who were working for a financial services company called WMA (World Marketing Alliance).

Lorena already had her securities license (Series 7) and wanted me to obtain mine and join forces with those guys. They invited both of us to attend a huge rally in Denver. We met some of the upper level managers who were pulling in thousands of dollars a week.

On the drive back to Fort Collins, Lorena was trying to convince me to quit MMCA and join WMA. I told her I needed to think about it for a while and she got extremely upset and threw her hands up in disgust. Then she refused to talk to me for the rest of the trip home. This was very typical of her, as I would learn...the hard way.

Have I mentioned those red flags? I knew that couples argue but I should have noticed that Lorena's behavior was different than what I had experienced before. I'd had a previous relationship that had lasted six years during which we had lived together. Lorena was different but I wasn't looking at our situation clearly. I also told myself that she had given up her life back east to move to Colorado to be with me. I thought I owed it to our relationship to try to get along and I did the best I could.

A few times we had arguments and didn't say much to

each other for a day or so. Sometimes I was sure Lorena wouldn't show up for our marriage counseling session, but she always did. In front of Dave, she acted like nothing out of the ordinary had happened and we proceeded to get along as usual. I didn't want to set her off again, so I never brought it up in counseling. Another mistake.

At the conclusion of the classes, Rev. Williams sent a letter to Rev. Mike in New Jersey stating that we had completed the course and were approved to be married.

On some days Lorena had to leave early to commute. I would get up and fix her lunch. I would give her a goodbye kiss and send her on her way. On days that I didn't have an appointment, I tried to make sure there was something cooked for dinner.

Lorena was always good about taking care of the dinner arrangements before she went back to work. She'd usually cook on Sundays and try to prepare enough food to get us through the week. She also taught me how to cook. Prior to that, for me it was kind of catch-as-catch-can when it came down to dinner. I could handle breakfast and lunch.

In the meantime, Lorena had become very unhappy with the situation at U.S. Bank. She felt that her boss wasn't very supportive. She contacted TIARRA again and received another job offer. She accepted the invitation to attend the June training class in Denver.

We had decided to get married in New Jersey since all of our relatives were there. Our wedding date would be Saturday May 23, 1998 at the Morning Star Baptist Church in Woodstown. Although she knew she was leaving U.S. Bank, Lorena attended their big business, all expenses paid trip to Las Vegas in May.

I kind of thought it was wrong, but I didn't say very much about it. I learned very early with Lorena not to bring up any touchy subjects, because she would get extremely upset.

I was a little low on funds and Lorena agreed to pay for the wedding and the honeymoon. I didn't really like it, but figured I would make it up to her later. We made it very clear that we only wanted money for our wedding gifts since we were combining two households and had everything we needed to make a home for ourselves. All of the money for our gifts went to Lorena to help defray some of the costs of the extravaganza.

I asked Jimmy Lee Walker to be my best man. He warned me that he had been the best man for several of his friends and they were all divorced now. I had prayed for my mate and figured that since God had answered my prayers, there was no need for me to be concerned.

"Skimmer" put on a small barbeque during the week in his backyard in Woodstown for my bachelor party. A few of the Cowtown Rodeo gang were present and we had a great time laughing and telling old stories.

David Walker, our cousin, put on a huge fish fry in Mom's backyard for the rehearsal dinner. He paid for the entire function as our wedding present. A few of my friends from out of state also attended the occasion. Hap Kellogg flew in from California. Brad and Wendy Morris flew in from Kansas City, Kansas.

The wedding was grand. My brother David donated his services on the piano. My sister Patricia sang a solo. My brother Reuben also sang a solo. My niece and nephew, Tannah and Coley Morris, were flower girl and ring bearer. My other nephew, Michael Morris, served as one of the ushers. It was definitely a family affair and momentous occasion.

We held our reception at the Dutch Inn in Gibbstown, New Jersey. The dance afterward was a ball! Many family members said our reception was the best they had ever attended. The DJ was first class and played one hit tune after another.

Our first dance together was *I Finally Found Someone* by Barbra Streisand and Bryan Adams. Then the DJ cut loose with *Bustin' Loose* by Chuck Brown. You should have seen the people jump up and head to the dance floor. There was no hesitation like I've seen at other receptions or dance functions. After the reception, we hung out in the bar with a few family and friends.

Lorena and I spent the night at the Dutch Inn.

The next morning after breakfast we drove up to the Pocono Mountains in Pennsylvania for our honeymoon. We stayed at Caesars Pocono Resort which was designed for newlyweds and couples on their anniversaries. We met several other couples and got to know a few. We played basketball, rode the lake in a paddle boat, rode horses and played games at a video arcade.

We had a great time. But the best part was enjoying each other's company and getting to know each other better in a pleasant atmosphere. The rooms had a small pool and also a large champagne-glass-looking bathtub.

One sour note came out of the blue. Lorena again brought up the fact that I had slept with a lot of white women in the past. She had previously told me that she had had sex with a white guy named Gary after her divorce, while she lived in Chicago. I didn't hold that against her, nor did I bring it up to rub it in her face like she did with me. Lorena also told me that even her own family hadn't known that Gary was white because she'd never told them.

I thought bringing up my past again was totally uncalled for and a very low blow considering we were on our honeymoon. It shocked me that she would choose to put a damper on such a special occasion. But as I was to find out, this was something that Lorena would do often, whenever we argued and she was upset with me.

After we returned to Woodstown, on Saturday May 30, I was honored to be able to announce Cowtown Rodeo along with Dusty Cleveland. Grant Harris, the owner, had extended the invitation to me and I had readily accepted.

It was nice to pick up a paycheck after the conclusion of the rodeo. I even introduced my new bride to the crowd and asked her to stand up. Needless to say I was pretty proud to have been able to meet and marry such a beautiful African-American woman. I wasn't thinking about our problems, only about how lucky I was.

The next morning, May 31, Patricia and Mom gave us a ride back to the airport in Baltimore. We were upgraded to first class and rode back home in style. We both wore the T-shirts that we'd gotten from Caesars announcing that we were newlyweds and had spent our honeymoon there.

Ken Lett, with whom I'd attended the University of Wyoming, picked us up. He lived in a subdivision called Green Valley Ranch which was only a few miles from DIA (Denver International Airport). Ken was also working at TIARRA because I had given his name to a job recruiter in 1993 after the *Rocky Mountain News* had published a story about my financial services and bull riding careers.

Lorena started her training class at TIARRA in Denver on Monday morning June 1, 1998. One of the last things she did before she went to bed the night before was to fax her resignation over to U.S. Bank. She had taken a two week vacation and had been paid the entire time we were gone for our marriage and honeymoon.

At the time I didn't realize she had done this. It turned out to be just another example of one of her plans to put something over on someone, regardless of rules or policy. She had known that she was not going to return to U.S. Bank, but chose to work the system and get paid in the process.

I had been studying quite a bit for my securities license. Lorena had convinced me that I could do a lot better if I were to obtain it. I took and passed the exam in Denver on June 24. It happened to be another major milestone in my life that took place on my birthday.

Next, I studied for and passed the Series 63 examination. I registered and became a licensed representative with the NASD. (National Association of Securities Dealers). The name has since been changed and is now known as FINRA (Financial Industry Regulatory Authority). The test and registration cost me about $650. I joined the financial group called World Marketing Alliance and attended a few meetings in a Greeley, Colorado office.

Meanwhile, Lorena was commuting each day about seventy miles each way to work. It took a toll on her and we discussed it. She wanted to move to Denver. Her argument was she had been willing to move about nine hundred miles to be with me. I should be willing to move a mere sixty miles in order to make her life a little better.

I really didn't want her to have to deal with slick and icy roads during the winter, and so we made a decision to move to Denver. I didn't want to leave Fort Collins since I'd lived there for twelve years and was very comfortable. I'd made a lot of good friends in Fort Collins and had pretty much already decided that I could've been comfortable living there for the rest of my life.

Sadly, in August I put my home on the market and it sold right away. The first agent and potential buyer that visited wanted to purchase it. I closed on it in late September.

Lorena and I made regular trips to the Denver area on the weekends. Because I had quite a few clients in northern Colorado and Wyoming, I wanted to stay on the north side of the city. We looked at several homes in the Northglenn and Thornton area. Finally, we made an offer on a beautiful four bedroom brick home in Northglenn. It worked out fine because we were able to close on that home and start moving in a few days before I sold and closed on my home in Fort Collins.

Lorena had convinced me that because I was involved in commission sales it would be a lot more difficult for me to qualify as a home buyer. So we decided to put the home in her name only to start. Then later we planned to add my name to the deed and mortgage.

I recruited many of my friends to help with the move. Bobby Wilson, Gerry Strom, Carlos Washington, and Clarence Gipson were all retired from the rodeo circuit like me. Bobby was a truck driver by trade and he brought up a big rig for the move. I paid a moving company to move the large heavy items such as the refrigerator, freezer and Lorena's piano.

I got involved with a company based in Fort Worth, Texas called Farm & Ranch Healthcare. They specialized in selling health insurance to clients in rural America. In October, I drove to Fort Worth and stayed there for about five days and attended some intense training sessions. I was able to spend a day or so visiting with my sister Rosalyn Hairston and her family who lived in Fort Worth. On my drive down, I'd stayed overnight in Amarillo and visited my cousins Roland and Vera Shorter.

Back in Colorado, I made a serious effort to make a living selling health insurance products and spent quite a bit of time on the road and making phone calls. I stayed in cheap motel rooms and ate inexpensively. I did okay, but not near as well as I'd hoped. It wasn't so much the road that bothered me. I just never made the income that I'd imagined I would.

In late October, Lorena made the startling discovery that she was pregnant. We were both shocked because I had been using condoms. We had talked about the possibility of having children and raising a family multiple times during our courtship, engagement and now during our short marriage. We had decided to get to know each other and spend some time together before making a decision about having children.

Lorena didn't take it very well. I heard her crying many times in the morning before she left to go to work. She'd break down and sob, "I don't want to be pregnant! I don't want to have a baby!" On other occasions telling me, "I hate this house, I hate my job, I hate Colorado and I hate living with you!"

We decided to go back to New Jersey for Christmas and the New Year's. By this time it was very apparent that she was pregnant. I arranged for someone in my family to pick us up at the airport in Washington, D.C. Lorena got upset saying, "Don't you think that someone in my family would like to pick us up for a change? Why does someone in your family always have to pick us up?"

I reminded her that when she was home for the holidays

in 1996, she had to pay a man thirty dollars to take her back to the Philadelphia Airport, because she couldn't find anyone in her family to do it.

It really didn't matter. She still was upset for no reason at all. I figured I was doing both of us a favor by finding someone to pick us up. Lorena didn't see it that way at all. My sister Patricia picked us up and took us back to the airport at the end of our stay in New Jersey.

We spent a few days at my mom's house in Woodstown and the remaining ones at Lorena's mom's house in the Elmer area. Lorena insisted that we spend and eat Christmas dinner at her sister's home in Dover, Delaware. I didn't like the idea, but as usual she had to have her way. If Lorena didn't get her way, she'd act out and would throw a fit.

While driving to Delaware, Lorena and I got into another argument. Her mom, who was so meek and mild, sat quietly in the back of the car during our disagreement. Lorena acused me of starting it saying, "You have to get into an argument with me on every holiday, don't you?" Lorena had started an argument with me on Thanksgiving Day, as well.

We were only with my side of the family for a little while on Christmas Day and that was well after dark. I gave my mom and my sisters and brothers a group family picture that we had taken together on our wedding day in late May. I could tell they were a little disappointed that I was in New Jersey for Christmas, and only spent less than thirty minutes with them.

We returned from New Jersey with a few Christmas presents that were intended for our coming baby. Lorena got increasingly upset with the increasing size of her body. She thought she was very unattractive to me looking like that. It didn't bother me at all. I figured she was being overly self-conscious.

On Easter Sunday, Lorena did a little cleaning around the house and then we were going to go over to Ken Lett's home for dinner. Lorena had a nasty habit. Whenever I was standing in the kitchen and she wanted to open a drawer. Instead of saying, "Excuse me," she would pull the drawer out, hit me in the leg and then expect me to move out of her way. Most of the time, I'd just move.

I got tired of it and on that particular occasion, I just stood there and ignored her. Lorena then accused me of trying to keep her from eating when she was hungry. She had a poached egg on a saucer and was trying to get a fork out of the drawer.

Lorena got upset and tossed the saucer into the sink and shattered it. It really shocked me and caught me off guard. I had no idea that she could lose all self control and throw an object across the room. This is a perfect example of how far off our communication skills were and in the next year or so, the incidents of violence would escalate. Again, I was in it and could neither understand nor do anything to diffuse it.

After smashing the saucer she went on a verbal tirade and told me that she wasn't going over to Ken's so I needed to call and cancel. We were also invited over to Mike Bond's future in-laws' home in Aurora. We had plans to go there for dessert. So I had to call and cancel our engagements telling them that because of the pregnancy Lorena wasn't feeling well. It was all a big lie just to cover up for her abrupt change of mood. I didn't know what else to do.

As it got closer and closer to Lorena's due date, she got increasingly irritable. She didn't want to have sex because she feared we might somehow damage the baby. During one of our conversations she accused me of cheating on her.

"Since you and I aren't having sex, and I know how much you enjoy it, I know you must be getting it somewhere else."

I said, "How in the world can you sit there and say that I'm cheating on you when you know everywhere I go? I go on appointments and come home every day, unless I stop at the health club to work out. I can't believe that you would say that to me. That's one of the worst things you could ever say to your spouse, to accuse them of cheating when you have absolutely no reason, whatsoever, to think that."

JUSTIN

It finally sank in that that Lorena was extremely insecure. It was a very low blow. I had no intentions of cheating on her. Having sex with someone else outside of my marriage was the farthest thing from my mind. It hurt to be accused of cheating by someone I was in love with. Despite her sometime irrational behavior, I loved her and our marriage and the child we were expecting. I tried to tell myself it was the pregnancy that was affecting her hormones or something.

In February, we also found out that we were going to have a boy. We debated on several names. Lorena wanted Jeremy. I mulled over naming him Abraham Jackson Morris, III. Lorena didn't want another Abraham in the family and insisted that that tradition had faded away. I still wanted to somehow keep the tradition going and so we settled on making the baby's middle name the same as my first—Abraham. Finally, we agreed to name our son Justin Abraham Morris.

When we were living in Fort Collins, Lorena and I had set up a joint checking account in order to pay our bills and expenses. When we moved to Northglenn we set up a new checking account. We sat down and figured out what our monthly expenses would be. Then we agreed to put equal deposits into that account. We paid the mortgage, groceries and all of our living expenses directly out of that account. We made sure there would always be a little extra in the account so we didn't bounce a check.

In late April, Lorena asked if I was going to the bank soon to make a monthly deposit into that account. I said no, but I'd be going in a few more days. She offered to write a check from her own personal account to put into our joint account. I told her not to worry about it and that she could write the check later.

A few days later, I approached her and asked her to write that check so I could go and deposit it.

She looked and me and responded, "Fuck you, fuck this, you're nothing but a fucking piece of shit!"

I was flabbergasted, to say the least. We hadn't even been arguing that day. All I did was ask her for something that she had offered to give me a few days before. And yet she blew a gasket when I asked her for the check.

It was to mark the first time that Lorena cursed at me. Little did I know it was just the beginning. I couldn't believe that she'd use the "F" word on me. I couldn't believe that such vulgar language and foul words could come out of her mouth. Now I realize that what I consider vulgar language is pretty common usage these days, but in my family and following the way I had grown up, that sort of language was extremely offensive to me. I didn't use it and didn't expect to hear it very often, and certainly not from the woman I'd married and directed at me, to boot!

Lorena's doctor at the Rose Medical Center decided that Justin would be delivered with a cesarean procedure. The delivery date was set for Saturday, May 15, 1999.

A woman friend of the doctor requested to watch the birth and received permission from Lorena. Before the delivery the doctor and nurse stuck a long nasty looking needle in Lorena's back in order to numb the lower part of her body. They made a slit in the upper part of her pelvic area and it started bleeding. The woman almost fainted. She left the delivery room and never returned. The sight of blood didn't bother me. I had seen my own and others' on many occasions because of my rodeo career.

When the doctor was pulling Justin out of his mother's womb there was a very loud snap. Justin came out screaming. I didn't realize what had prompted it until much later when the doctor told that he had to break Justin's arm. At first, I thought he was kidding me. But somehow Justin had gotten stuck. The doctor said he had less than a minute to get oxygen to the baby's brain. If he didn't, Justin would have ended up brain damaged. So in order to prevent that from happening, the doctor had snapped his arm in order to get him out as quickly as possible.

Justin's arm was pinned to his clothing. The doctor said it would heal in only a few weeks because he was a baby and would grow very rapidly. We had to give him liquid aspirin to help with the pain. Justin was also born with a thick full head of hair.

JUSTIN

Right after Justin was born, Lorena had surgery to remove a few fibroids that had been giving her trouble and causing her pain for a few years. I was given permission to film the entire surgery with my VHS camera. I set it up on a tripod and then watched the entire delivery and surgery from close range.

It is hard to explain how exciting it was for me to meet my son, to watch him come into the world, broken arm and all. The miracle of his birth was something that touched me very deeply and I was committed to helping my beautiful little boy explore all the possibilities the world had to offer him.

I stayed with Lorena for most of that day. And what a long and exhilarating day it had been! I had wondered for years if I would someday experience the joy of becoming a father. I was grateful that except for the broken arm, Justin was fine. I was also thankful that Lorena's surgery was successful and she was resting peacefully.

Finally, exhausted, I headed for home.

My family from New Jersey had been calling because they were very concerned. We didn't have cell phones back then. They were all relieved when I called them that night to say that everything was okay. I finally grabbed something to eat and crashed out in bed.

Lorena and Justin were discharged a few days later and came home.

I knew it was going to be a very stressful time for Lorena having to take care of Justin while she was recovering. I stepped up to the plate cooking all of the meals and cleaning up around the house. Lorena decided to breastfeed Justin.

She had to get up often in the middle of the night because Justin woke up and was hungry. It was a few weeks before he slept for most of the night.

Lorena gave me a list of things to do around the house. I set about doing them and it took me a couple of days to get most of them accomplished. I missed one item on the list and didn't mop the upstairs bathroom floor. This upset Lorena.

I learned the hard way that it was fruitless to go out of your way to try and please the woman. She only noticed what you didn't do, instead of what you had done.

Lorena's mother, brother and sister-in-law flew out to Colorado to see Justin. Then a couple of weeks later both of her sisters came out and spent a few days with us.

On the way back from the airport, I shared with them that Lorena had really been acting out around the house. Lorena's older sister told me that Lorena had experienced multiple problems in her first marriage, as well. Marie told me that Lorena had destroyed every wedding present from her first marriage or thrown them into the trash.

She also told me that soon after Lorena's marriage to Samuel, she had flipped out and been out of control. All of this happened the very first day after they'd returned from their honeymoon. Lorena had gone around the house throwing and breaking up things.

In desperation, Samuel had called her family and asked for some help and damage control. Lorena's mother, father, both sisters and their husbands got into a car and drove over in order to help and calm her down. One of Lorena's sisters said that while Samuel was on the telephone, you could hear Lorena in the background cursing up a storm.

I was shocked to hear this. Sitting there in the car, I wished that someone had pulled me off to the side to inform about Lorena's past problems. I felt betrayed because it was obvious that her family had known about her erratic behavior and had left me to find out for myself. I felt as if her family had been glad, or even anxious to pawn her and her issues on me.

Her sisters only stayed for a few days. The problems between Lorena and me proceeded to escalate.

During the month of June I'd celebrate my first Father's Day and later my forty-third birthday. Lorena had purchased two greeting cards for those occasions. I happened to see them by accident and had glanced at them. Both days came and went. Lorena didn't acknowledge either occasion. I also never received the cards. I know, without a doubt, that she'd had a change of heart and had thrown them away.

I took up the task of fixing Justin's baby formula nightly and putting the bottles in the refrigerator. One time Lorena got upset at me and told me I was stupid. Then she went off in a tirade saying, "You're stupid, stupid, stupid." This was all because I had fixed the bottles, gotten distracted and accidentally left them sitting on the counter for awhile. Lorena had often warned me that it was dangerous for the baby if the bottles weren't refrigerated right away.

I paid attention while Lorena fed Justin. The trouble was she was so protective that she wouldn't let me feed him. It was as if she was afraid that I'd drop the poor little guy or something. I now realize it was just part of her controlling behavior. But I always marveled at him, thinking, wow that's my son. I felt extremely blessed where he was concerned.

Because Lorena was acting so horrible, I called pastor Dave Williams in Fort Collins and asked for some advice. He told me that there was a possibility that Lorena was bipolar and was suffering from some form of postpartum depression. I'd never heard either term. I honestly believe it was worse than depression. It seems to me, now, that it may have been postpartum psychosis.

Rev. Williams suggested that we come to Fort Collins for a review session since it had been over a year since our marriage counseling. We went to the church and met him in his office.

I went into a diatribe chronicling Lorena's bizarre and irrational actions since Justin had been born. I told Dave that she had called me stupid on multiple occasions. Again, I realize this is common these days, but it was not common for me and it hurt me deeply.

When it was Lorena's turn to reply, she looked at me and then looked at Dave and said, "I never called him stupid."

Naively, I was astounded that she could sit there in church and lie like that.

We didn't speak to each other on the drive back to Northglenn. We also said very little to each other for the next couple of days. When we finally talked again I told Lorena, "I can't believe that you sat there in church and told Dave that you have never called me stupid."

Lorena in turn replied, "I never said that when we were sitting in church with Dave."

This was so bizarre to me.

Lorena's behavior continued to worsen and get even more outrageous. I called my mom and asked her to come out for a few days to help me. She agreed to fly out to visit for a few days. The night that she was to arrive we were cleaning up the house and Lorena got upset and threw a plastic cup across the living room at me.

Our wedding photos had been placed on her piano. She got upset and took them off and hid them somewhere in the house. That night when I was lying in bed trying to go to sleep, Lorena came into the bedroom, raised a pillow and smashed me in the head. I, of course, never saw it coming. I opened my eyes and told her that she had better knock it off.

I called her doctor at Rose Medical Center and he agreed to call and speak to Lorena. She got extremely upset after she found out that I had called him. I recommended to Lorena that she go and get some professional help. She was in total denial and refused. For this reason and several others I tagged her with the nickname of Cleopatra ("The Queen of Denial").

The verbal barrages and attacks began to come more and more often. "I hate you, I hate this house, I hate living with you, I hate my job, and I hate Colorado." Other times she would get upset saying, "I hate you, I hate you, I hate you."

These attacks seemed to me to come out of left field and I could never seem to predict what might set her off. The events always occurred after Justin was asleep in his crib. Lorena seemed to time them so she wouldn't go off and harm him. But they came on a regular or should I say an *irregular* basis.

Desperate for some sort of support, I resorted to regularly calling my family members and telling them what was going on in our home. One time, Lorena's mom called out of concern and told both of us to get on the phone. Lorena was eating dinner and refused to talk to her own mother. I talked to her mom, but she realized that Lorena wasn't going to budge, so we terminated the call.

Even Lorena's sisters told me that it was good for me to be around Justin as much as possible because they felt he was able to sense that his mother was extremely moody and this would upset him. They told me Justin really needed a stable parent in his life at this very critical time

I called my sister Patricia and she agreed to call Lorena. We had separate phone lines and our own personal phone numbers. Patricia called one evening and I could tell that Lorena was getting extremely agitated by the tone of her voice and her responses.

She was talking to Patricia on a cordless phone in the basement. Lorena pitched a fit and disconnected the phone. Then she ran upstairs. Patricia called her right back. Lorena's phone on the main floor rang.

In retaliation, Lorena ran over to the phone and violently jerked the phone cord out of the socket. Then, Patricia called me on my phone and we talked for awhile.

During another phone conversation with her oldest sister, I overheard Lorena tell Marie that she had absolutely no remorse for any of the things that she had said to me, and that she would never apologize.

When Lorena still lived in Chicago she had given me a picture of her participating in a fashion show. She was strutting down a runway catwalk. I'd had the photograph framed. During another one of her tirades she screamed at me a few times, "I curse the day that I met you. I hate you, I hate you, I hate you!"

My response was, "The truth is you hate yourself."

Upon hearing this, Lorena ran into the bedroom and took

the fashion picture out of the frame. Then she tore it up into several pieces and scattered them in the hallway. At the same time she was saying something about hating herself.

Lorena left the house to cool off. This was something she did often. She would simply say that I needed to watch Justin because she was leaving. Then she would just walk out the door or else go and take a short drive. Of course these were actually peaceful times I could spend with my son.

In bed that night, Lorena told me that she really didn't like herself. She said that she had always hated her name, but there was nothing she could do about it but live with it. She also told me that during her marriage to Samuel she had contemplated suicide.

She said, "I had made a decision that if I remained with Samuel, I was going to commit suicide. I decided that I was either going to leave him or kill myself. I was going to hang myself in the garage, so that when Samuel opened the garage door, he would see me hanging from the rafters."

Oddly, Lorena hated her name. I wonder why she never changed it. She had been named after her Aunt Lorena, who later passed away at the age of ninety. She liked her aunt but despised the name.

I once ran across an article in one of Lorena's files that she had saved. It was about an African-American businesswoman who was very successful. Years later, it was discovered that she had lied on her resume about having a certain college degree. I think the woman had dropped out of school but claimed she had received a master's degree. She had a very lucrative position in her company until she was exposed and lost her job

The woman had committed suicide. I always wondered why Lorena had saved this article. She probably saw herself in the same situation and would commit suicide if things went terribly wrong for her in her business world and career.

My mother had told me very early—right after Lorena had started acting out—"Whatever you do, don't hit her. She wants you to hit her. If you hit her, I guarantee that when the police come, you'll be the one that'll be arrested."

I started writing letters to Lorena's sisters, hoping they could either influence her or help me figure out how to deal with her. One lived in New Jersey and the other in Delaware. The sister who lived in New Jersey responded that all they were hearing was my side of the story.

"We really don't have any proof that Lorena is saying and doing all of these horrible things that you say."

This was a shock after what Marie had told me that day on the way from the airport. It made it pretty obvious that they didn't want to get in the middle of another one of Lorena's messes.

One Sunday afternoon Lorena flipped out again and went into another one of her tirades. I called my mother and left the cordless phone off of the receiver. Lorena was ranting and raving and cursing up a storm. At one point she said, "We used to have a good marriage until you fucked it up!" My mother listened intently and heard most of what Lorena said.

Afterward, Mom was so upset that she called Lorena's aunt and spoke to her about Lorena's behavior. The aunt was Lorena's father's sister. Later on, Mom said the woman had broken down and cried while they talked.

I wrote a few more letters to Lorena's sisters. I asked them to call and talk to my mother if they didn't believe the horrible things that were coming out of Lorena's mouth. They never did. I guess because they knew I was speaking the truth.

Things between Lorena and me were deteriorating. She frequently told me that she hated me.

"You never amounted to anything. The only thing that you are any good for is sex. All during your riding career, all you were was a rodeo bum. I married a bum."

In desperation, I reached out to anyone in Lorena's family who would listen to me. I even called her aunt, her brother and sister-in-law. I also called the pastor who had performed the ceremony during both of the times that Lorena had been married in Morning Star Baptist Church.

Rev. Mike agreed to call and speak with Lorena. After he called her, she really got upset, claiming that I was telling everyone about our personal life. My response was if she weren't saying all of these things to me, then I wouldn't have anything to tell. I wanted a solution.

The ironic thing about Lorena's behavior was whenever we went to her company's picnics and functions, she glowed and told everyone that I was a former professional bull rider. She seemed so proud and boastful of me in public, but behind closed doors was so vicious and nasty. Go figure. Obviously I couldn't.

Lorena suggested that we start to go a marriage counselor. I didn't want to go and felt it would be a waste of my time and that's exactly what it turned out to be. The only reason I agreed to go was because if it would help save my marriage, then I felt it would be worth it.

We went for a few sessions and all the while I didn't feel we were making any progress, but I continued to attend. After awhile, Lorena became so upset that she refused to go any more. The marriage counselor convinced me that I should still attend the sessions, even if I came alone.

Even while I sat there in front of her and vented about all of Lorena's bizarre behavior, she yawned as if she wasn't even interested. I'm sure that the only reason she wanted me to continue the sessions alone was because she would still collect the fees from Lorena's insurance company.

Then the marriage counselor told me that if things got so out of hand that I should call the police and have Lorena arrested. I really didn't want to call the police. My sister Patricia was encouraging me to step up to the plate when she said, "You continue to call home and talk about Lorena's actions, but what are you going to do about it?"

We took Justin along with us to the marriage counseling sessions. Most of the time, he would sleep through the sessions as long as he wasn't hungry.

I spent as much time as possible with Justin. I was really trying to get to know him and make a good father-son connection.

Before Lorena went back to work she found a daycare provider in Thornton, Colorado. By that time Justin was so used to being around his mother that the separation anxiety really got the best of him. Justin would bawl and cry non-stop when she dropped him off. The daycare provider couldn't handle it. She called Lorena more than once to come and get Justin during the day. Lorena returned from the hairdresser one Saturday afternoon and was totally beside herself. The beautician had convinced Lorena that the daycare woman might harm Justin, so Lorena pulled him out and never sent him back there again.

After she returned to work downtown, Lorena found a daycare center located downtown. She would take off for her lunch break and visit Justin to make sure he was okay. She continued to go overboard as far as worrying about someone else spending any quality time with her son. It was ridiculous.

Justin settled down at that new place. The child care staff loved him but as her behavior continued to errode, I was becoming increasingly concerned that Lorena might flip out and hurt Justin. The woman was already prone to violence and throwing things was becoming a pretty common occurrence.

Living with Lorena was becoming more and more unbearable. Every weekend, without fail, she would find something to complain about. I was getting sick and tired of it. She was miserable and unhappy and there didn't seem to be anything I could do about it.

One of the things Lorena started to complain about was that I was involved in a commission sales career with no regular hours and thus no guarantee of a dependable paycheck. She harped and harped on me about how she needed some help raising Justin and wanted me to have a regular job instead.

After a lot of contemplation, I finally gave in, figuring it was in the best interest of my family. I didn't want to leave the flexibility of my sales career. I enjoyed my work.

I applied for a few positions and landed an interview with Jackson National Life Insurance Company as a telephone representative in the phone center. Lorena really supported me and even offered to coach me before my telephone interview. We talked and she felt that I really didn't need her coaching because I was ready to go. I thanked her and appreciated her trying to help.

After the initial telephone interview, I was asked to come in for a regular interview. A couple of days later I was given an offer and accepted it.

I was told I would start at the beginning of September. But then in August I was called and asked if I could start the following Monday. I gladly accepted and that weekend I purchased a few new clothing items to spruce up my wardrobe.

Lorena was still on maternity leave. When I arrived home after my first day at work she had already cooked dinner to show her appreciation of me taking a major step in our lives.

The next weekend I was sitting in my office at home and doing things at my desk. Lorena walked into the room and sat down in my lap and told me how pleased she was with me for trying for and getting a new job. It really made me feel great. She hadn't been that nice to me for months. I figured we were finally on our way to recovery.

But that didn't last very long. Within a couple of weeks Lorena was acting out again and yelling, screaming and cursing. I had called my family members several times and they suggested that I secretly tape Lorena's tirades.

I set up a tape recorder in the closet of my home office and waited until the right moment. It wasn't long. Within a few days I had several minutes recorded of her ranting and raving. Lorena was just downright nasty.

When Justin was born, he didn't really favor either one of us as far as looks went, or maybe I just couldn't see it. He was a baby, and a cute baby (of course!) but I guess to me small babies don't really show a great resemblence to either of their parents. It was never an issue for me. But it surely was to Lorena. One night we were both sitting on the couch and looking at some of his baby pictures.

Lorena asked, "In your opinion does Justin look more like you or me?"

I said, "To tell you the truth he really doesn't look like either one of us. Besides who really cares? He's our son, and to me that's all that really matters. I love him."

That was all Lorena needed to start another stupid argument. I was so sick and tired of arguing with her over such trivial things that I got up off the couch and left the room.

The very next evening, Lorena started arguing again about whether Justin looked more like her or me.

"Lorena, who cares? It really doesn't matter to me who he looks more like. He is our son. Okay?"

Lorena said, "Even if he looked more like me, I wouldn't expect you to admit it."

Finally exasperated and totally frustrated, Lorena jumped up off the couch and grabbed her head as if she had suddenly been hit by a bolt of lightning. As she walked away she shouted out, "You can go and fuck yourself!"

I was utterly shocked and totally dumbfounded. Again, the languge thing is a big deal for me but how could such an outburst have resulted from our conversation?

Another time we got into an argument in the basement. Lorena stormed upstairs. When she was in the stairwell she screamed at me, "You can suck my cunt!"

I followed her upstairs. By then she was in the bathroom with the door still open. I asked her what she'd said.

"You heard me! Suck my cunt! Suck my cunt! Suck my cunt!"

Again, I was utterly shocked.

Lorena always seemed to be on her worst behavior on the weekends. Somehow, she must have managed to maintain a charming and business-like demeanor at work but when she came home it was another story entirely. She went back to work at TIARRA in September after several months on maternity leave. During the week we didn't see much of each other since we were both working and she was so busy taking care of Justin.

Lorena took Justin with her five days a week and then picked him up after work. Lorena got him dressed and ready each morning. My job was to prepare his baby nutrition bottles each and every night. I could only spend quality time with Justin after work or else on the weekends.

But on the weekend, Lorena never seemed to be at a loss to find something to complain about. She was never satisfied. Even little things irritated her. As an absurd example, she had a metal letter opener with her initials on it. One time I used it without her permission and she got extremely upset. Afterward, she took it and hid it in her closet in the bedroom. She was like a little child.

Lorena insisted that Justin's formula bottles be warmed up on the stove in a pan of heated water. The process took a lot longer than just sticking them in the microwave for a quick fix. Whenever I suggested that method she would throw a fit. After all, she always wanted to be in charge and make all of the major decisions...that would be major decisions like how to heat the bottles! One time Justin was throwing an early morning fit because he was hungry. Lorena put one of his bottles in the microwave oven to quickly heat it up. If I had done that she would have thrown a huge tizzy fit. Every time *I* suggested putting a bottle in the microwave to stop Justin from crying and to speed things up, she got upset.

On Sunday morning September 29, 1999 she started another verbal fight. In the midst of the fight she said, "You make me sick."

I responded by telling her, "You're already sick." And I didn't say that just to be mean. I honestly believed that the woman was mentally ill. It must have taken awhile for it to sink in. A few minutes later when I had my back to her, she walked up behind me and slapped me extremely hard in the shoulder.

"That's for telling me that I'm sick."

It surprised me and caught me off guard. I turned around and told her that she had better knock it off.

Things finally got so bad that I left the house and went down to the Northglenn police department. I spoke to an officer on duty, but I didn't file a police report about the incident.

Lorena was in a very foul mood all day. She had even gotten to the point where she would cook and when I went in to eat, she'd throw a fit and say that she didn't cook anything for me. So we started buying and eating our meals separately.

I went to the store and bought some chicken for dinner. I was cooking, basting it on top of the stove. We got into another verbal altercation. At that point she went outside and violently slammed the door to the garage. There was a covered breezeway between the house and the garage. As hard as she slammed the door, I couldn't believe that the window pane didn't break.

She had told me multiple times to pack my things and to get out. I had made it very clear that I wasn't going anywhere. If she was so adamant that one of us leave, then she could take the first step and move out.

So Lorena announced that she was going to move out. During the course of all of this drama, I asked her why she'd wanted to get married in the first place. She certainly didn't act like she really wanted to be in another marriage or that she cared anything for me.

Then she went on a binge. Lorena filled up four large empty trash cans with things. She threw away good tools and several other items that were stored in the garage. At one point, I went outside to see what she was doing and she turned and glared with a wild look and said, "Get out of here! These are my things. If I want to throw them away, then I'm going to throw them away." I went back in the house but later on I went out to assess the damage that she'd done.

The stress and the pressure of a newborn baby had gotten to her. Lorena had previously smoked cigarettes like a locomotive. After she found out she was pregnant she'd temporarily halted that practice. Soon after Justin was born I had gone outside looking for her one night and she was hiding on the other side of the garage puffing away. She obviously didn't want me to know that she had started smoking again.

After a few weeks, I put an ashtray and cigarette lighter in the area where she smoked to make it more convenient whenever she felt the urge to light up. I found the broken ashtray in one of the trash cans.

I went through the trash cans and retrieved many of the items. I locked the tools that I'd found in my pickup truck. When Lorena returned to the garage and discovered all of the things that I had rescued, she got very agitated and upset.

She demanded that I tell her where I had hidden them.

I told her no and that those items were considered community property. I wasn't just going to sit back helplessly and allow her to throw them away.

By that time it was starting to get dark outside. Lorena came back into the house ranting and raving. I went back into the garage to see what she had done. I checked to see that the tools were still locked in my truck. Lorena got extremely upset because she couldn't find them, and I refused to divulge where they were hidden.

When I came back into the house she had taken the large frying pan full of my chicken and hidden it. I asked Lorena several times where it was and she refused to tell me. Her excuse was that since I had taken something that belonged to her, she was going to take something that belonged to me. Tit for tat.

This seems so bizarre when I write it. But it is hard to see the situation clearly when you're in the middle of it. The frustration with the irrational behavior of someone you think you know is so disorienting when it's happening. You're hurt, confused and angry. I didn't know where to turn or how to deal with something that made no sense to me.

Finally, I went outside and found the frying pan with my chicken still in it hidden on the ground in some weeds on the side of the house. I wondered, how gross could she get?

Even after I knew where my food was, I asked her what she had done with it. She refused to tell me. I grabbed my stuff and headed back to the police station again. I had had enough of such foolishness.

This time I spoke to a different officer and told him that I had already been there once before. I asked him to call Lorena on her telephone and talk some sense into her. Because she refused to answer her phone, he offered to follow me back to the house. I told him several times that if he did, I didn't want Lorena arrested.

After a lot of discussion, he assured me that he would only talk to her and wouldn't arrest her. When we arrived at the house, Lorena was in the bathroom giving Justin a bath. The police officer asked her several times to come out and discuss what was going on. In the meantime he had also called for backup. To my surprise three more police officers showed up at our house.

Lorena refused to come out and talk to him. Finally, an older veteran showed up and he wasn't in the mood for any back talk. Lorena finally came out of the bathroom.

"You don't have any right to come into my house and act like you all own this place."

"I'd like to know what's going on here. So you take a seat on the couch so we can talk to you."

Lorena gave the guy some more lip.

"Ma'am, I'm asking you to have a seat on the couch."

Lorena still refused.

Then he said, "I'm asking you to have a seat on the couch and that is an order."

Lorena just stood there, continuing to defy him, showing her anger and belligerence.

"That's it, you're under arrest. Hand your son over to his father and place your hands behind your back."

Lorena gave Justin to me and the officers placed her in handcuffs and led her out the door.

As she was leaving she said, "Thanks a lot Abe."

I had to give a statement and I told the officers that earlier in the day my wfe had struck me in the shoulder.

Lorena was first taken to the Northglenn police station where she was eventually charged with domestic violence, failure to obey and obstruction of justice. In the state of Colorado a charge of domestic violence carries an automatic thirty day restraining order.

Later that night, she was transported to the Adams County Detention Center in Brighton, Colorado. I called a few people including my mom in New Jersey and Rev. Dave Williams in Fort Collins. I took her purse along with the keys to the house and gave them to the neighbors, Andy and Jan Maes, who lived right across the street.

I also called Ken and Cindy Lett. They offered to come and get Justin and take care of him for a few days until I knew what was going to happen. Lorena had been taking Justin and picking him up from the daycare center in downtown Denver. I didn't know when she would be home and thought at least Justin would have his usual routine the next day.

After they left I didn't sleep well at all.

First thing, the next morning at around 5:00 a.m. and then again at about 6:00 a.m. Lorena called me at home and asked me to come and pick her up.

"Are you just going to leave me out here all day long?"

"Lorena, you have a thirty day restraining order against you. I'm surprised that you even risked calling."

Later, I received a phone call from the sheriff's department telling me that if I was contacted at all by Lorena to give them a phone call. They would immediately go and arrest her again for violating the thirty day restraining order.

When I came home from work, Lorena was in the house. She had been given some tokens to use on a bus ride home. Then she had gone across the street and retrieved her purse from the neighbors.

Lorena said she was terrified to be in the house knowing

that she was violating that restraining order. Even the sound of sirens made her very anxious and nervous. Knowing that she wasn't allowed there for the next thirty days, she needed a place to stay.

I called an old friend, Richard Wilson, who had an extra bedroom. Richard lived alone and I was hoping Lorena could stay with him. Richard said we could come over to his place and was willing to listen to our dilemma.

Lorena followed me over there in her own car. All the while, I was thinking that if she somehow ended up in a motor vehicle accident, she surely would be arrested again for being in my presence, And yet she had somehow convinced me it was now my problem because I was the one who had put her in that position. Of course she had put herself there by refusing to do as the officer asked when he wanted her to sit down on the couch, but in her mind I was the cause of all the trouble.

At the last minute for some unknown reason, Richard declined and said he was uncomfortable having a married woman living in his apartment. Maybe he felt that he would eventually try to put the moves on Lorena. I really don't know why, but Richard said he didn't want her staying there. In retrospect he may have somehow sensed how volatile she was, though she behaved well when we were with him.

So we left and Lorena went and got a motel room. A couple of days later, she called me at work at Jackson National Life Insurance and identified herself as a Mrs. Brown.

She had employed the services of an attorney in an effort to get the thirty day restraining order dropped. I had to be willing to make an appearance in court on her behalf. I told her attorney that if the judge wasn't willing to drop the restraining order, that I'd be willing to move out of the house for the thirty days so Lorena would have a place to live.

In court that Thursday Lorena pled guilty to the domestic violence charges with the stipulation that they would be wiped off of her record in six months, as long as she kept her nose clean. Lorena was also court ordered to attend counseling with a therapist because of the violence charge.

At the time Lorena was a licensed and registered financial representative with the NASD (National Association of Securities Dealers) a very highly regulated industry. Because of the arrest, she was required to report it to the NASD, but I found out later that she never did. As usual, she was creating a reality for herself that didn't quite fit with the "other" reality the rest of us lived in. As far as she was concerned, rules, laws and civil behavior were for other people. Not Lorena.

After work on Friday, I stopped at Ken Lett's home and picked up Justin. His daughter Sheena had been taking care of him. Every time I showed up during the week Justin recognized me and lit up like a Christmas tree. He'd also kick his legs in jubilation because he recognized his daddy. Sheena said I didn't owe her anything for helping us out, but I paid her anyway.

After Lorena's sister Marie found out about all of the problems we were having, she talked to me on the phone.

"Anything that you strongly value and can't replace, you'd better get out of the house. I know my sister and I'm warning you. I guarantee that she'll throw your things into the trash."

I had several rodeo action photos on the walls in my office. I immediately took them down and took them across the street and asked my neighbors if they would temporarily hold onto them for me. A few weeks later, I went across the street and retrieved them, but I never hung them up again in that house. I didn't trust the woman.

Things settled down for a few weeks until Lorena approached me and asked me to help her pay for her attorney's fees. I refused. I felt it was her own fault and the penalty for her behavior over the past few months. Besides, if she had listened to the officer and done what he'd asked, she never would have been arrested in the first place.

After her arrest, Lorena agreed to resume marriage counseling. She told the marriage counselor that I had had her arrested and the marriage counselor chastised me. It really infuriated me because she had previously told me that if Lorena had continued acting out, I should call the police and have her arrested. And here she was getting on me in front of Lorena and acting like she'd had nothing to do with it. I lost all respect for the woman. All the counselor was interested in was a paycheck.

Lorena had made Justin the beneficiary of her IRA before he was born. It had not been accepted by the holding company because the beneficiary had to be a living person. She'd asked me to sign off on the form and I'd refused. Declaring that as the last straw, she informed me that she was going to find another place to live and move out. She no longer wanted to live with me.

Lorena spent the next few weeks looking for an apartment but didn't seem to find anything that suited her.

In October we got into another argument and she informed me that she was going to file for divorce. I really didn't believe her. A few days later, she said that she had already gone to an attorney and filed. Later, there was a knock at the door and I was served with the papers.

In the state of Colorado you don't have to have a reason to file for divorce. All you have to do is file. Colorado is considered a "no fault" state when it comes to dissolution of a marriage.

Several times I tried to persuade her to drop the divorce, but she refused. I made it very clear that I didn't want it. Even though I realized that it was a longshot that Lorena and I would ever be close again, I still thought we should try and work things out for Justin's sake. Lorena told me that the only way she would drop the divorce was if she would to be able to quit her job and have my income totally support the family.

I didn't think I earned enough to be able to pay all of our expenses which included two car payments and a mortgage. Besides, at that point I wasn't all that thrilled to step up to the plate and financially support her considering all of the verbal, physical and emotional abuse that I'd had to suffer for the past few months. Of course she knew this. She had picked a condition she was sure I wouldn't agree to.

The Class of 1974 at Woodstown was planning a 25th anniversary reunion. Lorena and I had both graduated in that class. We had planned to go, but then she changed her mind. I never found out why but I believe part of the reason was because she had been given six months of probation, which I suspect meant she couldn't leave the state.

Lorena forfeited her fee for the reunion dinner but she didn't want me to attend either, inisting I should remain in Colorado, and help her with Justin, even though I had already paid for my airline tickets.

Despite her protests, I went to New Jersey. I attended the Thanksgiving football game and then the reunion on that Saturday night. I didn't tell anyone that Lorena had filed for divorce. I was still very upset to think about the end of my marriage. I dreaded what might become of my relationship with my son. I had enough divorced friends to know how custody situations could escalate into disaster.

I wanted to take Justin so he could meet my family, but Lorena refused to let him go. I know she wasn't concerned about Justin traveling with me, she just wanted to put more pressure on me and was using Justin as a lever to attempt to control me.

When I was in New Jersey, Lorena's aunt Rachel found out I was visiting my mom and called to talk to me.

She said, "Although I'm related to Lorena, I'm on your side. Life is too short to have to deal with all of that nonsense. Lorena's nerves are shot. But whatever you do, don't let her know that I talked to you because then she probably won't ever speak to me again. You go on ahead and get your divorce. You'll be much better off without her."

Sad but true, I didn't take her advice.

I found it amazing that we had only been married for seventeen months and Lorena had filed for divorce. Justin had been born exactly fifty-one weeks after we were married.

Lorena was bound and determined to get rid of me. Finally, she realized that I wasn't going anywhere, despite her yelling and screaming at me to get out, which she had begun to do frequently. Then she decided that she was going to move out. I had told her if she wanted someone to move out it had to be her.

All the while I was bonding with Justin. As he got older and more mobile I would play on the floor with him. He loved to be in his little swing. We could put him in that swing and he'd get so excited. He had the cutest broad little smile.

I would also take Justin on baby carriage rides. I would take him down the streets and take the turns like I was driving a racing car. Justin loved it. He would smile and kick his legs whenever I took some wild and quick turns.

We didn't own a computer or have Internet access at home in those days so on most Sunday mornings Lorena would resort to going back to work because she could use the computer there to help her search for available apartments. She wouldn't even ask me if I had any plans. Lorena would get up and say, "You need to watch Justin. I'm leaving for awhile." She wouldn't even tell me where she was going, but I figured it out on my own. It wasn't that difficult. She had no idea how happy I was for the peaceful time with my son and I certainly never mentioned it.

Lorena's birthday was in December. Despite the way she had treated me on my birthday in June, I acknowledged her birthday, gave her a nice greeting card and called and left a very nice message on her work phone.

Later that month, we got into our usual weekend argument. It was just like clockwork. Lorena couldn't go more than three days without starting some kind of disagreement. She seemed to thrive on the conflict. I suppose it gave her a chance to blame all her dissatisfaction on me and to make herself feel like she was the reasonable person in our situation.

Late one Friday night she got so bad that I left the house and went and spent the night with Richard Wilson in Westminster. By then we were sleeping in separate bedrooms and Lorena never even knew that I was gone. I came back the next afternoon. Lorena figured I had gotten up early and played racquetball.

Our bedroom was downstairs in the basement. Since Lorena and I weren't getting along and the guest room was upstairs, it gave her a good excuse to sleep there so she could be closer to Justin since he never slept through the night.

That day Lorena was especially furious because she had made an appointment to get the heater fixed on her new car and was unable to reschedule it when something came up. She turned it into an attack on me, though I had nothing to do with it.

"You don't care if Justin gets sick in my cold car."

As usual this came out of the blue, related to nothing that was going on.

Then one Sunday morning in December Lorena was wearing a pair of purple sweatpants. As she was walking away from me, she pulled her sweatpants and panties down to her knees showing off her bare butt and said, "You can kiss my ass!" Then she left to go to the TIARRA office.

I was shocked and it greatly upset me. I broke down and cried after she left. I was very hurt and dismayed. I was so upset that I called my mom in New Jersey. I knew she would be in church, but I didn't care. I called right in the middle of the service and asked the man that answered to please go and pull her out of the service. I'm sure the congregation saw him go and get my mom and tell her that her son in Colorado was calling and needed to speak to her right away. I didn't even feel like waiting until Mom was out of church. That's how bad I felt.

I told Mom exactly what had happened and I broke down and cried again. Mom said to me, "Pack up some things and just leave."

I did just that. I had enough things packed in my car by the time Lorena returned. I called Richard Wilson and asked if I could stay with him for a few days. Later on that night I simply walked out. I should've been gone long before that. There's no doubt in my mind that most men would have checked out long before I did.

A few days later Lorena called and left me a voice message at work saying that I had a lot of nerve walking out on her right before Christmas. She also said, "I don't want you to come back and Justin doesn't want you to come back, either."

I didn't return home until the next Friday after work. Lorena was already home by the time I arrived because I had to go to Richard's and collect my stuff. Lorena had parked her car in the middle of our two car garage so I couldn't get my car in.

I spent quite a bit of time working in my office that evening. Of course Lorena had to stop by and add her two cents worth. She said, "I want you gone before the night is over because you aren't allowed to stay here anymore."

I had no intention of leaving.

Eventually, I went downstairs and went to bed.

Although she continued to insist that I leave, I refused. We said very little to each other and she did her best to avoid me.

Lorena even tried to keep me from having any contact with my own son. She continued to sleep upstairs and I slept downstairs. She didn't want me to have anything to do with Justin and so I didn't bother to stir things up. I just let her have her own way, as usual. It was the only way to get along, but there is no way to explain what a surreal situation it was.

Then it was Christmas. I don't know what came over Lorena, but first thing on Christmas morning she brought Justin downstairs and handed him to me as if to say "Merry Christmas."

She didn't say anything, just simply gave him to me without uttering a word. She hadn't let me near him and now I found that during that week someone at the daycare center had taken Justin's long hair and braided it into cornrows. It took a little getting use to.

Later that day, Richard Wilson had made a big dinner that

included prime rib. He called and invited us over. At first Lorena didn't want to go, but she finally relented and went and enjoyed a great homemade Christmas meal. She behaved as though nothing was wrong between us, but after we came home she reverted to her usual behavior.

I continued to write letters to her sisters, even though I knew they would tell Lorena exactly what I said about her bizarre behavior. Eventually, they told her that they didn't care to receive any more letters from me.

I had been in close contact with Rev. Williams about my personal situation. He had recommended that I get back into church. Lorena and I had visited a few churches when we first moved to Northglenn. Then we had both stopped going.

I had liked the morning service at New Hope Baptist Church in Denver and decided that I'd go back. So I'd get dressed on Sunday mornings and go alone because Lorena refused to go to church.

None of the arguments we had were about our finances. We always had an ample supply of money in our joint checking account to take care of all of our household expenses. But one Sunday morning I was dressed to go to church and we got into another argument. This one continued out into the garage. Lorena had strapped Justin into his car seat and attempted to back her car out. As she backed up, I reached out and grabbed her car door and opened it. I did it to make her stop.

Frustrated because she had to get out to close it, Lorena stormed around to the passenger's side of the car and screamed at me, "I hope you DIE on your way to church!"

As the year 2000 approached everyone seemed to be worried about Y2K. I wasn't worried at all. Lorena was a little worried and asked me to stock up on several gallons of bottled water. In the weeks preceding the new century it was amazing how empty the shelves were after the bottled water was frantically purchased.

Lorena told me that her sister Marie was so paranoid that

she was going to fill up the bathtub to use for drinking water just in case her faucet temporarily stopped producing water. I thought it was so silly.

Lorena and I didn't do anything that New Year's Eve. We didn't even have a toast to ring in the new year. She even went to bed before midnight. I stayed up until just after 12:00 a.m. and then I went to bed.

A few weeks later Lorena and I got into another argument at home. I was holding Justin in my arms. Lorena got upset and demanded, "Give him to me."

I refused to hand him over to her.

Again she demanded, "Give him to me."

I refused again. Then Lorena got upset and punched me twice in the shoulder. I told her that I was calling the police again on her for domestic violence.

The first thing out of her mouth was, "When the police arrive I'm going to lie to them. I'm going to show them the divorce papers and tell them the only reason you called was to get back at me because I filed for divorce."

I was pretty surprised that she would hit me again after spending a night in jail.

Then she changed her approach and begged and pleaded with me finally saying, "Look Abe, if you don't call the police, I'll give you this house as well as everything in it. Please don't call the police. Besides if I get arrested again, I'll lose my securities license and then I'll lose my job."

I'd never intended to call the police, but I'd bluffed in hopes of getting her to stop and think and calm down. As frustrating as it was to try to deal with her, I didn't want to see the woman arrested again. I knew the outcome the next time would be a lot worse. A year later, I would find myself wishng that I had called the police that day.

In January of 2000 Lorena convinced me to help her move the big bed to the upstairs bedroom. I didn't want to sleep on that small uncomfortable guest bed and so we started sleeping in the same bed again.

One of the most bizarre episodes occurred on a Sunday morning. It was around 6:30 a.m. I was sound asleep next to Lorena when she woke up screaming. She was making these weird animal-like sounds. She was lying on her back and she started kicking the bed with both feet. Then she flipped over to her stomach and started pounding her pillow with both fists. She kept screaming and making strange noises. Then, all of a sudden she leaped out of bed and headed down the hallway.

Lorena grabbed her head with both hands and in the process was still screaming. She went downstairs and I could still hear her screaming while she seemed to be going through some of our stuff that was packed in boxes in the laundry room. It sounded as though she was looking for something. You could hear the noise of her going through things—crash, boom, bam.

I finally put on some sweats and was going to make my way downstairs to see what the heck she was doing. By that time she was on her way back to the bedroom and I met her in the hallway. She was still screaming and holding both of her hands to her head.

"Lorena, Lorena what's going on?"

Lorena refused to answer me. She went back into the bedroom and quickly put on her sweats. Then she grabbed her purse and headed outside for the garage. She never uttered a single word to me.

Lorena got into her car and drove away. I went downstairs to see what she'd done. She had gone through the boxes with our wedding gifts and some of them were strewn all over the floor. I don't remember finding any broken items. I never could figure out what she was doing or what she had been looking for—or what had prompted the episode.

She returned to the house about thirty minutes later

without a word about where she'd been, what she was doing or what had upset her.

Later on that evening, while she was eating her dinner at the kitchen table, I asked her what that weird display was all about. At that time we weren't eating as a family. It was every man for himself based on Lorena's decision. She had cooked her dinner and was eating alone. She refused to answer me and completely ignored me.

Finally I said to her, "You're losing your mind, aren't you?"

Her only reaction was to raise her hand and her middle finger and flip me off.

During another one of our knock down drag out verbal fights Lorena said to me, "After we get divorced you can go back to being a whore just like you were before we got married."

Again, this was out of the blue, not related to any comments or discussion.

Despite Lorena's behavior towards me I enjoyed spending time with Justin. Sometimes I would play with him in his crib.

I doted on my son. It was a joy to watch him grow and navigate his way through his life. I could tell right away that he was attached to me. He would always light up whenever I was in his presence. To say that I was one proud father would be an understatement.

I felt that God had blessed our marriage with such a charming little boy. He was the joy of my life. Even when I was away from him I could still picture him.

Justin at the time had chubby little legs. He would often kick them with glee. Sometimes I'd make fun of him and mimic his baby sounds back to him. You could tell he'd perk up his ears and wonder why I was teasing him.

We had a scheduled meeting between us and the attorneys in late January. It was to be in downtown Denver at Lorena's attorney's office. That morning I asked Lorena, "So are you going to drop the divorce suit?"

Her response was, "I still don't know. Let's see what the attorneys have to say." It was all a big game. Now that she had filed for divorce, she knew she had the upper hand. Lorena no longer would have to move out. If she chose, I could be forced to move out per a court order.

During the conference I told my attorney that Lorena had hit me twice a few days before. He told me I should've called the police.

I also told him that Lorena had sold her Priceline.com stock which was a violation. After a divorce filing neither party can do any financial transactions without the other party's knowledge or consent.

Lorena told her attorney that she wanted me out of the house. Then the attorneys haggled over my visitations with Justin. I was given ten days to be out of the house with a February 1 deadline. Lorena had known she wanted me out of the house when we'd left that morning, but hadn't had the guts to tell me.

We had traveled in separate vehicles. Lorena had taken the day off work. I had taken the morning off and planned to go to work that afternoon.

During the conference Lorena and her attorney insisted that I pay her a certain amount of money for child support, but Lorena didn't want me to have any visitation with Justin at all.

When my attorney, Gary Filosa, saw that she wasn't going to give in, he said, "No judge in the country is going to accept that kind of an arrangement. We'll see you in court. Abe, get your things. We're leaving."

Her attorney stopped us. We worked out an arrangement that I'd pick Justin up from his daycare on Wednesdays. I would have to take him home by 8:00 p.m. the same night. I would pick him up on Sunday mornings at 9:00 a.m. and Lorena would come and get him from me at 5:00 p.m.

I was allowed to leave my truck and two dogs home. I was

required to clean up the yard on Sunday mornings when I picked up Justin.

After the conference I saw Lorena in the lobby of the building where we'd met. I ignored her, but I noticed that she had worn her wedding ring, as if she were proud that she was married. I found this very strange.

On my way back to Jackson National Life, I called Mom on my cell phone and told her the disappointing news. After work that evening I didn't speak to Lorena. After all, she was forcing me out of my own home.

The first thing out of her mouth was, "So does this mean that there will be no chance for a reconciliation between you and I?"

One thing I'd learned about dealing with Lorena was that it was impossible to figure her out. She had instigated the divorce. Despite what she'd said to me before we went to meet with the attorneys, she had had them insist I leave the house. Now this?

I made arrangements to live with Richard Wilson. He could use the extra money since he was living in a two bedroom apartment. Richard didn't have an extra bed, so I took the bed out of the guest room.

The night that I was moving for some strange reason the back door to the house somehow locked after I had gone outside for the last time right before I left. We had lived in that house for over a year and a half. This had never happened before. I figured it must have been an omen.

Lorena proved to be nasty throughout our separation. Even over the most petty things. Soon after I was kicked out of my home, I realized I had forgotten to pack my shampoo. The next time I returned Justin I asked Lorena permission to go downstairs to my bathroom and get my shampoo. She refused. So I asked her to go downstairs and get it for me since she didn't want me in the house. Again she refused.

Lorena couldn't leave the state until her six months probation was completed in April of 2000.

She also had to get my permission to take Justin out of state because we were separated. One night when I dropped Justin off, she asked permission take him back to New Jersey. The only reason I said yes was to try to get on her good side and hopefully resolve our disputes.

After I returned to Richard's place I gave it some more thought and decided against it. Every time I asked her to do something, it was an automatic "NO." Why should I continue to be so agreeable? I called her at home and told her that I had changed my mind. She didn't answer her phone so I left her a voice message.

I also called her at work and left her a voice message there. Afterward, she claimed that she had already made her reservations and was going to go to court if necessary to be allowed to go. My attorney convinced me not to fight it, but I knew it wouldn't help my situation any. Lorena had lied in order to get her way. She'd succeeded. She would continue to lie.

Meanwhile I continued to bond with Justin. I only got to see him twice a week but I really was always excited the night before and anxious to see him the following day. I'd pick him up from the daycare on Wednesdays and from Lorena on Sunday mornings. Justin and I would go to New Hope Baptist church.

Lorena was constantly conniving and orchestrating the proceedings during our separation. I kept trying to get her to drop the divorce and she kept coming up with excuses not to.

One morning as I was driving out of the parking lot at the apartment complex, Richard came outside and flagged me down. He said Lorena was on the telephone. I figured something was wrong with Justin so I went back inside. She said Justin was sick and that she needed to go to work. She asked me to call in sick and watch him for the day.

I said sure, if I was allowed to spend the day at the house.

She threw a fit as usual saying, "I don't want you in this house." Again reluctantly, I consented and called in sick and went and picked up Justin and took him back to Richard's place.

I figured that my gesture would gain some favorable points with Lorena, but I should have known better. And looking back, I was such a fool to give in to her so easily. It meant absolutely nothing to her.

It is easy to see now how many things I did just trying to appease her. Of course now wish I hadn't. Many friends and family members told me to just let her go. I'd always had the wrong impression—that Lorena was something special—and I didn't want to let my marriage go without feeling like I had given it a decent chance. I definitely came out on the short end of the stick for trying so hard. I have a lot of regrets about that but a person can only do what he feels is right at the time.

Lorena asked me to take her to the airport for her trip to New Jersey. I really didn't want to, but consented anyway. At least I would get a chance to see Justin off. On the way I asked her who was picking her up in Philadelphia. I saw a receipt that she had rented a car and I was curious to see what she'd say. As usual she blew a gasket. Here I was going out of my way to take her to the airport after being kicked out of my home and she was yelling at me for nothing. Instead of firing back, I tried not to argue with her.

Reluctantly, I picked her up at the airport a week later. When Justin saw me waiting at the gate, he got excited. Too bad I didn't receive the same reception from Lorena. She acted as if I was obligated to pick her up. This was back in the day when people could go all the way to the arrival gate and wait for you.

Whenever Lorena would come over on Sunday afternoons to pick up Justin, she would walk into the house and say, "Hi" to Justin, acting as if I didn't even exist. She would act so excited to see him, even though she had spent most of the week with him and had just seen him that morning. It seemed to be just one more way for her to be rude to me.

We had several phone conversations during the evening hours. It was one complaint after another. After awhile I would take the phone away from my ear and wouldn't respond until I couldn't hear Lorena talking anymore. I did this multiple times and she was never aware that I wasn't listening to her gripes.

Most people would've been able to sense that the person on the other end of the line wasn't really listening to them. But, not Lorena. She was so engrossed in her monologues that she never picked up on it.

Justin was a pretty sharp little boy. One Wednesday when I was going to return him to Lorena, I told him that it was time to go. He started crying and screaming for no apparent reason. As I drove the car he continued and wouldn't stop. I pulled the car off of the road and asked him what was wrong.

Justin was only about ten months old and he couldn't tell me. But he knew he was headed back home to be in the house alone with his mother. I was totally dumbfounded at Justin's reaction. I never told Lorena because I knew she would get upset.

Another time I asked Lorena again if she would be willing to drop the divorce suit. She said that she would only if I was willing to sign off and not be able to claim any proceeds from any of her retirement plans, IRA's, stocks, bonds or anything else that she held in her personal financial portfolio.

Soon after her trip back East, Lorena decided that she wanted to move back to New Jersey. I was totally against it. She proceeded to work on me.

"If something happens to both of us, then Justin is going to be alone, especially if he doesn't get to know his relatives back East. I want him to grow up and get to know Michael, Tannah and Coley."

They were my young nephews and niece in Woodstown.

"Besides Abe, you don't have any real close friends out here. How often do your friends call you on the telephone? The biggest reason that you came out here was to rodeo and you don't compete anymore. My mom is getting older and I want to be able to spend more time with her. You know she isn't going to be around forever."

I made it very clear that I didn't want to move back to New Jersey. I came up with all the reasons why I didn't want to move and Lorena had a rebuttal and/or response for each of them.

"If you really cared about Justin and want to be a good father to him, then you would go with us. I don't want Justin to have to grow up without his father. Do you want Justin to grow up without his father? I want Justin to get to know both sides of our families."

During another discussion, Lorena suggested that we go through with the divorce and then in two years get married again. How strange is that? I told her that she must be crazy if she thought I would agree to do that. What would be the point? It made no sense and seemed like a very strange idea. I told her that if we got a divorce then that was it for me. Forget about getting married again.

Another time, Lorena suggested that we stay married but go through a process called a "legal separation." I had never heard the term before. I asked my attorney about it and he was totally against it.

Then Lorena wanted to give marriage counseling another try to help resolve our problems. This time we agreed to see a man. We met in his office. The first thing out of Lorena's mouth was, "I don't feel loved."

As usual I was shocked. Imagine that—Lorena saying that she didn't feel loved. After all she hadn't said one single positive thing to me in over eight months and often told me how much she hated me. Yet she could set her lips and utter the words, "I don't feel loved." Go figure.

I had reactions to some of her statements. The trouble was she couldn't handle the truth. Lorena was extremely upset and visibly shaken after the session. Challenging Lorena's version of reality in front of a third party was something she just couldn't handle. We never went back.

Lorena knew I was very concerned about her mental state and concerned that she might flip out and hurt Justin. So she called my work number at Jackson National Life and told me that she was going to call me each morning and report that Justin was okay. Lorena was making a subtle threat that she knew would worry me when she also told me that if for any reason she didn't call me, I needed to be concerned about the welfare of my son.

Lorena was such a jealous person. When I told her that Justin was saying "Dadda" she got extremely upset. Little did she know that it is a lot easier for babies learning to talk to say the letter "D" compared to the letter "M" for Mama.

After several weeks I made the heartbreaking decision that in order to save my marriage or at least be close to my son I would be willing to leave an area that I loved and move back to New Jersey.

Lorena started going through stuff in the garage and throwing away things that she thought she wouldn't need or want to take back to New Jersey. The problem was she wasn't only throwing away her personal items, but had started throwing away mine, too. Memorial Day was that Monday so I suggested we have a cookout on our gas grill. When I went over to the house I got extremely upset that many of my personal items had been thrown away.

We got into a big argument and I told Lorena that she needed to be on medication for all of her bizarre antics. I was standing in the garage when I made that statement. Lorena approached me carrying Justin in one arm and raised her other hand as if she was going to strike me. I just stood there and looked at her as if to say I know that you aren't about ready to hit me again.

Sure enough, she slapped me as hard as she could right in the face. I just glared at her and didn't say a word. As I stood there she raised her hand and struck me again on the side of my face.

I told her that I was going to call the police, and that she was going to be arrested and go back to jail again. Lorena knew she was wrong. She begged and pleaded with me not to call the police on her.

She said, "If you call the police on me and I am arrested, I'll lose my securities license. Please don't call the police."

I was so upset. I thought the very nerve of this woman to slap me in the face. One of the reasons I hadn't reacted was because we were standing in the garage and she was holding Justin. If I had done something to Lorena, she could have dropped him on his head. I didn't want to take that risk.

I didn't call the police that day. It would prove to be one of the biggest mistakes of my life.

I had applied for a job at TIARRA in the summer of 1999 before going to Jackson National Life. After receiving my resume, I was told that a husband and wife couldn't work in the same department. We would have been classified as in the same department but I would have been taking incoming calls in a phone center. Lorena would meet clients and have one-on-one sessions. We would have had different jobs, but TIARRA classified them both as under the umbrella of the Counseling Department.

Lorena made a few calls to the TIARRA home office in New York City. She found out the same policy didn't apply to the New York office. I applied for a telephone counseling phone center position through their Human Resources in NYC.

During her visit to New Jersey, Lorena had taken a day and visited those TIARRA offices. They were located in mid-Manhattan. She wasn't all that impressed with the city, but she was bound and determined to move back East. She told me several times that she didn't want to have to go through the extensive training program with another company.

Lorena had had several jobs in the financial services industry and each was like starting all over again. The training program at TIARRA was very intense and lasted about three months. She asked for and was given permission to transfer to the New York office.

My first step in coming onboard with TIARRA was a telephone interview with a woman in New York City. She liked what she heard. I was then scheduled to be interviewed by a man in Denver who was in charge of the call center.

My personal interview went very well. I was tendered an offer and asked if I could be in New York City in about two weeks. I told the woman in New York that it was impossible for me to pack and move to that part of the country in less than three weeks.

The training class was to start on June 12. I was hired by the New York office with the stipulation that I would train in Denver, and then transfer to New York. The training class in both cities would start on the same day.

An official offer sheet was faxed to me at the office at Jackson National Life. I had to sign it and then fax it back to New York City. I really liked my job at Jackson National Life. I especially liked a lot of the people that I worked with and it was very hard for me to resign.

I would receive a $10,000 increase in my salary for going over to TIARRA. Deep down inside I didn't want to change jobs, nor did I want to move back East. But for the sake of my family and trying to maintain a relationship with my son, I'd decided to do it.

As far as the relationship with Lorena went, there were just too many issues and wounds to heal. I knew it would never be the relationship I wanted. My focus was on trying to be the best father I could for Justin, even if it meant going back to New Jersey.

During our separation, Lorena had called me and said that my dog Kato had been laying around and was obviously in a lot of pain with his hips. I knew I'd have to put him down. I didn't want to see him suffer anymore.

I came back to the house on a Saturday afternoon and picked him up and took him over to a veterinarian's office. I fought back the tears because I knew that I'd never see him again. Kato was fourteen years old at the time. He'd had problems with his hips for years but he'd lived to be a grand old dog.

Sydney, my other dog at that time, was about sixteen years old. About a month after I put Kato down, Lorena called and said that Sydney had somehow disappeared. I asked her permission to come home and spend the night just in case Sydney showed up in the middle of the night. Lorena refused. In looking back now, I honestly believe that Lorena let Sydney out on purpose and then lied to cover it up.

In the meantime, our two attorneys went back and forth on many of the settlement issues. Lorena had come up with another outlandish proposal. She wanted to get divorced and continue to live together in New Jersey as if we were one big happy family.

Lorena agreed to drop the divorce suit only two days before it was going to be final. I'm sure she knew that if she didn't, I wasn't going to move back to New Jersey.

I'm now also sure that her attorney told her that the judge wasn't going to allow her to take my son and move out of the state of Colorado. After she dropped the divorce, I asked Lorena permission to move back into our home. She refused. How in the world did she expect us to try and work this thing out if she refused to live with me?

Lorena said that she didn't want to live together until we were in New Jersey. I thought this was ludicrous. I told her that I wasn't willing to move back to New Jersey and live with her unless we made the effort in Colorado first. Then she came up with a proposal that I could "transition" back into our home.

Lorena said I could stay overnight on Tuesdays and Thursdays, but she didn't want me there two nights in a row. I told her that she was ridiculous, and that I wasn't willing to be going back and forth to Richard's apartment. I was either going to move back in for good or not at all. She never changed her mind, and so I never lived in our home in Northglenn again.

When I told my mom that Lorena refused to let me move back into the house she said, "There's no way that you should move back to New Jersey and expect to live with her if she won't let you live in that house in Colorado."

Like many before me, I should have listened to my mom.

Lorena had also asked me to contact the ministers at New Hope Baptist Church where I attended in order to have Justin be a part of a baby dedication ceremony.

I approached Rev. Katherine Farley after service one day. I was sure that there was no way I was going to stand up in front of the church and profess my honor to be the best father possible and to raise my son in a good Christian home, when the two of us couldn't even get along and weren't living in the same household. Lorena was a hypocrite to want to go through with the ceremony.

Lorena refused to even attend church. I'd carry Justin to church every Sunday. I'm sure some of the women wondered who was this man bringing his cute little son to church alone. It had to be a very unusual sight.

I continued to pick Justin up every week from the daycare center on Wednesday afternoons and from the house on Sunday mornings. Although our time together was limited, we were still enjoying each other. I was looking forward to when he would be a toddler and we could play ball.

Justin, like all babies, was at the stage where everything he picked up went into his mouth. One Sunday afternoon during a visit with me at Richard's place he picked up and put a rock in his mouth. Luckily I caught it in time before he could choke. It really gave me a scare.

During the time that Lorena was packing and deciding what to keep and take back to New Jersey, she threw numerous good items into the trash. There were many things that Justin had outgrown. Instead of taking them down to the Salvation Army store and giving them away, she just threw them into the trash can. It was such a shame and a waste of precious articles.

Lorena even threw good tools away. There were wrenches, saws, levels—you name it. I even had a lawn chair that an ex-girlfriend had given to me for a birthday present years before. Lorena was aware of where it had come from and wasted no time throwing it away when I was no longer living in the house. Every time I went back over to the house, something of mine that I wanted to keep turned up missing because she had thrown it in the trash.

I started to work for TIARRA in early June. Lorena had already been given permission to leave Denver and transfer to the New York City office. She would only work for three more weeks in Denver while I was in training.

We had very little contact while at work. I kept my distance from her. We only met for lunch one time and as usual she got upset and acted out. It just wasn't worth the hassle of trying to deal with her. The slightest little thing would get her all bent out of shape.

I was astounded at the rapport that she maintained with her fellow employees and co-workers. They all thought the world of her. They spoke very highly of her. She was so good at charming those around her that she wanted to impress. I couldn't figure out how she managed it.

One time, Lorena came over to my desk and asked me when I was going to come over and mow the lawn. I only mowed the lawn out of the goodness of my heart. Deep down inside I had no desire to cut the lawn after I was no longer living there. She left with her usual comment. "You don't care about me and Justin. All you care about is yourself."

My thoughts were, you certainly don't care about me since you had me court ordered out of my own home.

My birthday in June came and went. We were separated and still planning to move to New Jersey. I thought Lorena would at least go out of her way to wish me a Happy Birthday, especially since she'd neglected to do so in 1999. You'd think I would have learned what to expect by then.

Once I went to talk to Lorena at her desk. Right away, I noticed the little blue fan that I'd had on my own desk in my office at home was now perched on hers. I didn't even say a word to her about it.

We had had problems with our sprinkler system. Lorena asked if I would take off work early on a Friday afternoon in order to be at the house so a repairman could come by and work on it. Like a fool I agreed. It wasn't okay for me to live there, but it was perfectly okay for me to come over and see that things got fixed whenever it was an inconvenience to her.

The cable wires to fix the sprinkler system had to be run over the roof. Because I wasn't around, Lorena had to go up on the roof and do the best that she could. Again she asked me to come over and fix the cables. While I was there she made a comment, "Anyone else wouldn't want to have their wife up on that dangerous roof on a hot day trying to mess with those cables."

Lorena put our house on the market. I figured it wouldn't take long to sell. After we had moved there in September of 1998, people (probably realtors) were always stopping by and taking pictures of our home. It was one of the nicest in the neighborhood.

The house sold quickly. Since my name wasn't on the house, I wasn't at the closing.

At the end of June, Lorena and Justin went back East to meet with a realtor and find a place to live. We didn't even travel together. We made plans to meet on the New Jersey Turnpike. We missed our connections and Lorena went on to an area in Union County to look at a few places.

She had done a lot of leg work on the Internet in order to narrow down the search. Lorena had taken into account the accessibility to the train station from which we would commute to mid-Manhattan. Also we had to consider daycare and the quality of the facilities for Justin.

Lorena had met with a realtor on a Sunday. I joined them on a Monday and spent the entire day looking at homes. We narrowed it down to a home in Rahway. At the end of the day

Lorena got upset for some unknown reason and started yelling at me again.

We spent that night at her brother's home in Pemberton, New Jersey. As we slept Lorena woke me up with another one of her bizarre escapades of kicking the bed, punching the pillow and screaming in the middle of the night. I was convinced that it happened often and that I had nothing to do with it. She was a very troubled human being.

The next morning I drove back to my mom's house in Woodstown then flew back to Colorado the next day. The Greeley Stampede was in progress and I remember some guy at the airport parking lot making a smart comment to me about my cowboy hat.

He said, "If you go up to the Greeley Stampede with that hat on they'll let you in for free." Then he started laughing to the group he was traveling with. Irritated, I pulled out my PRCA Gold Card and told him that the reason that I could get in to the rodeo for free was because I had earned the privilege.

Lorena had about three weeks to pack up things and get ready to move. She insisted that she wasn't going to pack any of my things and wanted me to come over after work and help her. Every time that I stopped by there, more of my personal items had disappeared.

The day before the movers showed up, we both stayed up all night packing. We knew ahead of time that we wouldn't be able to take any plants on the trip. I had had some plants for over twenty years, since my college days. I hated to get rid them.

When my father died in February 1998, people had given the family a lot of houseplants. When it was time to leave, all of us children decided to take one home as a memory of my dad. It really hurt me now to just give it away or leave it out in the sun as Lorena had done with her plants. Remember, those were the same plants that had been so important to her that I was watering them in a rest stop when I moved her to Colorado in August 1997.

Because I would be driving back to New Jersey, Lorena

had me take a few of her smaller plants over to Richard's and asked me to bring them with me when I made the cross-country trip. I ended up giving a lot of my plants to my friends. I also gave away an expensive western print to someone else along with lariats, brand new filing cabinets, a freezer, a washer and a dryer.

Lorena didn't want me to keep my little Nissan pickup truck, either. I didn't want to sell it. My brother Reuben didn't have a vehicle so I told him that if he flew out to Colorado, he could use it. He brought his wife out and they drove it back.

Lorena didn't want me to take some of my furniture to New Jersey. For some unknown reason she wanted me to leave behind two dressers, some tables, a couple of chairs and a big old desk. Her reason was that she felt I should get rid of the old and upgrade to some new stuff.

I was okay with my older furniture. I asked her if I got rid of the old stuff, was she willing to help me buy some new stuff since it was her idea. Of course she blew up.

In the end, I agreed to leave behind my dressers, knowing it would mean that I wouldn't have a place to put my clothes once we got to New Jersey. But as long as there was no inconvenience to Lorena, she didn't really care.

I refused to leave my big desk behind though. Lorena finally gave in on that issue. When the movers were taking out my desk Lorena commented, "Gosh, Abe, your desk is so dusty. It looks like you haven't dusted it off in awhile."

We worked all day Friday and into the early evening getting our things out of the house and garage. At the end of the day, I took Justin and went over to Richard's for the night. Lorena wanted to do some more cleaning and opted to come over later.

She was going to fly into Philadelphia on Sunday afternoon. We spent all day Saturday at Richard's place. Lorena had sent her car back East with a motor vehicle escort service because she didn't want to drive that far with Justin in tow.

I took her and Justin to the airport on Sunday morning.

Lorena was late as usual and in jeopardy of missing her flight. Again she was upset and very agitated and argumentative. The ticket agent assured her that she could get on the flight and let her go through a special door to speed the security process.

Lorena told me that it was fine for me to leave. I knew that she wasn't going to make the flight. Instead of leaving the airport, I simply sat at the curb and waited for my cell phone to ring. Sure enough about twenty minutes later, she called saying they had missed the flight.

On the way back to Richard's she was nasty. She told me that she was going to lie to her relatives and tell them that she wasn't traveling until Monday so they wouldn't know she'd missed her flight. She had no problems telling another lie.

Later when we were at Richard's place, Lorena was vacuuming his floor. Somehow, crawling across the cord, Justin accidentally unplugged the vacuum cleaner. Lorena screamed at him, "Justin why don't you get out of the way!" It was totally uncalled for. There was no need to be screaming at an innocent little child. He had no idea that he was going to pull the cord out of the socket. Justin was simply trying to navigate his small body around the living room.

This was another example of Lorena not being able to handle the stress in her life. That night she got upset and started yelling and screaming at me.

"Just because you're moving back East with me doesn't necessarily mean that we're going to stay together. I can just as easily file for divorce in New Jersey again."

Somewhere in the process of her yelling and screaming she also said, "You can suck your own dick!" And as usual I just stood there and took it.

At that stage of the game it seemed too late to turn back. Our home in Northglenn had been sold. What was left of my personal possessions and property were already well on their way to New Jersey. I'd always had second thoughts about going. This pretty much confirmed that it would only be a matter of time before Lorena and I were separated again. I felt more sorry for

Justin than I did myself. He was an innocent little child and had already suffered verbal abuse from his own mom. It would only get worse.

On Monday morning Richard took Justin and Lorena back out to DIA. I had to go to work. Although they were on a standby status, they were able to board the plane and head off to Philadelphia.

My training class didn't end until August 28, which was a Friday. The original plan was for me to finish training and then take my call components. These were live calls in which a seasoned veteran would listen in to make sure that we were giving the client the correct information.

The calls could be a little stressful, especially with someone sitting next to you watching and monitoring your every move. I didn't have a lot of prior computer experience, so I was very nervous.

I wasn't going to be heading to New Jersey until the middle of September. Lorena called and said that she was overwhelmed in trying to raise Justin alone. She now had about an hour commute each way to and from work.

I sympathized with her although I wished I hadn't. I didn't want to move back East, especially after the way she'd treated me in the past year since Justin was born.

Begrudgingly, I went to my supervisor and was given permission to leave immediately following my written final examination on Friday afternoon. I was told I could take the call components portion while I was in New York City. Besides, it had been a few weeks since I had seen Justin. I didn't miss being around Lorena but I sure missed my boy.

I had most of my things packed before I went to work on Friday morning. I always rode the bus to and from work, except on the days that I had my visitations with Justin.

Everyone in my training class knew I was leaving. About a week before, they had taken me out to lunch as a going away present. I really appreciated their generous concern and thoughts. I had made some friends and I knew I'd miss them. But my family was more important and I knew I needed to move on.

Richard tried to convince me to stay one more night and get a good rest before striking out. I wanted to leave and at least get to Kansas before I pulled in for the night. Normally, I probably would have just stopped at a rest stop overnight. Ever since the death of Michael Jordan's father, I had avoided staying and sleeping in the car overnight.

As I drove past the Denver Coliseum where I had ridden several times during my PRCA career, I broke down and actually started crying. They weren't just little tears, either. They were huge tears and I just couldn't control my emotions. I figured it was probably the last time I'd ever see that building. The realization that I was leaving an area that I had grown to love since August 1974 hit me like a ton of bricks. I couldn't believe that I had let Lorena talk me into moving back to New Jersey.

I stopped in Colby, Kansas and got a motel room for the night. I drove hard all the next day and spent the night with my cousin Lucille Liggins and her husband Tony on a military base just outside of St. Louis.

The next day, I made it as far as West Virginia and settled in for the night. The drive was fine. My little Saturn ran great though it had a tendency to burn oil.

I drove the rest of the way home to my mom's house in Woodstown. I arrived very late at night and put in some earplugs and slept on the couch.

I wanted to spend a little time with my family before heading to North Jersey. When I called Lorena to tell her I was in Woodstown and wasn't sure when I would be home she got upset and hung up the phone on me. Lorena didn't want me around, and then would pull a stunt like that. Her explanation was I was acting like my family in Woodstown was more important to me than she and Justin were. At least my family was happy to see me.

I was already at the house unpacking my stuff when Lorena and Justin came home. I hadn't seen Justin in over a month. Lorena acted very happy to see me and we gave each other a hug and a kiss.

Justin was so excited to see his daddy. I took him out of his car seat and lifted him over my head several times. He still couldn't talk but he could say "Dadda".

I didn't have to report to work until Wednesday morning so I spent the next day just getting acclimated to the new house and its surroundings.

On Wednesday morning we dropped Justin off at the daycare center and caught the NJ Transit train to New York City. All of the trains stopped at Penn Station which was in the basement of Madison Square Garden.

Then we got on a subway to the Lexington Avenue stop. From there we walked a few blocks to the main office at 485 Lexington Avenue. All the time I was asking myself how in the world I'd ended up in there.

I absolutely hated everything about the city. It was dirty, noisy and very crowded. Sitting at my desk, I noticed that my eyes and nose burned because of the air. Riding the subway I felt like a cow on my last ride to the slaughterhouse. The subways were so crowded in the morning rush hour and commute. I couldn't understand how anyone could possibly get used to that environment. One of the saving graces was that at least we could get away and escape back to New Jersey at the end of the day.

But even Rahway was unlike any other place I'd lived before. The sky was a constant haze and there were no clear afternoons and sunny days like I'd been used to in Wyoming and Colorado. Even the air seemed to have a constant funny odor to it. It wasn't fresh. I didn't think I'd ever get used to the humidity, either. Colorado's climate is very dry.

I didn't like anything about where I was living and working. I asked myself many times why I'd let Lorena convince me to move. Before I left, my friends had told me that I would be back, sooner or later. I told them I was going for my family and that I would only return to the wild, wild West to visit. Of course in retrospect, they obviously knew more than I did.

I also found the people to be very rude in my new surroundings. I had never before been around so many people that kept to themselves. They'd neither smile nor make eye contact. They would push you from behind and step on your feet, and wouldn't bother to say excuse me. Walking down the sidewalk, they would bump into you hard and just keep on going. I knew I'd never get used to it. After awhile I learned how to walk down the street. If someone came towards me and I was on the right side edge of the sidewalk, I would purposely ram right into them and keep on strutting. I refused to get out of their way. I simply got tired of the rudeness. This was out of character for me and looking back it was probably a manifestation of my general discontent.

I never really felt all that comfortable in that new office, either. The first week I was there I was introduced to my new supervisor. We had a team meeting and I wasn't even invited to attend. At the very least, I felt I could have met and got to know some of the other people I would be working with. I felt ostracized from the very beginning.

The only thing I liked about the New York City office was they had an in-house cafeteria. The food was very reasonably priced and was actually good with generous portions. It was cheaper and much more convenient to eat in the cafeteria than to fix and take a lunch from home. The company had a system whereby your meals could be deducted directly from your paychecks so carrying money wasn't an issue. Some people would buy both their lunch and dinner from the cafeteria.

Life at home in New Jersey wasn't much better. It hadn't taken Lorena very long to revert to her old ways. One of the first arguments we had was over my rodeo career memorabilia and newspaper articles. She discovered that I had brought a box full of them.

"Why did you have to bring that stuff from Colorado? You should've thrown it into the garbage. It's just a bunch of junk. It's not worth any money."

"I'm not throwing my rodeo stuff into the garbage."

Lorena got upset saying, "I'm your wife. My opinions should matter to you."

I loved homemade chocolate chip cookies and perfected my own recipe. I baked cookies frequently. Friends and relatives have often told me they're the best cookies they've ever tasted. They have also encouraged me to go into business and market them myself like Famous Amos.

I would usually eat one of those cookies a day. Lorena got upset at me one day and remarked, "What kind of a role model are you being for Justin by having a cookie each day?"

This baffled me. There was something wrong with eating a cookie? I wasn't overweight and didn't need to watch what I ate.

Another argument we had was over some new furniture. Lorena wanted to buy a new dining room table. One Sunday afternoon, at her request, we went to a furniture store and picked out a table. When the time came to pay for it Lorena wanted me to pay for half of it. I refused.

When we had sold our home in Northglenn Lorena had gone to the closing alone. You'll remember she had managed to have that house only in her name because at the time I was in commission sales and it was easier (so she'd said) for her to qualify for the loan on her own. She had received a very large sum of money ($24,000—which I didn't find out until 2004) for the sale but refused to disclose the amount of that check to me. I told her to buy the new table with the proceeds from the house money.

To this she responded, "I'm not going to tell you how much the check was for, and I'll never tell you how much the check was for. You can just forget it."

I said, "That right there is part of the reason that you and I don't get along."

She refused to listen to my reasoning that legally half of that money was mine. We were supposed to be living and acting as a family and she was withholding money that was our money and not just her money. We left the store and she yelled and screamed at me on the ride home.

On another occasion, she was downstairs and we got into an altercation. There were just words exchanged. For no apparent reason she ran over to the window and jerked the curtains off down, mangled the hanging rods and threw them onto the floor. I watched her in utter amazement.

Lorena was also having problems with Justin. He didn't respect her authority and was giving her fits. Right off the bat she told me that Justin never slept through the entire night until I showed up in Rahway. Once I was there, he slept soundly. I really don't know the reason why. My guess would be that Justin wasn't totally comfortable around Lorena because of her erratic behavior and her yelling and screaming fits at night.

Lorena started complaining that she needed more help with Justin. She said that the mornings were the most critical times. In order to help her out, I started getting out of bed earlier in the mornings. She was all for that.

It was all in vain. I asked what I could do to help her in the mornings, and she said "nothing." She wouldn't let me help with Justin. It was impossible to please her. It was "damned if you do and damned if you don't."

Lorena said Justin would pull off his socks in the mornings after she put them on. He would also kick at her when she tried to put on his shoes. He was becoming a little terror with her and she couldn't handle it.

At dinner time, she would put food into his mouth and although Justin was hungry, he would spit it back out. This really frustrated her. One time he had her in tears and she went upstairs and laid on the bed.

"You go feed him and see what he does to you," she said.

I fed him with no problems. Not only did he eat the food that I gave him, but he wanted more. Lorena hated the fact that Justin was so easy with me. It really got to her emotionally.

Bathing was also another traumatic time for Lorena. Justin loved the water. He was very cooperative until it was time to get out. Whenever she would lift him out, he would kick loose and throw a fit. This happened over and over again, and Lorena would have to spank him in order to make him quit and behave.

Finally, in frustration Lorena asked me to come up to the bathroom when it was time to take him out of the tub. She would loudly yell, "Daddy, Daddy time to get out." As long as I was standing there and Justin saw me, he never acted up.

Brushing his teeth in the morning was also another task that upset Lorena. Justin either refused to open his mouth and let Lorena brush his teeth or he would spit the toothpaste out or onto the floor.

Almost in tears she said, "You come and brush his teeth."

Again I had no problem, though this was the first time she'd allowed me to do it. He was very cooperative with me. I'd say, "Open up," and he would. I brushed his teeth as if I'd done it many times before, when in fact Lorena had kept me away from my son as much as possible, insisting on doing everything herself.

She was extremely jealous of the way that Justin acted with me. On the weekends Justin and I played in the backyard or else we took walks together. Sometimes we would play basketball on the backyard patio. I would use a trash can and have Justin drop a ball into it. Every time, I would clap my hands and say, "Yea," as if he had just scored a basket. Justin quickly got the hang of it, and would clap his hands as if he were shooting a long range three point shot at the buzzer.

Spending time with my son was so important to both me and Justin. Watching him grow and change was amazing. I was so proud of him and couldn't help wishing that we weren't caught up in the web of his mother's volatile behavior.

Lorena was so over-protective of the little guy. She was always complaining that I played too rough with him, but I was careful and never once did I make Justin cry from romping around on the floor with him.

Lorena would take Justin to the daycare center because I had to be at work at 8:00 a.m. I caught the train at around 6:30 a.m.

in the morning. It was about an hour and fifteen minute commute from our house to work.

I would pick Justin up from the daycare center after work at 5:30 p.m. Lorena complained that she didn't like Justin staying at the daycare center so long each day. He was one of the first children there in the morning and then one of the last ones to leave.

She insisted that I ask my supervisor to put me on a later shift at work. I thought it was a ridiculous request and so I never bothered, although I had to constantly hear about it from her. She also suggested that I get rid of my car, even though it was already paid for.

"We can live just fine with only one car. Then we can both pay for my car." When I resisted she said, "Every time I come up with an idea for the good of the family, you are totally opposed to it."

I thought the suggestion was ludicrous. We worked different shifts and left the house and returned at different times each day. What would I do with no car? The fact that I wouldn't have a car would also severely limit my options to return to the West. Lorena knew exactly what she was doing.

I look back now and suspect she had plans to end our relationship and leave me with absolutely nothing, including transportation. She seemed to be working toward that goal as she methodically disposed of everything from my original house in Ft. Collins to my truck, my dogs, plants, furniture and many personal momentos. And she did it so skillfully that it was years before I could see the overall picture of what I'd let her get away with.

Justin was sick on a couple of days. Lorena insisted her job was too important to miss a day of work. So I was the one who called in sick. Another time the daycare called Lorena and said Justin was sick and to come and get him. Lorena came to my desk and insisted that I ask to leave work early and take him to the hospital.

I stepped up to the plate, doing things that most husbands

wouldn't think about doing. Lorena hated to go grocery shopping. We'd usually go on Sunday afternoons. I decided to help take the pressure off of her. I'd do all of the grocery shopping. Lorena would make up a list and I'd go to the store alone.

Before that, when we shopped together, we'd go into the store and she'd start making comments about all the shoppers. It was as if she hated to be around other people. She'd make the same kind of comments whenever we traveled in or out of airports.

In order to try and save some money, Lorena convinced me to switch to all generic cereals because they were much cheaper than the name brands I liked. There were some cereals that she liked, but of course she refused to switch, saying that the generic cereals just didn't taste quite the same. So there wouldn't be another argument, I made the switch. Lorena never did.

I also did all of the dishes. I'd cook on occasions, but Lorena did most of the cooking. Once she got upset at me and threw the yellow gloves that I used to wash dishes into the garbage. Throwing things in the trash seemed to represent her disdain for the object she was disposing of and more importantly, for whatever or whomever was connected to it. When I asked her what happened to my gloves she told me she didn't know. I looked everywhere for them. I should have known to look into the trash first, because that is exactly where I found them.

One morning we got into another argument. I was on the main floor and Lorena was upstairs. She came downstairs swinging a metal hanger at me. I took it away from her.

Another morning I was upstairs and she was on the main floor. There was a nice pottery bowl that she had on her piano. In her emotional state she grabbed it and hurled it upstairs against one of the walls. It shattered with a loud clang-a-lang-a-lang.

During another morning argument she got upset when I was eating a bowl of rice chex cereal. She ran over to the table, and before I realized what she was doing, she grabbed my bowl and ran into the kitchen and dumped the contents into the sink.

I got up from the table and never said a single word. There

were many times that I just didn't want to deal with her wild behavior. I fixed myself another bowl of cereal and started eating my breakfast again.

A few minutes later, Lorena came back downstairs and dumped that bowl into the sink as well. Again I didn't say anything to her. I fixed myself yet another bowl of cereal and went downstairs to the third level of our home and ate my breakfast sitting at my desk. To this day I don't understand if she did these things to start a fight or to try to force me to get violent with her. It never made any sense to me.

During another stupid argument in the morning she berated me as being ugly and stupid. She also told me, "The only reason I married you was because I was lonely. I never loved you. I loved Samuel, but I never loved you. The only reason that Harriet loved you was because you have a big dick."

Harriet was the woman with whom I'd had a long term relationship before I met Lorena.

"You're ugly. You look just like a monkey. You smell like a monkey. So from now on your name will be Monkey. I'll just refer to you as Monkey in the future."

It was just one argument and fight after another, none of them based on anything. She seemed to pick something out of thin air and make an issue of it. One Sunday morning Lorena was upset again. She came at me swinging and punching at me. I blocked every one of them, at the same time telling her that I had warned her about putting her hands on me.

I grabbed her and threw her on the couch in order to try and calm her down. She acted like a dog with rabies. Her eyes were wild and huge. She was trying to do anything possible to get at me. Lorena dug her fingernails into my hands and wrists. I still have the scars.

Then she grabbed the silver necklace that my brother Reuben had given me at Christmas in 1996. Once she had a solid hold on that, I knew she was going to rip it off of my neck. I gave in and came to her to prevent this. I ended up laying on her with my chest and then she bit me and I don't mean just a nip.

A few days later when the scars were healing and were very visible, I went outside in broad daylight with my shirt off and used my VHS movie camera to film my chest and hands.

I had a trunk in the basement with a lock on it. I'd put the lock on before the movers picked it up in Colorado. It had some money and an old coin collection that I'd had since I was a young kid. I had lost interest in collecting coins but still kept them. I figured I'd pass it on to Justin someday. I stashed the VHS tape in that locker, just in case I ever needed some evidence.

Lorena often made remarks about the lock on that trunk. Was it locked because there were things in there that I didn't want her to see? As if I didn't have plenty of reasons not to trust her.

Another major altercation occurred on a Sunday morning. We had a verbal disagreement. She got upset and went down to the third level of our house.

I heard things being thrown around and headed down to investigate. As I was coming down the steps, she ran over to a clock radio that my mom had given me while I was still in college. It sat on top of the television. Lorena jerked the cord out of the wall, hurled it across the room and hit me right in the shin. I really didn't see it coming until it was too late.

Then she grabbed a cordless telephone and threw that across the room, hitting me with it. She was on a rampage.

Then she said, "Go back upstairs. Go back upstairs. Unless you go back upstairs I'm going to stay down here and break up all of your stupid stuff."

Next she grabbed one of the bookcases and slung it over, spilling the books out across the floor. Then she ran over to my desk and with one sweeping motion knocked off as many things as she could.

She was still ranting and raving and acting like a woman possessed. Then Justin came to the top of the stairs and she picked him up so he wouldn't tumble down them. Even with Justin in her one arm, she was still trying to inflict as much damage as possible.

I had finally seen enough. I grabbed her and wrestled her to the floor, at the same time making sure that Justin didn't get dropped in the process.

I held her down and told her that I wasn't going to let her up until she cooled off.

She tried to get up and finally said, "Okay let me up. I promise I won't break up any more of your stupid stuff."

That wasn't good enough for me and I said, "I'm not going to let you up until you say, 'I'm not going to break up any more of your stuff, not your *stupid* stuff'."

Lorena finally gave in and said, "Okay I'm not going to break up any more of your stuff."

Then I let her up.

This was the last straw for me in a situation that had never been right. I told her that I was going to pack my things and go back to Colorado. "It's impossible to live with you. I really don't know why I took the risk and tried to work things out. If it wasn't for Justin, I wouldn't have done it."

"Go on back to Colorado. I can tell you right now that I'm not going to try to talk you out of it or try to get you to stay here. I'm going to file for divorce and when I do I'm going to go to court and lie to the judge and say that you stole my jewelry box and all of my jewelry. I'm going to lie to the judge and say anything that I can in order to bring you down!"

She took a walk down the street so she could cool off.

The room was in shambles. I vowed not to pick up a single item from the violent whirlwind. Later on that day Lorena went back downstairs and cleaned up.

At one point, the alarm clock that Lorena used on her nightstand quit working. I let her use mine, but told her she would have to wake me up, because she always got up before I did.

She was always upset with me so she took it upon herself to get back at me one morning. Instead of just pushing me lightly and waking me up, she came in and started hitting me saying to wake up.

I hated being startled awake at 5:30 a.m. I reached out and tried to grab her. Lorena jumped out of the way and flipped out. She ran out of the bedroom. Then as I was getting out of bed, she ran back into the room and bull rushed me.

We tussled around and fell onto the floor with the blanket still wrapped around me. She started yelling out of the bedroom for the neighbors to call the police.

I let her up and went on about my business of getting ready for work.

Of course she yelled and screamed and ranted and raved. Lorena reached into her jewelry box and took something out. She ran into the bathroom saying, "I'm going to flush my wedding ring down the toilet." She slammed the door and flushed the toilet.

After this incident, I took my wedding band off and didn't bother to wear it for a while. A few weeks later my cousin, David Walker, got married and we were invited to his dinner and reception. Lorena wore her wedding ring. I didn't even comment. I just acted like she had been wearing it all along.

Lorena took a company sponsored trip to Boston to conduct one-on-one counseling sessions with a few professors. It was an overnight trip during the week. After she returned she divulged to me that she had met some guy during her stay in Boston.

I never suspected that Lorena would cheat on me. At the time I really didn't care about any of her outside infidelities. I didn't even ask any questions concerning what else happened after she met this stranger in Boston. I had no idea why she'd felt so compelled to confess this to me.

Things at work weren't going well for me. I failed to pass my call components. Kenneth, my supervisor, called me into his office and gave me a few options. He said I could choose to take them over again, or else choose to be demoted to the ATS Unit.

Kenneth said if I took them over again and didn't pass,

then I would automatically be terminated from the company. I told him it was personal and that I hadn't moved all the way from Colorado just to be terminated.

A couple of weeks later, I took them over and failed again. I wasn't terminated, but was demoted to the ATS Unit. I was told that I would have to stay there for at least a year before I could try to go back as a telephone counselor.

I was devastated. I probably got a little foggy, but I wasn't going to cry about it. I had way too much pride to cry over that job. It didn't mean that much to me. I'd always felt out of place working in a phone center environment and sitting in a little cubicle. I was a people person and needed to be out among them. I was more cut out for sales than giving out information over the telephone. At times I also felt a little inferior. I wasn't a computer genius and often had difficulty navigating the systems, but, I always possessed great communication skills.

Other than spending time with Justin, there was absolutely nothing that I liked about living in North Jersey and working in New York City.

I certainly hated living with Lorena. She constantly complained and was verbally and physically abusive. In the mornings I told her she looked nice in her business attire. She never complimented me on anything. It was just one fight after another.

She often told me how stupid or ugly I was. She also told me that all I had amounted to during my professional bull riding career was a "rodeo bum."

Consequently, when I told Lorena that I had been demoted she got extremely upset. Getting demoted meant I would have a major cut in my salary. All during my trials at work, she certainly didn't help with her constant bickering at home.

Lorena said that it was going to put more pressure on her to pick up more of the household bills. I totally disagreed. Even with the pay cut, I was still going to be able to pay my half of the bills with no problem.

"You always depend on me to take up the slack," she accused.

Lorena earned about $25,000 a year more than I did. I think she liked the fact that she earned more. It made her feel superior and in control of our financial picture. And she'd always had this obsession about me inheriting her nest egg. It was never "our" nest egg, always *hers*. She felt she had earned it over the years before we ever met, and didn't want to pass away and leave it all to me. The fact that if she died I would be raising Justin alone and he would benefit from that money didn't seem to be part of this particular argument. Lorena mentioned that her sister-in-law had told her I just wanted to be with Lorena to hold on to that so-called "gravy train."

On Friday morning December 8, 2000 Lorena came to my cubicle at work and said she had been involved in an automobile accident. She had been hit by a large trash truck owned by the city. Her car had received some severe damage, but luckily, she was fine. Justin hadn't been in the car. She had already dropped him off at the daycare center and was on her way to the train station when it happened.

Lorena said the worst part of the accident was the airbag inflating and hitting her in the face. She said it stung like crazy. She told me we would have to ride home together because her car was going to be in the shop for a few days.

She insisted that she could drive my car and asked to drive it to an eye doctor's appointment on Monday. She had never driven a stick shift. I told her that it was a lot harder than it looked, but she insisted. So before I gave her the keys to my car, we went to an empty school parking lot to practice.

Lorena was horrible. She insisted that I allow her to drive us back home. She kept stalling because she was letting out the clutch too fast.

We stalled at an intersection and she got all flustered. I jumped out of the car in traffic and ran around to the driver's side and took us home. Only then was she finally convinced that she couldn't drive my car, though she still insisted that if she hadn't panicked, she would've been okay.

One Saturday night Lorena was down in the basement looking for the Christmas decorations. She came upstairs a little miffed saying, "I can't find a lot of our Christmas decorations."

I knew it was a deliberate ploy. I responded, "Of course you can't find them. I don't even know why you're pretending to look. You know good and well that you threw them away in Colorado, right before we moved." Man did she get upset when I said that! It was true and she knew it. Lorena was probably upset that I had the audacity to challenge her. I was tired of playing her silly little games.

Lorena went into another one of her rages shouting, "Eat my shit!"

It was typical.

Later on that night when we were lying in bed, Lorena informed me that she was going to purchase another bed and move into the spare bedroom upstairs. She said she was no longer interested in being intimate and having sex with me. She was going to start sleeping alone, so I wouldn't be bothering her.

The truth was, she was still having sleeping fits during the night. It seemed like about every two weeks she would wake me up in the middle of the night screaming and kicking the bed. I believe that she wasn't willing to deal with whatever that was about, or even willing to talk to me about it, and that was the real reason she wanted to sleep alone.

Then she said, "You're probably disappointed I didn't get killed in that car accident."

I thought it was a horrible thing to say. It didn't seem to bother her, because she had opened her mouth as usual and just blurted it out.

Then she said, "I'm going to file for divorce again. I got myself into this mess, and so it's up to me to get myself out of it.

It's just a matter of time before we'll be divorced. Tick tock, the clock is ticking."

The next day was simply a carryover from the previous one. Lorena was absolutely nasty and unbearable the entire day. We argued throughout the day. I reminded her that she had thrown away many of our personal possessions and she got even angrier.

At one point she'd had enough and went outside and started smoking her cigarettes again. At least she didn't want to smoke in front of Justin.

Another time she was downstairs looking through our things. Many of them were still packed in boxes and sitting on the basement floor. We hadn't yet taken the time to sit down and go through them.

I was upstairs sitting on the couch with Justin in my lap watching an NFL football game. I could hear her going through boxes downstairs. I got off the couch and yelled into the heating vent that, "I don't know why you're downstairs pretending to look for something that you already know isn't here."

She yelled back, "I wish you would stop yelling, the neighbors are going to hear you." I knew the neighbors couldn't hear me if I was talking to her via the vent and with all the doors and windows closed.

Later, I was sitting at the table and munching on some leftover pizza for lunch. I told her that I knew about her past history of tearing up the house the first day home from her honeymoon with Samuel. I also told her I knew about that eight-page letter that Samuel had written to her mom. I told her she obviously had problems and needed to seek out professional help and get back on some medication so she wasn't in this constant state of agitation. At that point Lorena went off of the deep end again. She leaped out of her chair at the other end of the table and ran toward me.

Lorena swung her arm and in the process purposely knocked over the glass of punch that was sitting on the table. The grape punch splashed all over me and Justin, who was sitting in my lap. Justin was as surprised as I was and we both just looked at her. Then, Lorena grabbed the gallon container and went in the kitchen and dumped the remainder into the sink.

I changed Justin's stained and wet clothes and my own. There was just no way to deal with her when she was like that.

I decided to do the grocery shopping on that Sunday afternoon. Lorena refused to write out a list and give it to me. When I asked her to give me the checkbook, she got upset and threw it and hit me with it.

Later that evening, we were in the kitchen. She had thawed out some hamburger and I figured it was for our dinner. She was going to fry it and I asked what she was cooking. Lorena really got upset saying, "This hamburger is for Justin." She was starting to mix more solid foods in with his baby food then.

"Well you don't have to get so bent out of shape. All I did was ask you a simple question. What do you expect from me? I'm not some kind of a mind reader."

Then Lorena shocked the heck out of me. She picked up the frying pan with both hands and violently slammed it into the counter top. It left a huge dent in the side of the frying pan. I was speechless. She took another frying pan out and threw the dented one into the trash. I took it out later just in case I needed to use it for evidence to show how violent she could be.

I also said, "This is one of the major reasons that you and I don't get along. You try to hold and keep important information from me."

There were some razor blades on Lorena's dresser that were being used to scrape stuff off of walls around the house. Lorena ran into the bedroom and grabbed them shouting, "I'm gonna get my razor blades," hinting she would hurt herself, which was a common threat. With that she went into the bathroom and locked the door for about fifteen minutes. I guess when she figured out that I wasn't going to do anything to try and stop her, she came back out. I wasn't going to buy into the escapade. It was just one more bid for attention that couldn't be satisfied.

Because Lorena still didn't have a vehicle, we decided to carpool to work the next morning. She was going to leave work early to rent a car to use until hers was repaired. She had an eye doctor's appointment the following afternoon. During one of previous exams the eye doctor had told her that she was showing signs of glaucoma.

That night we got into another argument. I asked her again about the amount of the check she'd received for selling our home in Colorado. Again she told me that I might as well forget it because I was never going to find out. I told her that it was a big family financial matter.

Lorena reiterated her plans to get a divorce and also to begin sleeping in the spare bedroom. I asked myself over and over why I had made the trip to New Jersey.

The next day was Monday December 11, 2000. Lorena was bitter and nasty again first thing in the morning. There were several mornings that I would say "good morning" to her or else tell her how nice she looked and she'd completely ignore me.

I had taken my shower and was eating my breakfast at the table. Lorena went downstairs and when she walked by I just casually looked at her.

She saw me looking at her and screamed at me, "Don't you look at me!" She kept going. I hadn't said a single word to her. Then as she was walking upstairs she said, "You can eat out of my ass!" I thought this was an over reaction on her part, especially since I hadn't even said anything to her all morning.

I calmly finished eating my breakfast and then I went upstairs. She was in the bathroom. I stood well outside the bathroom door and told her, "There's no reason for you to be so nasty and hateful first thing in the morning. I haven't said anything to you at all, much less anything to warrant that kind of language."

She said, "So what are you going to do about it? What are you going to do about it?" Lorena came out of the bathroom and charged into me, pushing me and slamming me hard up against the wall in the hallway.

I was shocked and the move caught me off guard. I certainly wasn't going to stand by and have her push me around. I had told her several times to keep her hands off of me, but obviously those words meant nothing to her.

In order to protect myself, I grabbed both of her wrists and pushed her into the bedroom and onto the bed to try and calm her down. She went berserk kicking at me.

Lorena was flailing around on top of the bed and going crazy. All I was trying to do was stay out of the way of her feet and calm her down. She rolled around and kicked at the lamp that was on my nightstand. It hit the floor and shattered.

By then the bed was all torn up. The sheets and the mattresses were in disarray. I was determined to hold on until she quit. She was still yelling and screaming and thrashing around like a fish. I never said a word during the entire event. My biggest concern was that she didn't kick me. Eventually, we both fell onto the floor.

The bed had been pushed over exposing the bent up frying pan that I'd hidden the night before. Finally, I decided to release my grip on Lorena's wrists and let her up.

As I got up and started to leave the room, she reached and grabbed that frying pan. I knew that she was going to throw it at me. I ran back at her just as she was cocking her arm, and snatched it out of her hand.

In her disgust and rage she ran over to her dresser and lifted her wooden jewelry box up over her head. It was reminiscent of Shaquille O' Neal going in for a thunderous dunk shot. Lorena violently slammed the jewelry box down onto her dresser. It shattered and her jewelry scattered all over the bedroom. I reached down to pick up a few items.

Lorena screamed at me, "Don't you touch any of my stuff!"

So I stopped. As I walked out of the bedroom, I accidentally stepped on my full length mirror that had fallen onto the floor. I didn't see it and it was too late.

Then Lorena said, "See what you did? You broke your own mirror."

I took the frying pan and left the room. We didn't have time to try to clean up anything and we both needed to get out the door to work. Lorena came downstairs and sat on the couch.

She said that if we were going to get to work on time that we would need to hurry up and get ready. Then she asked me to go upstairs and get Justin out of the bed.

As I was going back upstairs she told me to, "Shut up," even though at that moment I wasn't saying anything.

I told her, "No." She kept insisting that I had better not say another word to her. I refused and kept on talking.

Then she said, "Now I'm going to call the police on you. You go on to work by yourself. You better leave so you aren't late. I'll come on later."

This made no sense since her car was in the shop but I was too angry to think about it. I left. I honestly didn't believe that she would call the police on me, especially after all she had done to me, and then begged me not to call the police on her.

"Just as soon as you walk out of the door, I'm going to call the police."

Eventually, I got myself together and left for work. I went downstairs and hid that frying pan in my green rodeo equipment bag that was in my walk-in closet. I should've taken it and put it in the trunk of my car.

I really didn't think much about Lorena's threats, although I didn't trust her. I didn't feel as if I'd done anything wrong, much less anything that warranted calling the police. In retrospect, I realized that I should've called the police on her. She was the one who had stormed out of the bathroom and rammed me into the wall, precipitating the whole thing.

I went on to work. Usually I went straight to the daycare and picked up Justin after work. I didn't know if Lorena had gotten off work early and picked him up so I went home first.

They weren't there, so I went to the daycare center. Lorena showed up while I was there and very sweetly and in a very innocent tone said to one of the staff workers, "We got our wires crossed, and so we both came to pick up Justin today."

I waited in the parking lot and followed her home. Lorena had gone to the grocery store and bought a few items.

The bedroom and the mess had all been straightened up as if nothing had ever happened. I kept my distance from Lorena and went downstairs. The only thing Lorena said to me was to ask if I had the checkbook. I gave it to her and thought nothing of it. She was unusually quiet because she expected and knew that we were going to have company later on.

At about 7:30 p.m. the doorbell rang. No one ever came to our house. Wondering who could it be at that time of the night, I looked out the window to see two Union County deputy sheriff's cruisers parked in front of our house.

Lorena let them into the house. It was only then that I realized that she had indeed called the police on me that morning. Instead of waiting for them to come downstairs, I went upstairs to see what they wanted.

They had paperwork with them and promptly informed me that Lorena had called and reported domestic violence and that she had taken out a restraining order against me. I would have to leave the house until further notice.

They gave me about fifteen minutes to grab some clothing for the rest of the work week. Lorena quickly grabbed Justin and took him upstairs to a bedroom so he wouldn't see the police escort me out of the house.

I wasn't under arrest, but I had to leave.

The police officers made me give them my key to the house. I told them my side of the story, but I'm sure at that time they didn't really care to hear it. They had a job to do and that was to get me out of the house. I went into my closet to show them the bent up frying pan that Lorena had tried to hit me with. It was gone. Lorena had gone through my stuff and found it and had disposed of it.

I didn't have a lot of options. There was a hotel close by but they wanted $80 for one night. So I chose to drive the hour and forty-five minutes to Mom's house.

The paperwork said I would have a mandatory court

appearance on Friday December 15. After the day at work, I arrived at Mom's at about 11:00 p.m. I was dog tired. I got up at about 4:30 a.m. the next morning and was back on the road for the two hour drive so I could make it to work on time.

The next day, I made some phone calls and made an appointment with an attorney in Linden, New Jersey. I told him my story over the telephone, and he recommended that I go to the courthouse first, and take out a restraining order against Lorena.

Next, I met with him and he agreed to represent me for a $1,000 retainer fee. On Thursday, December 14, Lorena celebrated her birthday by receiving paperwork from Union County stating that there was also a restraining order in place against her.

After we arrived at the courthouse the next day, I met with my attorney for a few minutes. He informed me that in the state of New Jersey if Lorena refused to drop the restraining order, then it became permanent and lifetime.

He went in and talked with her for a few minutes before we went into the courtroom. I asked him if he explained to her that the restraining order could become permanent. He said that he didn't. He approached her again to chat with her, but before he could, we were asked to come into the courtroom. I felt very uncomfortable and not at all confident in my attorney.

Lorena had lied from the very beginning. According to the paperwork that she had filed with the court, she said that I had cursed her out and started a big fight that morning. Lorena also said I had verbally threatened her with bodily harm. She said all of the right things to make me look like the bad guy. She also said that I had hit her on several other occasions in the past as well.

In court she said that I had thrown her to the floor on one occasion while she was holding Justin, and in total disregard of his health and safety. She sat there in the court room so cool, calm and collected as if she had been preparing for this moment for a long time. Lorena wasn't going to miss out on the chance to bring home the Oscar with her award winning performance.

She told the judge, "I fear for my own safety as well as that of my child."

My attorney was given a chance to cross examine Lorena. Lorena started to get frustrated trying to respond. He asked her if I had left bruises on her, why didn't she take pictures of them? Of course the truth was they never existed. I had never struck her. I hadn't even restrained her with enough force to leave any marks on her.

He asked Lorena about the jewelry box. Lorena said that it was somehow broken in the fight. I was gaining confidence in my attorney as I could see he was determined to press Lorena which would probably cause her lies to unravel.

Seeing that Lorena was starting to break down, the judge said, "Okay I'm going to put a halt to this questioning."

Just as he was about to get the truth of what was really going on in this case, he quit. It was so sad that I had paid an attorney $1,000 to help me and the judge refused to even let the man do his job.

The judge asked if there had been any other prior physical altercations in the home. I answered, "Yes." But I didn't get the chance to mention it was Lorena who was the attacker in every single one of them. I'm sure the judge naturally assumed that I was the aggressor.

The judge's response was, "The two of you can't continue to live in the same home anymore." Then the judge asked Lorena if she wanted to drop the restraining order.

Lorena's response was, "No."

"Are you aware that if you refuse to drop the restraining order then it will become permanent and lifetime. Are you sure this is what you want to do?"

Lorena again responded with a "Yes."

"I'm going to ask you again. Are you aware that the restraining order will become permanent and life time. Are you sure that this is what you want to do?"

Again Lorena's response was an unequivocal, "Yes."

So the judge asked her a third time. This time Lorena had a little more time to think about her answer. She hesitated and looked at my attorney as if she wanted to talk with him before responding. But the judge spoke up and said, "It's too late now, I've already made my decision."

Then the judge looked at me and said, "You will have to move out of the home. You'll be given about thirty minutes tonight to remove some of your things from the house. A police escort must be present. Later on you'll be allowed to remove the remainder of your property, as long as the police are present."

I asked how long before I would be allowed to get the rest of my things. The judge said it should be in about two weeks.

The next item on the agenda was for a Christmas visitation with Justin and what time I would be able to spend with him in the next few weeks. The judge came up with a plan for me to pick up Justin and then return him to Lorena at her sister's home in Carneys Point, New Jersey.

The judge court ordered both Lorena and me to attend anger management classes. I needed to attend anger management classes as much as I needed to attend Alcoholic Anonymous. In the last ten years I'd had less than ten beers. I had never had a problem with alcohol or anger in my entire life. The judge's decision felt like she was processing cattle. It gave me the impression that she didn't really care about the facts. All the judge seemed to want was to hand out a verdict and get the case off of her docket so she could move on to the next one.

The only person who needed anger management classes was Lorena and she needed a heck of a lot more than that to help straighten her out.

Another item up for discussion was the child support payments. I told the judge that I had recently been demoted and had no idea what my weekly salary was going to be because it hadn't been adjusted yet. The judge agreed to put off the child support calculation until my new salary was in place. The judge also said that since we both worked for the same company, I wasn't allowed on the sixteenth floor where Lorena worked. She gave us permission to communicate about Justin and said it could be either by e-mail or the phone as long as it pertained to concerns about Justin only.

Next, the judge questioned me about why I had obtained a restraining order against Lorena. At first she sounded like she wasn't going to allow it, until my attorney gave his input and then the judge let it stand.

After our case was decided we waited outside in the hallway until we were given some paperwork. My attorney approached Lorena and asked her if she was going to go home or to work.

I had driven all the way to North Jersey and preferred to get my things and go back to Mom's house as soon as possible. Lorena said she was going to work, which meant I couldn't get my things until about 7:00 p.m. I had hidden a spare key in the shed outside. If I wasn't afraid that I'd be arrested for going back onto the property, I would have gone home and gotten my stuff and left. Ever since Lorena had been arrested in Colorado, there was no doubt in my mind that she wanted me to have that same kind of a jail experience.

I was forced to wait about ten hours before I could go back home and get some more of my things. I went to the daycare center and picked up Justin. He and I went to the mall to kill some time. I could only wonder what was going to become of my relationship with Justin.

That night I went to the police station about the time that Lorena would be home. The police called her but she didn't answer. An hour later they were still unable to reach her. They were getting irritated with me for continuing to ask them to call. Finally, I asked them to just follow me over there.

The police rang and rang the doorbell and Lorena wouldn't answer the door. They knocked so hard that the nextdoor neighbors came to their front door because of all of the noise. I told them that Lorena had gotten me kicked out of my home and that I was no longer allowed to live there.

Finally, after a great deal of noise on the part of the police, Lorena answered the door and let us in.

I made sure that I grabbed my rodeo memorabilia that was in plain sight. I always knew that Lorena would throw my rodeo photographs into the trash at the first opportunity.

I loaded my car up to the hilt. It was so full that I couldn't even see out the back window. The primary reason it was so packed wasn't that I needed all of these items right away, it was because I was trying to save them from being thrown away.

I remember getting on the highway and trying to change lanes. I was accustomed to using my mirrors but my passenger side mirror was blocked by the things in the front seat. I put my signal light on and finally managed to ease over into the other lane to get onto the New Jersey Turnpike.

I wanted to cry. What was going to happen to Justin?

On Monday morning, I resumed the routine of getting up at about 4:30 a.m. and driving to North Jersey and catching the train just so I could maintain my job. It was killing me. Lorena didn't care. She had gotten what she wanted.

One day, I saw her in the hallway on my way to the cafeteria. Lorena spotted me before I saw her. What really caught my eye was that I saw someone turn around and go the other way. Then I realized that it was her. She had probably been on the lookout for me.

I guess Lorena thought I was going to try to talk to her to reason with her. The thing that always surprised me about Lorena was that she always seemed to believe I would keep coming back to her. She always thought men were standing in line to get her number for a chance to go out with her. If they only knew what I knew, they would've been stampeding in the opposite direction.

After a week or so of that grueling schedule, my Aunt Vester Bowens called a cousin, Lisa Watkins, who lived in Jersey City and arranged for me to live with her during the week. I would come back to Mom's on the weekend then drive to Rahway on Monday mornings and then go to Jersey City after work.

On work days I'd leave early so I could eat breakfast as well as lunch in the company cafeteria. I had to re-arrange my entire schedule. I would take a different train into the city Tuesday through Friday.

My cousin Lisa told me that Jersey City had the highest

rate of car thefts in the nation. My car still had Colorado license plates on it. She said it stuck out like a sore thumb. Lisa convinced me to buy a device for my steering wheel. She said that most thieves wouldn't bother the vehicles that had one.

It was such an inconvenience living like that, especially since I hadn't deserved to be legally removed from my own home—for the second time—in less than a year. But I knew I had no one to blame but myself. I had let Lorena talk me into all this and I was reaping the results of a very bad decision.

It was extremely cold in December 2000, and it gave me more of a reason to hate being in New York City. Colorado was much drier and the cold there never had the same bite to it. I remember waiting on the street corners to cross. It was brutal standing there and waiting for the light to change. That wind would cut right through you.

I informed my supervisors at work of my situation and they had me go to speak with a crisis counselor off site once a week. I really didn't have a good reason to stay on the East coast anymore. Even my mother told me that my best bet was to pack my things and head back to Colorado.

I knew if I left I wouldn't see Justin as much as I wanted to, but I didn't trust Lorena at all. I knew the first chance she got, she would have me arrested and put in jail to give her a better chance of gaining full custody of Justin.

I finally made the painful decision to go back to Colorado. A few calls were made and I was approved to transfer back.

I went to the courthouse in New Jersey in order to make arrangements so I could get my personal property. I was told I had to file a motion and then it would be approximately six weeks before I could return to my home to retrieve my property.

I got extremely irritated and said that the judge had told me I could go back in a couple of weeks. It didn't make any difference to the people at the courthouse. I asked to speak to the judge in person, but she refused to see me. I realized right then and there that the legal system really didn't care about me.

When my Uncle James Pope back in Woodstown heard about the outcome of my court case he remarked, "You didn't have a chance when you went into the courtroom. You are big, black and athletic looking and that was all the judge needed to see. You were defeated before you ever even opened your mouth."

And to tell you the truth, I agreed with him one hundred percent.

One Saturday, I drove out to Elmer to visit Lorena's mom. She told me that I should just get myself a place to live so I could be near Justin. I responded by telling her that I didn't move all the way across the country to live in some rinky-dink apartment. I didn't like anything at all about residing in North Jersey.

The last day I was at work in New York City, I was told that I could go home early. I stopped by the daycare center to say goodbye to Justin. Of course, he had no idea that I was leaving. I remember watching him eating a cookie and I was very sad not knowing when I would see him again.

I talked to my cousin David Walker and my mom called Lorena to see if I could come up on a Sunday afternoon to get my things. Unfortunately for me it snowed on Saturday night and the roads were pretty slick. David was going to drive and bring along his big pickup truck and a trailer. We would've been able to get most of my stuff out of the house.

My cousin Jimmy Lee Walker and my brother Reuben and I went to Rahway to get my things. I wasn't allowed at the house. They dropped me off at the train station because it was a very cold day. They came back a few hours later with the little Nissan truck that I had let Reuben take from Colorado. It was packed full of my things. I had told them to get as much as possible, but to leave the books for last. That proved to be a bad decision. They were astounded at how many of my things they had to leave behind because there wasn't enough room.

At that point, I made yet another huge mistake. I should

have contacted the phone center in Denver and delayed my trip because I wasn't able to get my things. Instead, I had agreed to show up by Monday of the next week.

I left on a Tuesday afternoon in January 2001, driving back to Denver. Before I left, Mom gathered everyone in the living room and prayed to God for my safe trip. As we assembled, the song in the background was *I've Got a Long Dusty Road* by Mahalia Jackson. I thought how fitting, considering my current dilemma.

I never bothered to notify Lorena that I'd made a decision to go back out West. I didn't see any point. It was pretty obvious that she didn't care about me at all. All she really cared about were the child support payments. In one of her fits of rage in New Jersey, she had commented to me that because of my life insurance policy benefits I was worth more dead than alive. Obviously she'd meant it.

I left and this time the tears were for my son Justin.

I drove as far as Ohio before I stopped and got a motel room for the night. I was dog tired. It sure had been a harrowing experience living with Lorena. Looking back, it hadn't been worth it. I still wondered why I had taken so much abuse from her. But of course there was only one answer: Justin.

I had a lot of things to think about as I drove westward. Many times I had wondered if Lorena would be the last woman I would have in my life. I was forty-four years old. I'd had every intention of honoring my marriage vows and now I was alone.

Even when we were separated for the six months in Colorado, I'd been faithful to her. I knew there were very few men who would have, but I had to live with myself and that was most important to me.

I stopped a few times for gas and meals. I noticed an entirely different demeanor among the people in the midwest. I got some smiles and even a few, "Hellos," from strangers. That, to me, was reassurance that I was headed in the right direction. After being traumatized by the attitudes of the people in New

York City, it was a welcome change.

I drove through a stretch of freezing rain and it left a layer of ice on my windshield. I had to stop a few times in Missouri and scrape it off.

In June 2000, I had attended a friend, Mike Sinclair's wedding in Wyoming on my birthday, June 24. I'd told another friend, Steve Buhlke, that I was moving back East. He'd told me, "You'll be back, I know you and I know your heart. You'll be back." I'd assured him that my heart was with my son and that I would never return to the West.

Well here I was, back again and happy to be there. I arrived in Denver and stayed with Richard Wilson again for a few days. I saw an ad in the *Denver Post* and called a guy named Ethan. The ad said "roommate wanted; looking for a Christian man or woman." I called at about 11:00 a.m. on a Sunday. The woman who answered the phone said Ethan was still in bed asleep. Another sign which I ignored but later proved to be a warning. Ethan was lazy.

I didn't have a lot of time to make a decision about a place to live. Richard said I could have the bed back that I had left there when I'd moved out in August.

Ethan lived in his own home in Northglenn, Colorado. I would have my own bedroom upstairs. Ethan had a bedroom upstairs. Another woman named Sybil lived downstairs.

When I moved in, Ethan told me that he attended church every other week. It turned out to be a huge lie. I ended up living there for two years and three months. I only remember Ethan going to church one time.

He had an in-house photography business. Ethan photographed couples, mostly at weddings. He was very good at his trade, but only utilized it during the warmer months. Otherwise, like an owl he slept most of the day. Ethan also sat around the house drinking. It soon became obvious that he had an alcohol problem.

I returned to work in downtown Denver. Many of the employees I'd worked with before were shocked to see me back and asked why. I really didn't want to talk about it with the people I worked with. Deep down inside I was deeply hurt and emotionally drained.

For a few weeks all I did was listen to calls with other people. My computer and the system hadn't been set up yet for me to be taking calls on my own.

I didn't hear anything at all from Lorena until about six weeks after I had been back in Denver. She called on my direct line at work on February 27, 2001.

I said, "Hello."

"Abe, this is Lorena. Justin needs …" That was all that I heard. I was so angry and disgusted by all the stuff that she had done to me that I instantly disconnected the call.

Lorena called me right back and left me a long message saying that Justin needed a lot of different things and that I shouldn't expect for her to pay for these by herself. She needed some money for child support.

Well, I needed a place to live. But thanks to her, I no longer had one. My current living situation meant nothing to her.

She also said, "Abe you need to call Verizon and get the telephone switched over into my name. I tried calling them, but they refused to make the switch because the phone is in your name."

I ignored Lorena and her voice message. I also refused to call her back. I had enough new challenges in my life to be concerned with now.

When I approached my supervisor Agatha about my new salary, she gave me the runaround. In a phone call before I'd left New York City, she had told me what my new salary would be. Then one day Agatha called me into her office and pulled out a piece of notebook paper with a dollar figure and some other notes written on it. She got very angry when I insisted that wasn't what she'd told me over the phone. I have an excellent memory. But I didn't have any written documentation to prove it. From that day on, I looked forward to the day that I no longer was a part of corporate America and especially that organization.

A few weeks after Lorena's initial call to me I had a funny feeling that she had taken it upon herself to contact Verizon. I called the corporate office for Verizon in New York state. I gave them my home phone number in Rahway and asked whose name was on the account.

I was told by a customer service representative, "That number is listed to a Lorena. Morris."

"So how did her name get on my account?"

"Sir, it has always been listed on this account."

In an angry tone I said, "No it hasn't. So I would like to know how Lorena's name got put on my account."

"Sir, may I put you on hold please?"

I was put on hold for about five minutes, before the representative came back on the line.

"Sir, I apologize for the wait. It looks like on February 28, Lorena Morris called us and reported your death. So at that point we switched the phone number into her name."

Lorena had done a lot of heinous things in my time with her but this took the cake.

What made it worse was that Verizon had taken her word for it over the telephone, and hadn't even requested a death certificate. Maybe they'd felt sorry for her as a poor widow in her time of bereavement. Surely, she had to be going through a lot with a one and a half year old child to raise alone. And she'd lost her beloved husband. Poor lady.

In order to prove that I was still alive, I had to fax a copy of my driver's license to their legal department for Verizon to put my name back on that account.

I contacted the attorney in New Jersey who'd gone to court with me and asked him to subpoena the records from Verizon to show the amount of deception Lorena was willing to go through get what she wanted. He refused and said he would only do it if I paid him another $250 fee. I asked him about the $1,000 that I had already paid him. Surely there had to be some more money left in that retainer account. He told me the $1,000 fee was for the one day in court only. If I wanted him to do anything else, it was going to cost me more money.

We ended the conversation with him telling me, "Look, I told you what it would cost to get me to subpoena the records. If you aren't willing to write me another check, then my advice to you is to go and get another attorney."

He disconnected the phone call. I thought to myself, "What a jerk!" I knew I would never talk to that man again.

Because Lorena hadn't been receiving any child support payments, she had gone back to the Union County Courthouse to try and get them to put some pressure on me. After what she had done to me, I wasn't going to willingly mail her one red cent.

Lorena had thrown all of my mail into the trash except for a commission renewal check for $372 from PFL Life Insurance Company. She had cashed my personal check and pocketed the money. In most states this would qualify as theft. But Lorena was quickly learning that she could get away with any and every thing that she did.

Union County Court didn't have my new mailing address, so thanks to Lorena they started sending all court correspondence to me at my work address in Denver. It was kind of embarrassing to receive these notices of mandatory court appearances in my mailbox at work.

My first court appearance was scheduled in March 2001. After I had already made my airline reservations it was cancelled and scheduled for a later date. It cost me $50 to change my reservations through the airlines, but the New Jersey court system didn't care. All they really cared about was that I was in court and on time for the appearance whenever they decided to schedule it.

Our court date was reset for April 23, 2001. The purpose was to establish the child support. Before I traveled to New Jersey, I was required to fax the court copies of my pay stubs.

Before I went to court, I visited one of Lorena's best friends from high school, Sharon. She lived right next door to my mom in Woodstown. Mom often watched her girls when Sharon needed a babysitter.

Sharon had been at our wedding in May 1998. I knew that she and Lorena kept in touch and I was sure that Lorena had already told her that we were separated and I that had moved back to Colorado.

Sharon told me, "Lorena said that you moved out and went back to Colorado and she didn't even know that you were leaving. She told me she went downstairs and a lot of things were gone from your desk. She said, 'Abe didn't even have the decency to say goodbye to his own son'."

I told Sharon, "Obviously she didn't tell you that she called the police on me and had me kicked out of my own home."

I went to my mom's house and retrieved the paperwork to show Sharon that Lorena had taken out a restraining order against me. I had a feeling that things wouldn't be much better when I got to the courtroom.

In court the judge asked me if my salary was a certain figure per month. She already had my pay stubs and I confirmed the amount. The judge asked Lorena what her salary was. Then she said she'd take a short recess and come back with her decision.

When she came back she said, "Your child support payments will be $285 per week." I was shocked. When Lorena had filed for divorce in the state of Colorado, my child support payments had been calculated at $150 per week. I'd had to write Lorena a check for that amount weekly.

I questioned the judge as to why such a high figure. She told me that she had figured out my child support based on two different calculations. One set it at $285 per week and the second set it at $320 per week.

The $320 per week was based on a one-time $24,000 commission check that I had received when I left PFL Life Insurance Company in early 2000. Lorena had found a copy of that check in my files and convincingly lied to the court saying that it was a check I received annually. The judge had figured that $24,000 check into one of her calculations.

When I tried to explain this the judge said, "If you would like to argue about it, then I'll set it at over $300 per week." Then she glared at me and said, "Now do you want to argue about it?"

So much for a fair and equitable legal system. That judge was biased from the time I'd first set foot in her courtroom.

I complained to the judge that Lorena had been calling and harassing me about things other than issues that involved Justin. So the judge changed the restraining order to say that phone calls between us were no longer allowed. In the future, we could only communicate via e-mail. And those e-mails were only to contain information concerning Justin. No other information or communication would be allowed.

Lorena then said, "I want permission from you that Abe Morris not be allowed to have any overnight visitations with our son Justin."

The judge's response was, "Permission is denied. That is his father. And your son needs to get to know his own father."

I asked the judge permission to return to my home in Rahway to retrieve some more of my personal items.

Lorena lied to the judge saying that I had removed all of my personal property when Jimmy Lee and Reuben had gone to the house on December 29.

"There is nothing else in that house that belongs to him," Lorena insisted.

After we debated back and forth the judge was finally convinced that I still had a lot of things in that house. She gave me permission—with a police escort—to go back to the house for fifteen minutes to remove more of my personal property.

Lorena said she was going to work right after court. So that meant I would have to wait several hours for her to return to the house, just as I had last time.

Then the judge asked, "Is there anything else that either one of you would like to bring up?"

I said, "Yes. Lorena cashed one of my personal checks from

PFL Life for $372 and spent the money."

I showed the judge a photo copy of the front and back side of the check.

She asked Lorena, "Why did you cash his personal check?"

Lorena got all flustered and said, "I cashed it to use it for the daycare expenses."

Then the judge said, "Then I'm going to move the child support payments back one entire week in order to compensate him for the money that you spent. Instead of the child support payments starting today April 23 they will not officially start until April 30."

I hadn't seen Justin for a few months. I asked and was granted permission by the judge to go to the daycare and pick up Justin for a few hours.

When I went to the daycare center the staff refused to let me take Justin off of the premises. Lorena had lied and told them that I no longer had joint legal custody. She said she had gained sole custody of Justin through the court system. I had to go back outside to the car and show them the paperwork from the court. They photocopied it and put it into Justin's file.

The weather wasn't too bad in late April and so we went to a nearby park. There were a lot of high school kids practicing for the upcoming track season. Justin was glad to see me and stayed real close while we walked around.

That night I had to go through the routine again of going to the police station and showing them the paperwork so I could go back to my home. When I had left in December there were about twenty boxes of my things in the basement. They were labeled and hadn't been touched since our move from Colorado. Those boxes contained books that I had collected and kept over the years. Some of them had been autographed by the authors. A few of them were out of print.

When I went down into the basement I stared in amazement at the empty space where my things had been stored. I couldn't believe that all of my boxes were gone. I didn't know if I was angry or just plain bewildered when I realized that all of my prized possessions had been thrown away. I wasn't even sure if I wanted to cry or what. How someone could just take things that belonged to another and simply throw them into the trash and not have any guilt feelings about it was beyond me.

I had saved a bowl that was loaded with Susan B. Anthony dollar coins. The bowl was gone. I had left some money in my desk drawer and of course it was also long gone. I looked into the kitchen cabinet and grabbed some plates that belonged to me.

Lorena screamed, "Those are my plates."

So the police officer made me put them back. Anything that Lorena didn't want me to have, she claimed was hers. I ended up leaving with only a handful of my things. It had been a complete waste of my time to wait around for so long, and come away with so little.

Soon after I returned to Colorado, I figured out that the judge had used the wrong figures in calculating my weekly child support payments. I called the Union County Courthouse in New Jersey. I was told to write a letter of explanation to the judge and fax copies of the check stubs to her.

I faxed the check stubs on April 25, 2001 and sent her a letter dated May 8, 2001. She in turn sent me a letter dated July 6, 2001 stating that the child support payments would not be re-calculated, despite the fact that I'd provided her with adequate documentation that her numbers were way out of line.

Meanwhile, I sent Lorena e-mails to try and arrange a visit with Justin. She refused to acknowledge or answer. Eventually, I had to contact the court. The judge sent Lorena a letter warning her that she was required to answer my e-mails concerning visitation or she would be subpoenaed back to court.

I didn't return to New Jersey until August of 2001. Cowtown Rodeo in Woodstown held a reunion of the cowboys and cowgirls of the bygone era. I planned to attend and thought it would be an opportune time to visit with Justin and take him to a rodeo.

I contacted Lorena and she refused to let me see Justin. She had found out about the rodeo reunion through one of her sisters. Lorena told me that the only reason I was coming home was for the reunion and not to see Justin.

She said, "If you really care about Justin, then you'll come home on a separate weekend strictly to see him and not for any other reason."

The woman was totally irrational. With the price of airline tickets, I guess she thought it was okay to just fork out money at will and hop on an airplane. The only time airline tickets and money were an issue with Lorena was when she was the one paying for them. Otherwise she didn't care.

I contacted the Union County courthouse and notified them that I had purchased airline tickets in order to come to New Jersey, and Lorena was refusing to let me see my son.

Lorena wrote a letter to the judge that was full of lies. She told her that the reason she had refused to let me see Justin was because she had already planned a trip that weekend so Justin wouldn't be available. Lorena tried to make it seem like she was reasonable and accommodating and that I was the one causing unnecessary problems.

The judge ended up doing a three-way conference call and I was allowed to have Justin for an overnight visit only. I told the judge that I would try to fly back to see Justin as often as possible. I would try for at least once a month, but I knew financially that wouldn't always be possible.

The judge then told Lorena to make sure that the third weekend was always left open for me to have Justin in case I came back to New Jersey. Any weekend was allowable, but I would be given special preference for the third weekend so there would always be a sure weekend that I could see him, no matter what the circumstances.

I flew into Philadelphia and then drove to North Jersey on a Thursday to pick up Justin.

Lorena had taken Friday off and I had to bring Justin over to her mom's house by 3:00 p.m. She had lied to the judge again, saying that she was going to take Justin on a trip after that which was a two hour drive. Actually, she stayed at her mom's house for the whole weekend.

When I dropped Justin off at Lorena's mom's home, Lorena wanted to speak with me in private. Justin went into the house with his grandmom. We went over to a small covered area and sat down to talk.

As usual Lorena always had to go first and get her two cents in. Every time I would try to talk, she'd interrupt me. Lorena wanted me to sign off on the mortgage and give her full ownership of the home in Rahway. I asked her what happened to all of my things and boxes that were in the house when I'd left in December.

Lorena hesitated and paused. She wouldn't tell me where my things were. The truth was they were all buried in some landfill in Union County. She was trying to pretend she still had them and use that for leverage.

Then Lorena said, "You agree to sign off on the house, and you'll get all of your things back."

I kept insisting that they didn't exist anymore, and that she knew she had thrown my things away. Finally, Lorena had had enough and exploded, or should I say imploded.

I got up to leave. Lorena came charging across the lawn in her mom's yard. Lorena was pointing her finger and screaming at me. "I'm finished with you. I'm finished with you. I'm going to file for divorce. I'm going to file for divorce. You're going to get screwed. You're going to get screwed. I'm going to beat you to a pulp until you have nothing left to show for it!"

I went back to my mom's house and celebrated the Cowtown Rodeo reunion that night with some old friends hoping to get a little relief from the situation with Lorena.

On Monday, she sent me an e-mail at work saying Justin had had some kind of fever and high temperature. Lorena said she was going to rush him to the emergency room at the hospital. She never did.

I responded in an e-mail back to her asking why, if Justin was having such an emergency, she hadn't called me at my mom's house. It couldn't have been such a life and death situation if she waited two days, and then sent me an e-mail after I'd returned to Colorado.

That summer, I received a letter from Lorena that she had her sister mail to me so she wouldn't be violating the restraining order. The letter stated that she was going to file for divorce. Lorena wanted me to make her the primary beneficiary of all of my life insurance policies.

I never responded to her letter. Lorena couldn't file for divorce until she had been a resident of New Jersey for a year. In August of 2001 she went to the Union County courthouse and filed for divorce.

The sheriff in Adams County, Colorado made a few attempts to serve me the divorce papers, but I was always at work when he came around. Finally, Lorena hired a process server who somehow got on my floor at TIARRA and delivered the goods. Because we were in the financial services and securities industry, strangers and unauthorized personnel weren't allowed on my floor.

Lorena had decided to act as her own attorney. She made some very unreasonable demands including that she would have sole legal custody of Justin and that he couldn't ever come to Colorado to visit me.

My next step was to find a New Jersey attorney to represent my case. I called several. Because of the background and the emotional overtones of the case, a few that I talked to weren't willing. I can understand that, now. My case has certainly turned out to be a mess, but I can't help believing that if I'd somehow had better representation in the beginning, a lot of the continuing problems would never have developed.

I had sixty days to file a response to Lorena's motion for a dissolution of marriage.

I talked to attorney Mark Schmidt and he agreed to represent me. I had to send him $3,000 for a retainer so he could get started on the paperwork.

On Tuesday September 11, 2001 there was the now infamous attack on the World Trade Center in New York City. I remember it well. My workout days during the week were on Tuesdays and Thursdays. I was on the afternoon shift that didn't start until 12:15 p.m. I didn't like the shift because there wasn't enough time to do anything in the mornings before work, and not enough time to do anything in the evenings, either.

I didn't get home until a little after 10:00 p.m. most days so I would do my workout routines in the mornings before work. I had worked out at Bally's that morning and then gone over to BIGG'S, the supermarket, to pick up a few items. There was a television on and it was broadcasting images of the first airplane that hit the North Tower. I watched in amazement, thinking that an errant airplane had accidentally hit the building.

By the time I got home, Ethan was watching television and I watched the videos of the second plane crashing into the South Tower before I went to work. On my drive to the bus Park n' Ride, I heard about the missing airplane that had crashed near Shanksburg, Pennsylvania.

When I arrived at the Republic Plaza there was a mass exodus of employees leaving the building. Someone said to me, "You might as well turn right around and go back home."

I went inside anyway. I at the very least wanted my supervisor to see that I had shown up for work. She went around and recommended that we log on to our phones and take calls as usual. They would give us an update as soon as possible on whether we would be closing for the day.

Although we were only on the fourth floor, a lot of us were afraid because we really didn't know what was going on. We all wanted to go home as soon as possible.

My mom called me at work and asked if I'd heard about all of the things that were going on on the East coast.

Lorena's family knew that she worked in New York City but had no idea exactly where. For all they knew she could have been in one of the World Trade Center buildings. Her mom was in a panic and called her several times throughout the day, but with no success. Lorena's sister said she didn't even know the name of the company that Lorena worked for. Lorena had a cell phone, but never even bothered to give her own family members the phone number. I guess Lorena didn't think it was important.

Lorena's other sister was also in a panic. She had contacted my family because she had no idea which daycare center Justin was in or where. They didn't have a phone number for that, either.

My mom called me asking for information about Justin's daycare. My sister Janice was on standby and ready to jump into her vehicle and race up to North Jersey to pick up Justin before the center closed, if necessary.

It just so happened that Lorena didn't go to Manhattan that particular day. If she had, she probably wouldn't have been able to get back home. All major transportation had come to a virtual standstill. She had gone to visit a college in North Jersey.

It wasn't until late in the afternoon that Lorena's family and mine found out that she was safe. All day long she didn't even bother to call her own mother so she didn't have to worry. Later on, I heard that Lorena said that the World Trade Center was located in Lower Manhattan and her office was about five miles away in mid-Manhattan.

How in the world was someone that lived in rural South Jersey supposed to know that? I also heard that Lorena had commented, "What was the big deal about a couple of airplanes crashing into a couple of skyscrapers?"

Mom also told me that Lorena came to Woodstown sometime later and they were discussing the events of 9/11. She said that Lorena actually laughed about the disaster.

During the next couple of months, I wanted to go home for Christmas to see Justin.

For Christmas in 2001, I had to get a Consent Order through my attorney and the court. I was supposed to go to Lorena's sister's home in Quinton, New Jersey to pick up Justin. Before I left, Lorena called my mom's house and left a message.

"Abe, this is Lorena. My sister doesn't want you to come to her house. There is a church nearby. You come over to the parking lot of that church. We'll keep our eyes out for you. We'll bring Justin over there so you can pick him up."

Of course the phone call to my mom's house was a violation of the restraining order, but Lorena never cared about court orders, so she did as she pleased.

Someone suggested that I take along someone else as a witness. Otherwise, it would be their word against mine. In a court of law I already knew that I was bound to lose if Lorena lied again, so I took my brother David with me. When we pulled up in the driveway, I told him to get out and come up to the front door with me. I wasn't about to have a confrontation with anyone in Lorena's family and have them call the police on me.

When I rang the doorbell, there was a lot of noise and commotion from within the house. Her sister came to the door and asked in a nasty tone, "Didn't you get the message?"

I told her, "The Court Order said to pick up Justin at your house. It didn't say anything about a church next door."

She knew I was right. She apparently didn't want to get into an argument with me on Christmas Day. She said, "Hold on," and then closed the door.

A few minutes later she opened the door again and handed Justin to me. He was so excited to see me! Her sister came outside with the keys to the brand new Dodge Intrepid that Lorena was now driving to get Justin's things. It was very obvious that financially Lorena wasn't struggling at all.

Before I left our house in Rahway Lorena and I had talked about getting the old paneling taken off of the walls and doing some remodeling. We had discussed taking out a loan, even though Lorena continued to refuse to tell me how much we'd made from the sale of our home in Northglenn.

Lorena didn't want to take out a loan. In the spring of 2001 she received about $20,000 in a bonus check from TIARRA. She then used that money to get the remodeling done.

Later on, Lorena stated that after I left she had struggled quite a bit. Yes, she struggled so much that she had several rooms including both bathrooms in our house remodeled and painted, all of which she had done without borrowing any money.

My attorney and I responded to the divorce filing in writing to the Union County Court. He also sent some Interrogatories. They were a series of legal questions designed to make Lorena divulge her assets, and so forth. The information she disclosed in them would be legal and binding. Once they were sent to Lorena, she was court ordered to answer them in a timely fashion and return them to Mark Schmidt.

Our responses to the court were forwarded to Lorena and her new attorney, Shelly Martin. Mark assured me that Lorena would be a lot easier to deal with now that she had hired an attorney. Little did he imagine that Lorena would never be easy to deal with, even for the person who might be representing her.

Eventually Lorena did respond to the interogatories but she only answered some of the questions. Mark was not very pleased and sent Lorena and her new attorney letters threatening to file a contempt of court motion if Lorena didn't comply with the court order. Lorena ignored him and his letter. Mark never followed through. Lorena figured out sooner than I did that my attorney was full of a lot of hot air.

In the spring of 2002, I planned a trip back East so I could see Justin. As usual, Lorena wouldn't cooperate and my attorney wrote up another Consent Order and it went through the court system. More legal fees for me, just as Lorena intended.

When I picked up Justin from the Kindercare Daycare Center in Clark, New Jersey, Lorena had refused to send any clean clothes or diapers for the boy.

My attorney had charged me his usual fee of about $225 an hour to write up the Consent Order. The next time I tried to visit Justin he jumped the gun. Because Lorena wouldn't cooperate he asked, "Do you need me to write up another Consent Order?"

I said, "Why should I pay you to write up another Consent Order when the exact same verbiage is already on file with the Union County Courthouse?"

The first two visits that I had with Justin in 2002, Lorena refused to send any clean clothes for him. She claimed to care so much for her child, yet her actions spoke volumes. Lorena wasn't focused on Justin. She was focused on making as many problems for me as possible.

One of our visits was during the Easter holiday. I took Justin to a church sponsored Easter egg hunt. He collected and loaded up on eggs and other prizes. Afterward, we went downstairs to the church basement for a little get together that was specially designed to entertain the little kids.

Luckily, my sisters still had some old nice clothes from their boys that they hadn't gotten rid of yet. We were able to outfit Justin so he looked very nice on Easter Sunday.

Justin was starting to get older and more attached to me. He hated it when it was time to go back to his mom. At first he would just cry. Later on, as he got bigger, he would throw a fit and cry until he fell asleep on the ride back home. One time he threw such a fit that he actually somehow got out of his car seat. I had to pull over on the side of the New Jersey Turnpike and strap him back in. Of course this broke my heart. I felt guilty, as though

I were the cause of his distress. I badly wanted to find some way that Lorena and I could get along and ease the stress on my son. Unfortunatley, Lorena wasn't on the same page where Justin was concerned.

Living in Northglenn with Ethan still wasn't my cup of tea. But temporarily I was stuck there, and so I did my best to endure the situation.

One night Ethan and Sybil got into a knock down drag out fight during one of his drunken escapades. He called the police on her for no apparent reason and kicked her out. The next day Sybil packed her things and left.

I knew if push came to shove, he would do the same thing to me, so I never trusted him. It made my situation very unstable and I was unable to figure out a way that I could afford to move.

After Sybil moved out a black guy named Michael Branch moved into the upstairs bedroom and Ethan moved downstairs. Michael was cool. I liked him a lot. We had a lot of things in common. He worked for StorageTek, a sophisticated computer software company in Louisville, Colorado. He was a pretty sharp dude. Michael's story was unbelievable and very similar to mine.

His wife was also involved in an insurance career. She had also been arrested for domestic violence. They had a son who was only a year younger than Justin. His ex-wife also lived back East. He told me that she was bipolar, too.

There were many times that I figured God had put both of us together so we could share our stories of the problems we had seeing our sons. I could bounce stories off of him and he did the same with me. I learned a lot from him.

Then another divorced guy named Mike moved into the downstairs bedroom. Luckily, we all got along just fine. I liked Mike as well. We talked a lot and shared things concerning our personal lives.

Michael moved out after about a year and a half. Another eighteen months later, he was killed in an automobile accident in Northglenn. He was hit by a speeding police cruiser on an emergency call that wasn't using its flashing lights or warning siren. Tragically, Michael was on his way to Georgia to be there for a surgical procedure on his young son.

In February 2002, Lorena's mother passed away. She had been sick for quite awhile with cancer. She had been in and out of the hospital and was taking chemo treatments. She finally succumbed to the disease. She was a very nice and religious woman.

Lorena's mom's funeral was held at the Morning Star Baptist Church where her mom had been a member. The church is only about two hundred yards from my mom's house.

Mom and my sister Patricia had reached out to Lorena and volunteered to watch Justin during the funeral. Lorena declined their offer. Instead, she sent Justin to a local daycare center to be among strangers, rather than allow him to spend time with his own family members. It was such a shame.

One day I went on the computer at work and looked at Lorena's personal account. There was a form that she had signed and dated on January 28, 2001 stating that she was exempt from ERISA laws. She had blatantly tried to remove my name as the beneficiary of her TIARRA retirement account.

At first, I didn't say anything except to my co-workers about it. One day one of my supervisors came over to my desk and I told her about it.

Jane said, "She could be terminated for that."

Another day, I was in Agatha's office. We were having a heated discussion and I got upset and told her what Lorena had attempted to do. Agatha told me that she may have to report it to human resources. I got tears in my eyes and asked her not to because if Lorena found out I'd reported her, she would retaliate against me by hurting Justin.

A few days later Agatha came over to my desk and said that as a registered principal in the NASD, she was required to report that violation to the human resources department.

That week, I received a phone call at my desk and was asked to come up to the HR office. Anytime you are called up there it was considered serious.

I told the woman in HR stories about how emotionally unstable Lorena was and my concerns for Justin. About a week later, Agatha called me into her office and told me that I had violated company policy by looking at Lorena's personal account on my computer. For that reason I received a verbal warning and was placed on six month's probation. That meant I couldn't have any other violations within that time frame or I could be in serious hot water.

I was upset about the sanction. I asked, "So what are you going to do to Lorena for the blatant violation and lying under false pretences?"

I was told Lorena had been dealt with in New York and her consequences were considered confidential. Later on, I found out that she had been placed on a "suicide watch" by the company. I figured she must have put on a dramatic performance to warrant that reaction. Other than that Lorena got away scot-free as usual. I'm sure she wasn't even placed on probation.

In May, Lorena called me on the telephone at work and said she was going to come to Colorado for a company sponsored business conference in Colorado Springs. Whenever an employee is placed on probation, he or she isn't allowed to travel on any company sponsored trips. That is how I knew that TIARRA hadn't taken any disciplinary action against Lorena.

She offered to bring Justin to Colorado as long as I took a few days off from work so I could watch him. The truth was that Lorena didn't trust anyone with her child for long periods of time. The only reason that she agreed to bring Justin was more for her own satisfaction than to appease me.

JUSTIN

I hadn't seen Justin for a few weeks and I was always excited about any opportunity for us to be together since I had been court ordered out of my home and literally thrown into the streets. Justin and I had a very strong bond and he was always excited to see his daddy. All week long I anticipated his visit. I couldn't wait to see my son again.

I drove to Colorado Springs to pick him up on a Sunday morning. I met Lorena and as we were walking to the outside door of the hotel she said to me for no reason whatsoever, "I sure hope you don't go acting all crazy."

I instantly got belligerent and replied, "You're the one that acts crazy." My reaction indicated how deeply affected I was by everything that had happened.

I took Justin back to Northglenn with me. We had a great time together. On Monday, I took him downtown so he could see where I worked in a huge skyscraper. The building was the tallest in the entire state, Republic Plaza.

I took Justin around so a few of my co-workers could meet him. One of them took some pictures of Justin and me. I had no idea at the time but, the following year I would start to write an autobiography titled, *My Cowboy Hat Still Fits*. One of those pictures would be used in an article in January 2003 about me and the book in a Western style weekly newspaper called the *Fence Post* out of Windsor, Colorado.

Later on that afternoon we went to the park and played soccer. I could see right away that Justin was going to be an athlete. Even though he was only three at the time, he ran me ragged all over the field. I just couldn't seem to wear him out.

That evening we visited a few friends. We went over to the new home of Andy and Jan Maes who had lived right across the street from us in Northglenn. They were now living in Thornton. Andy gave Justin a nice felt cowboy hat.

Later that night I showed Justin a racquetball and a racquet. He was so mesmerized that he wanted to go and play. I said, "We'll go and play tomorrow."

"No, I want to go and play right now!" he insisted.

The next morning we went to a racquetball court. I couldn't believe how excited he got when I hit the ball against the front wall. I had let him use an old racquet that I had broken. It was a good thing, because he kept hitting the floor with the racquet as he was swinging it. He loved it.

I was supposed to have him back in Colorado Springs at 6:00 p.m. on Tuesday. We stopped and spent some time at the Professional Rodeo Cowboys Association (PRCA) Hall of Fame in Colorado Springs before I dropped him off at The Broadmoor.

Lorena was her usual hateful self when she approached Justin and me. As usual she said, "Hi" to Justin and focused her eyes and attention strictly on him as if I didn't even exist. She never said a word to me. She just took his hand and his clothes bag and walked away.

As Justin was led away he turned and waved goodbye to me. When Lorena noticed that Justin was trying to wave at me, she jerked him hard to interrupt his gesture. The sight almost brought tears to my eyes, but I was glad to have been able to spend some time with the poor little guy.

When I returned to work at TIARRA there was another voicemail on my phone from Lorena. She was very upset at the verbal barrage and exchange of emotions when I picked up Justin in Colorado Springs. She said she had gone to the bellman and the front desk personnel. They would be subpoenaed and would testify in a court of law that I was out of line and had threatened her. Another one of her lies, of course.

I wasn't too worried about her threats. My biggest concern was that she had again called me in violation of a court restraining order which forbade her to call me and leave me any kind of a message.

The summer of 2002, I had to return to New Jersey for a so-called early settlement case. This was set up to bring closure to our divorce case so it wouldn't have to go to trial.

My attorney and Lorena's attorney sat on a panel with two

neutral attorneys and hashed over the issues. I had sent several of my concerns to Mark before my trip back East.

After the conference Lorena and I were herded in front of a judge to hopefully settle the case that day. I had no idea that was going to happen. Before we went into the courtroom my attorney tried to convince me to accept a lump sum of $5,000 as a cash settlement from Lorena. I told him that he must be crazy.

There were two homes involved in this divorce case. I still didn't know the amount of the check that Lorena had received from the sale of our home in Colorado. Plus there was now equity in the home in Rahway.

Mark Schmidt told me over again and again, "I think $5,000 is a fair settlement. If I were you I would accept that and get this thing over with."

The judge got a little miffed. She was under the impression that we were going to settle the case. I still had several of my personal items left at that house in Rahway, and I wanted to get my hands on them before any case settling was done.

I felt as if I was being rushed and bamboozled, and I wasn't having any of it. I'm sure this made my attorney look bad in front of the judge, but I didn't care. He was also in the cattle processing mode, but I wasn't in the mood to be slaughtered that day.

My attorney also wanted me to settle for a weekly child support payment of $250. I was paying $360 a week at the time. He said, "You'll be paying $110 less a week than you're paying now. If this thing goes to trial then it will cost you a lot more than the $5,000 that we're asking for. I think it's a fair and equitable deal."

We ended up walking out on the proposed deal. I wasn't going to be pressured into agreeing to anything that I didn't have time to thoroughly think through. I certainly didn't like the idea of being blindsided when I thought all we were there for was to negotiate a settlement. I had no idea at the start of the session that their goal was to end the case right then and there.

I was very upset at the strong arm tactics of my attorney. He knew I was visibly upset at him. When we departed he asked,

"When are you going back to Colorado? I will get a hold of you next week."

From that point forward I should have tried to get another attorney to handle my case. Mark Schmidt didn't seem to have my best interests in mind. He had constantly ignored my requests.

I had badgered him to subpoena the phone records from Verizon saying that Lorena had called and reported my death on February 28, 2001. His response was that he didn't see that we had anything to gain from it.

Lorena was court ordered to submit a set of interrogatories to be used in our settlement case. At that point she still hadn't sent them back, even though they'd been court ordered.

Lorena had made a habit of picking up her phone whenever she got upset and calling and leaving me voice mails at work. I constantly complained to my attorney. He in turn had written letters to Lorena's attorney threatening to file contempt of court charges but he never did. He was charging me exorbitant fees for this lack of action.

Going back and forth to New Jersey for mandatory court appearances was a huge financial burden on me. Whenever I went back there, I would fly into Philadelphia. Then I would have to drive almost two hours each way just to pick up and drop off Justin. Lorena refused to meet me halfway on the turnpike.

A few times I had court ordered hearings in New Jersey on a Monday morning. I would ask Lorena to allow me to keep Justin one more day and bring him back and drop him off at the daycare center on Monday morning. This would've allowed me to spend more time with my son since my visitation time was already very limited.

Also, this would have saved me time and money. Why take two trips to North Jersey? It cost me gas, wear and tear on my mom's car, and turnpike tolls to make two unnecessary trips plus four hours of driving time. There was absolutely no reason to be so unreasonable but, as I was coming to realize, Lorena's main goal was to punish me. For what, I still don't know, unless it was for making the mistake of having loved and married her. Now that she had destroyed my feelings for her, she couldn't bear the fact that I still adored my son.

I could have dropped Justin off at the daycare center on Monday morning and then gone straight to court. Instead, I had to bring Justin home on a Sunday evening, turn around and drive all the way back to my mom's house in South Jersey. Then I'd get up early the next morning and drive right back again.

On top of all that, whenever I had a court appointment that didn't coincide with the third weekend of the month, Lorena refused to let me see Justin at all. Her excuse was always that it wasn't the third weekend of the month.

On one trip I tried in vain to see Justin before I left for Colorado. Lorena refused. So I stopped at the daycare center to see Justin on my way to court. Justin didn't know that I was coming so he was surprised when his daddy showed up at the door. He thought that I was coming to pick him up. So when I left without him, he threw a big fit.

Right after my court appearance was over, I stopped at the daycare center again to visit him. The staff called Lorena at home because I wanted to take him out for a few hours.

They wouldn't allow me to see Justin, even though I had joint legal custody of my own son. Lorena relented and came down to the daycare center to talk to me. The staff wouldn't even let me enter the building, and so I waited outside.

Lorena showed up and walked right by me as if I didn't exist, as she had so often done. She went inside and spoke with the daycare staff. Then she came over to the front door saying, "Let me talk to him."

Already upset because I had been in New Jersey for the entire weekend and she had refused to let me see Justin, I let her have both barrels. "Don't you say a single word to me. Don't talk to me. The restraining order says that you can't talk to me, so don't you dare say a single word to me!"

Lorena backed off. That was the first time since we had started dating that she didn't respond to me. I was surprised.

As she backed away she screamed out, "Call the police, call the police!"

One of the staff members came out to talk to me. At that point I knew I was outnumbered and out gunned. It was my word against the word of several women staff members. I knew if they called the police, I was going to be the one who would lose.

Although I could have waited peacefully outside, I said, "Look, I'll just leave."

It wasn't worth it to me to risk going to jail. I didn't trust Lorena at all. I knew she would lie to the police, and say that I was there threatening her and the daycare staff.

I thought it was a travesty that she could get away with stuff like that when at the same time it was fine for her to unlawfully collect my $360 a week for child support and not let me spend any time with my son.

My mom didn't trust Lorena, either. She had a huge silver medallion cross in a drawer in the kitchen. One time I was getting ready to take Justin back to Rahway. Mom gave me the cross and insisted that I wear it on the outside, so it was visible to Lorena when I dropped Justin off at the front door of the house.

One time I had dropped Justin off and was sitting outside in the car. He was standing in the front window waving goodbye to me. Lorena walked up and pulled him away.

When Justin was about three years old I bought him his first pair of little cowboy boots. He loved those black cowboy boots. I also bought him a cowboy hat that he wore home one time. Sadly it disappeared. We both knew that Lorena had thrown it away.

I also asked him if he wanted to have one of my trophy rodeo belt buckles. Justin chose the first one that I ever won at the University of Wyoming college rodeo in 1978.

He immediately claimed ownership of that buckle. I

would take it back to New Jersey with me each time I went to visit him. Whenever I asked whose buckle Justin was wearing he would say, "That's Justin's buckle." He hadn't yet learned to say, "my" buckle.

Sometimes I would point to the one he was wearing and say, "That's Daddy's buckle."

Justin would point to the buckle I was wearing and say, "No, *that's* Daddy's buckle!"

One Sunday afternoon he was wearing his boots and the belt buckle. When I told him it was time to go back home, Justin sat down on the living room floor of my mom's house and started taking off his cowboy boots. Then he wanted to take off his belt buckle. Young as he was, he knew what would happen to them if he wore them home.

I told him he could wear the buckle home, and just give it to me after we got there. He wasn't willing to take the risk because he was afraid I would forget. Justin wanted to take it off right then and there. So I helped him take it off and I brought it back to Colorado with me. He was such a sharp kid that it was amazing to see him think ahead at that age.

As Justin got older he would throw a fit each and every time that I took him back to his mother. I always felt so sorry that a little innocent child with his intelligence had to go through such separation anxiety. With no cooperation from his mother I just didn't know what I could do.

It was "like father like son." As Justin got older I gave him a baseball cap to wear when we were together. One time, I was taking him back to Rahway and I was wearing my cap. I took it off and set it on the front seat.

I watched in the rearview mirror as Justin quietly took off his baseball cap and set it aside as well.

I would play a cassette tape of my father singing *Nearer My God to Thee* with the Morning Star Baptist Male Chorus. There was also a song on there by Roosevelt Pope, my grandfather. The song was *On the Battlefield.*

Justin loved the tape. After awhile he would ask for the

tape and sing along with my dad. Eventually it broke, so I had to get my brother David Morris to make me another copy. Pretty soon it was our regular routine. Justin would get into the back seat and after we were on the road, he would say, "I want to listen to Granddad."

Then he would say, "Play again, Daddy. Play again."

On one occasion, Lorena happened to come to South Jersey to visit her mother and family for the weekend. She refused to come over to my mom's house to pick up Justin. I'm sure that after the way she had carried on since our separation, she was too ashamed to be seen by anyone in my family.

I strapped Justin into his car seat. He fought it the entire time that I drove him over to the Woodstown Acme where Lorena had insisted I meet her. Justin couldn't get himself out of the car seat so he started violently and repeatedly banging his head on the back of the car seat. I hated seeing him carry on that way. It hurt to watch him self-destruct and do that to himself. As I was driving the car I had to reach back with my right arm and try to stop him. I was afraid that he was really going to hurt himself.

When I arrived at the Acme I parked the car. As I was carrying Justin through the parking lot and toward Lorena's car that was parked right in front of the entrance to the supermarket, Justin was kicking and screaming as loud as he could.

Justin was saying, "No, Daddy I don't want to go. No, no!"

I got to Lorena's car. She said, "What's wrong with him?"

I said, "He doesn't want to go with you. Look at how he's carrying on."

When I put Justin down to open the back car door, he was still writhing and screaming at the top of his lungs. He started crawling on the pavement in an attempt to get away from Lorena. I could tell she was getting upset because we were attracting a lot of attention. It was embarrassing for her to watch Justin carrying on like that in public.

Then Lorena starting yelling at me, "I'm calling the police.

I'm calling the police."

I told her to go ahead and call the police. Whenever Lorena got upset at me her battle cry became, "I'm going to call the police!"

I hadn't done a thing to her other than try to give Justin back to her. I got Justin into the back seat of her car and he crawled down onto the floor and refused to cooperate with her. I walked away as she continued to fight with him right in front of the store.

My mom had told me that about a year before, Lorena had brought Justin down to visit with her mom for the weekend. Knowing that her mom wouldn't have any milk at her house for Justin, Lorena had stopped at a convenience store right before she got to her mom's house.

Lorena had unbuckled Justin from the car seat and gone into the store. When she returned, Justin was fighting her and refused to let her buckle him into the car seat again. The scene got to be so bad that a complete stranger had intervened and asked Lorena if everything was okay. The man had even offered to help get Justin buckled in again. How embarrassing.

Lorena made up the rules of engagement at will as we proceeded towards a final divorce. At one point she said that I was forbidden to set foot onto the property at Kindercare to pick up or drop off Justin.

There were two occasions when I dropped Justin off at the daycare center. When Justin realized that I was leaving him there, he threw a fit. He vehemently fought the staff members who were trying to restrain him.

The next time I dropped him off, the daycare center was ready. It took three of those women to hold him down while I walked out the door. I sure felt sorry for the poor little guy. It broke my heart to see him carry on like that, and to be held down against his will like he was a runaway slave or something.

On a couple of my visits back East, I asked my sister Janice to drive to Clark, New Jersey and pick up Justin and then pick me up at the Philadelphia Airport on the way back.

There were several times when I asked Lorena to give me permission to pick up Justin on a Thursday evening because I flew into Philadelphia that day. The answer was always a big NO.

She was in charge and always insisted that I pick up Justin on a Friday morning. I guess she felt it was better for Justin to spend time among strangers in a daycare setting than to spend a little extra time with his own father.

We had a scheduled court appearance in the fall of 2002. On my drive to court that morning I heard on the radio that after an intensive manhunt in the Maryland, Washington, D.C. and Virginia areas, the two snipers who had plagued that area and kept everyone in an emotional hostage situation had been captured. So of course that was the news all over the airwaves.

Even though that was the hot topic of the day, I certainly didn't care to discuss it with my attorney, who I was paying $240 an hour. It seemed like that was all he wanted to talk about while we were sitting in court awaiting our turn. I wanted to talk about the issues involving my divorce case, and not some breaking news that I had absolutely nothing to do with or control of. This was his way of keeping me off guard so I wouldn't complain about the poor service that he was providing.

We went in front of the judge for a while. The judge had the impression that we may be close to settling our case, and so he wanted us to go downstairs in the basement and discuss it with both of our attorneys. Provided we were able to come to some kind of conclusions, we could have been divorced that same day. Of course, we weren't even close to settling. The judge gave us permission to temporarily drop the restraining orders so we could negotiate and talk.

We were sitting downstairs at a lunch table. Lorena insisted that she be allowed to speak first concerning some of the outstanding issues. Everyone sat there and listened patiently while she had her say.

Then it was my turn to respond. As soon as I started talking, Lorena very rudely interrupted me in mid-sentence. So I stopped until she was done. I tried again to speak and she promptly interrupted me again. I tried to speak a third time and she did it again.

This time I pushed back from the table, and said to both attorneys, "See, this is a perfect example of why Lorena and I don't get along."

Mark Schmidt looked at Lorena and said, "You need to stop interrupting my client when he is responding."

At this point Lorena cut her eyes toward him and screamed out, "NO!"

Her attorney in turn said, "Yes, Lorena, stop interrupting him, we need to hear what he's trying to say."

Then Lorena focused her eyes on her own attorney and screamed at her, "NO!"

Needless to say we didn't get very much accomplished that day except run up our attorney fees.

After awhile, the judge came downstairs to check on our progress. The attorneys told him that there was no way that we were going to settle the case that day. As usual Lorena was in a very foul mood.

Later on that year, my attorney and I had a major disagreement over the telephone. I told him I wasn't satisfied with his services and all of his broken promises to file motions on my behalf.

I said, "You remind me of a college student that does a term paper, and then at the end of the semester never bothers to turn it in."

At the end of the conversation he said, "Look I'm not going to sit here and take this and listen to you tell me how to do my job. Next time you come back to New Jersey you get yourself another attorney."

I told him no. I wasn't willing to start the process all over again. I wanted to get a fair and equitable settlement offer and move on with my life.

I was enduring a lot of stress in my personal life.

I really didn't enjoy my job at TIARRA at all. The company had given me a raw deal concerning my reduced salary when I returned to Colorado. I was stuck on the afternoon/night shift which allowed little time to date or have a personal life.

I complained so much to one of my supervisors that one day he asked me if I seriously thought that I'd be able to maintain my current job. At that time, I didn't realize I was projecting such a negative attitude. He thought I was going to buckle under the stress.

After that, I went into an immediate shut down phase. I didn't trust him, and made it a point to never discuss all the things that Lorena was doing and getting away with. I never spoke about Lorena or my personal life with my supervisor again.

My attorney in New Jersey had filed a motion on my behalf. In a response from her attorney Lorena had sworn under oath that I had stolen her jewelry box. She had itemized the cost and value of it and what it contained.

Her list said I had taken a gold Wittnauer watch valued at $500.00 and also a pair of gold earrings that were given to her by her mother. She said I had stolen another watch valued at $350.00. Lorena also claimed to still have the receipts for these items some fifteen years after she'd purchased them, and wanted these things included as part of the cash settlement package when we divorced. Lorena wanted me to reimburse her $5,000 for the value of the items.

I was in a state of shock. I received the fax at work and we had a department meeting right after I read it. It must have showed on my face all during the meeting because afterward Agatha asked me to come into her office and close the door.

She started out by telling me that she knew that something was seriously wrong, and wanted to know what it was. I was so upset that I divulged everything to her about the recent fax.

How could I have stolen Lorena's jewelry box when two armed sheriffs had escorted me from the property on Monday December 11, 2000? In her anger, Lorena had smashed her own jewelry box that morning. Then she had testified in court under oath on Friday, December 15, 2000 that it had been broken during the fight. Now, it was a year and a half later and she was swearing under oath that I had stolen her jewelry box, and wanted me to compensate her for it.

As if that weren't enough, she had also asked the judge to issue a bench warrant for my arrest for stealing her jewelry. She was asking the judge to have me arrested and to go to jail for something that she knew she had done herself.

Lying under oath in the legal system was supposed to be considered perjury and punishable by law. But the system was failing. I'd dealt with a lot of people over the years of this dilemma. They told me to just let God take care of Lorena, that in due time she was going to get just what she had coming to her. I was told, "You just continue to do the right thing. She'll get her justice one of these days." Though I shared that belief, it wasn't much consolation when she was trying to get me arrested for something that had never happened. Nor did it help me deal with a legal system that continued to bend in Lorena's favor.

During all of the trips to New Jersey, Justin and I continued to be close, surprisingly close considering how young he was and how rarely I saw him. He would always sit in my lap or right next to me. If I got up and went down the hallway to go to the bathroom, he would follow me and try to open the bathroom door.

Every morning he would wake up at Mom's house and sit in my lap for hours watching television. I could always tell he really missed his father and longed to spend more time with me.

As Justin got a little older I taught him quite a bit about sports. We would always go to the park and play kickball or soccer. He loved to run and was always laughing. Justin was always happy to be spending time with me. I always felt the same.

It was times like those when I realized just how much he really missed me. One time my cousin Jimmy Pope had a cookout at my uncle's home. Justin was playing with the bigger kids and when they picked on him he came crying to me for comfort.

Later I was sitting on the couch and he walked toward me. I was in a playful mood so I held both hands out, teasing him and not allowing him to get too close to me. Man did he throw a fit and burst out crying. It broke my heart, I was only kidding with him. After that I knew I'd never do that to him again.

I was still renting from Ethan. In January of 2003 Mike moved out. Because we had gotten along so well, Mike asked me to move into his new place with him. I went over one night, but I decided I didn't want to have to start a whole new routine all over again so I respectfully declined his offer.

A teenage kid moved into Mike's old room. Because of our age difference we hardly ever talked. We had nothing in common and he wasn't there very much.

I continued to make periodic trips to New Jersey to try and settle my divorce case and to see Justin.

In January 2003 the *Denver Post* did a story on me and my first book *My Cowboy Hat Still Fits*. I had started writing the book in March 2002. At the time it was just what the doctor ordered to help me maintain my own sanity. It helped take my mind off of all the negative things that were occurring in my life and helped me to concentrate and relive the past positives. It was the best therapy for me.

One of my co-workers was an insatiable reader. The idea to write the book had begun when Treisha Kong told me that I had lived a very unique life and asked if I'd ever considered sitting down and putting it on paper.

I told her that I might write a book about my rodeo career. Once I seemed open to the idea, she hammered and hammered me. Finally, I sat down one day at the computer and started writing my story. I was able to focus on the manuscript, and it gave me a lot of incentive to keep going.

In a way that was the motivation I needed to get out of the bed in the mornings and get after it. Before I started writing, I would just fall asleep on the bus commute to and from work unless I engaged in a conversation with someone. For the most part I usually kept to myself.

After I started writing, during the commute I proofread my book and made corrections until I could get back on the computer again. At times I even shared some of my stories with other people. After letting some of my co-workers read parts of my book they'd ask, "Were you a journalism or English major in college?"

My answer was always the same, "No. The only time I wrote in college was when a term paper was due." Their feedback was always so positive and helpful to me. It takes me awhile for things to sink in.

I flew ATA for most of my flights back East. I'll always remember boarding the flights in Philadelphia and the song *Don't Know Why (I Didn't Call)* by Norah Jones was playing on several occasions. It was kind of sad and always made me think about Justin. I was always afraid that Lorena was going to flip out and physically hurt him. One time I was visiting my sister Roz in Fort Worth, Texas in October 2003. I heard that song and tears rolled down my face.

I met a woman named Laura Cutera on one of my connecting ATA flights from Chicago to Denver. She was a college professor at the University of Colorado in Denver. She sat right next to me. I was so tired that I planned to sleep the entire time.

I grabbed a pillow and a blanket and she asked for the same.

She spoke to me and I thought that would be the end of it. For some unknown reason, we started talking and I shared with her that I was a writer. She was also a writer. She wrote plays.

None of my work had been published yet, but I had a few stories that I planned to submit to publications and literary agents. I had a couple printed and carried them in my briefcase. She wanted to see them. So, soon after we took off I got up and pulled them out for her to read.

I was curious and peeked at her a few times, trying to get an assessment of what she was thinking about my stories. When she had read all three stories she looked at me and said, "I can see a movie coming out of this."

It sure made me feel good. The woman was a professional playwright and knew the literary industry well. My book wasn't even complete yet and she was already saying it was going to become a movie. It really gave me a boost.

Many others had told me the same thing. I did my best not to think about it. It was hard though. My personal life was in chaos and the book gave me hope of a brighter day ahead.

I became obsessed with the book, probably because it allowed me to forget the legal mess and how much I missed Justin. There were nights when I couldn't sleep and would turn to thinking about the possibilities for the book.

When I was writing I was trying to recall events that had taken place during my many years of rodeoing. It was difficult since Lorena had maliciously thrown away all of my rodeo entry books. I had kept excellent notes during my entire career in those books and now they were all gone. Having the back-up material and documentation would have made my writing so much easier.

In November 2002, I became a published writer when *The Rodeo News* out of LaPorte, Colorado published one of the stories from my book. The newspaper published a second story from my book in the December 2002 issue.

Then in January 2003 a newspaper out of Oklahoma called *Humps N' Horns Bull Riding News* published a story straight from my book. *The Denver Post* did a story on me and the secretary in my department sent it via e-mail to all of the employees in the Denver Phone Center at TIARRA. Until that day most of my co-workers had no idea who I was.

Another weekly publication from Windsor, Colorado called the *Fence Post* published a story about me and the book in January 2003. I also did a radio interview on 850 am KOA. Suddenly the book and I were getting a ton of publicity. It did a lot to raise my spirits and restore some self confidence.

I had finished the manuscript, but then faced the formidable task of trying to find either a literary agent or a publisher for my book. Friends told me that I'd better have some very thick skin.

Back at work, I shared my accomplishments with a former African-American co-worker who had been transferred to a different department. He told me something that really surprised and shocked me.

Harold said, "I'm going to tell you right now that this company doesn't want to see you be successful outside these walls. Do you also realize that you intimidate the people around here? You are a dark skinned guy. You're very athletic looking and you carry yourself well."

I never forgot what he told me and soon learned that he knew exactly what he was talking about. It was a very eye opening experience for me as I learned that some people who seemed to be in my corner before I started receiving all of the media attention were getting very jealous and started dropping like flies. I hadn"t expected that and it caught me off guard.

I continued to make periodic trips to New Jersey. By then Justin was starting to really like and understand the game of basketball.

Sometimes we'd go to the eight foot basket behind the Mary S. Shoemaker Elementary school for his benefit. Justin couldn't shoot that high so I would give him the ball and lift him up and allow him to dunk it. Then we would clap our hands and cheer. He loved it. This way he didn't stand around unable to participate. Justin loved sports. He liked them even better when he was able to be a part of the ongoing action.

In February 2003 I was in New Jersey to visit Justin. It was President's Day weekend and we got hammered by a Nor'easter. We got about twenty inches of snow. It started snowing on a Saturday evening and pretty much snowed all night. Everything on Sunday was cancelled including church services. So of course, I couldn't take Justin back to North Jersey. My flight on Monday morning was cancelled and the Philadelphia airport was closed. The kids all loved it because it meant school was closed.

Mom had invited us over for Sunday dinner. The roads were so bad that Patricia couldn't even drive over to mom's house. We bundled up like Eskimos in a blizzard and walked over there. Justin was still so little that I perched him up on my shoulders and carried him over to Mom's.

Lorena called my Mom later that evening and said, "I guess Abe isn't going to bring Justin home because of the weather." The New Jersey Turnpike had been closed due to so many accidents. I didn't talk to Lorena. I had no desire to. She told my mom, "It just started snowing here a few hours ago and we only have a few inches so far."

I knew it was another one of her lies. It had been snowing in New Jersey for several hours.

Lorena called my sister Patricia on Monday, wanting me to bring Justin back home. She asked to speak to me and I refused. Lorena still had the restraining order on me which restricted me from talking to her on the telephone. Besides, the roads were still pretty bad. I wasn't going to risk Justin's life and my own just to appease her.

I wasn't able to get out of Philadelphia until Wednesday. I had missed a few days at work due to the blizzard. Patricia agreed to take me back to the airport and then take Justin to the daycare center in Clark.

It broke my heart when I was dropped off at the airport

and Justin started crying saying, "Daddy, I don't want you to go."

When Patricia and Mom dropped Justin off at the daycare center, they said he threw a fit. The daycare staff called Lorena at work to tell her.

I experienced two big blizzards in early 2003. In March we got about thirty-six inches of snow. Our office was closed for a day. Like a fool I went to work on the second day. It was pretty dangerous. I walked down the street facing oncoming traffic. Whenever a car would approach, I would have to jump into the snow bank. You couldn't walk on the sidewalks because there was about four feet of snow on them. The snow plows had added to the thirty-six inches that were already there.

Most of my co-workers were snowed in and didn't come in. It was like a ghost town at work. Our supervisor closed our department and sent us home early.

It was truly amazing that so much snow could fall in one vicious storm. I think part of the reason I went to work was just to get out of the house, and also get away from Ethan and the other guys who were living there. I didn't enjoy being cooped up all day long again with that bunch.

There was so much snow that several flat roofs collapsed because the structures couldn't handle the weight. It would be weeks before the huge mounds of snow that had been piled up in the parking lots would melt.

In the spring I was still dealing with my pending divorce and still trying to maintain a relationship with Justin. Lorena was constantly calling me at work and leaving me harassing voicemails. And she was sending threatening and harassing e-mails to my work e-mail address.

We had a scheduled conference call with the two of us and our attorneys. I was at work when the call came through. Lorena's attorney proposed that we drop the mutual restraining orders. I was all in favor of dropping mine. My attorney told me not to make that decision right away and that he wanted to speak with me in private first. He recommended that I not drop the restraining order.

Lorena had proposed that we get involved in family counseling sessions with a Dr. Davis, whom she had previously taken Justin to see. I wasn't interested in any family counseling sessions. Besides, I couldn't see the purpose of having family counseling sessions. Once we were divorced we would no longer be a family.

I had been opposed to this for a long time. Mark Schmidt thought it was a good idea to be involved in these family counseling sessions saying, "You're always going to be a family." I thought this was ridiculous. If we were always going to be a family, then why were we spending all of this money on attorney's fees and getting a divorce?

Lorena had wanted me to travel to New Jersey for these sessions. Considering the costs involved and the inconveniences, I agreed to get involved and do the sessions via the telephone only.

Lorena admitted to throwing away our wedding photos. I requested that she contact the photographer in New Jersey and pay for duplicate copies. Lorena and her attorney agreed that she would send me the duplicate copies of our wedding pictures.

My sister Patricia had taken a lot of photos at our cookout in Mom's backyard and then the rehearsal at the church the day before the wedding. Lorena had also destroyed all of those. I wished I had kept them instead of trusting Lorena and putting them in with our other pictures and mementos.

During the phone call, I blasted Lorena for all the things she had been doing to me and for throwing my possessions into the trash. She apparently got upset, burst out crying, jumped out of her chair and left the room. Although we were on a conference call and she was in New Jersey, it was very apparent what was going on. You could hear her attorney Shelly Martin say, "Come back here, come back here. Okay, Lorena just left the room."

Meanwhile, my attorney had been pressuring me to accept some ridiculous settlement proposals. I balked at each one and refused to give in. They were all one sided and in Lorena's favor. There were many times I had to question whose side he was really on. I understand the lawyers were trying to achieve a settlement but very little consideration was ever given to my concerns. Lorena was the one who had both attorneys' attention.

We had been working for weeks so I could go back to the house in Rahway in order to retrieve the rest of my things that Lorena hadn't already disposed of. Finally, my attorney received permission from Lorena and her attorney that I could go to the house and get my things on Easter Sunday when I returned Justin.

My attorney assured me everything was in place. I gathered up friends and family. David Walker drove his pickup truck and we hauled a trailer, as well.

Before we went to the house I stopped at the police station to make sure that the paperwork I had was in order. The police informed me that although I had letters from the two attorneys, I would be in violation of the restraining order if I were to go onto the property without a policeman. The agreement hadn't been approved by the Union County court.

I was shocked and also upset at my attorney. He put my life and well-being in double jeopardy by telling me that everything was okay for me to go to the house.

We went to the house and I told Lorena that I would be in violation of a court order if I set foot on the property. Her response was, "Why did you have to go the police station first?"

I refused to get out of the vehicle. I had driven my sister's van in case we picked up a few items that I didn't want blowing in the wind or getting wet if it rained.

Lorena approached the van saying, "Look Abe, you can go ahead and get out and get your things. I'm not going to call the police on you."

Only a fool would've have listened to her at that stage. There had been three separate incidents where she had screamed at me that she was going to call the police on me since our separation in December 2000 and I didn't trust her at all. No one in their right mind would have.

I ended up walking away from the stuff. Lorena was

upset, as usual. I just couldn't take the risk that I would try to take something of mine that she objected to. I could vividly see her running into the house screaming, "I'm calling the police on you."

I was furious with my attorney at that point. I didn't want very much to do with him other than to get the divorce case over and move on. He'd done me one disservice after another and yet was charging me some huge fees.

He had tried to get me to sign a Quit Claim deed to give Lorena the house in New Jersey. I had refused. I wanted to get what was left of my property there and be compensated for the items that she had thrown away.

Lorena wanted to get the home refinanced. My attorney insisted that it was in my best financial interest to allow her to do so. I was no fool. Once I gave her control of the house she would have insisted it was her property and so anything on the property automatically belonged to her. I obviously couldn't count on the legal system to come to my rescue. They had already screwed me every which way but loose.

My attorney had sent me an overnight package in late 2002 outlining certain items that he thought I should accept. It was a complete waste of money to mail me packages overnight as if there were a sense of urgency. There was no sense of urgency on his part. I had badgered him to subpoena the records from Verizon. I had badgered him to get the answers to the interrogatories that Lorena was court ordered to fill out and return to him. Any time she violated a court order, he refused to challange her behavior.

The house and the living conditions were getting to me in Northglenn. Ethan and the new guy were just plain gross at times. They knew I wasn't happy with their behavior and one night Ethan came upstairs and told me I should consider moving out.

He said, "You really don't get along with anyone else in this house, and so you need to be gone by the end of the month."

I had now become accustomed to getting kicked out of the

place where I was living and didn't take the news very well. I stepped right up to the plate and said, "I'll move out when I find another place to live, but until then I'll be staying right here."

Ethan didn't respond, and so that was the end of the discussion. This all happened about the middle of April. I started looking for a place to live. I preferred to stay in Northglenn since I was so comfortable in the area.

I went to several places that had ads in the newspaper. One guy wanted me to fill out a whole questionnaire and asked for my social security number. I didn't mind him doing his homework and background checks on me, but there was no way that he was going to get my social security number.

I went to another place that had an ad in the newspaper. There was a house full of pit bulls and puppies. I would have the entire basement area to myself. The place was filthy. I was deathly afraid of pit bulls. There was dog poop all over the house. I left knowing that I wasn't going to subject myself to living in such squalor.

I told a few friends that I was going to have to move. The word got around. One of my friends, Bart Timmons, a retired African-American bull rider, called and said I could move in with him. I went over one weekend and checked out his place.

The only thing that I didn't really like was that he wanted me to sleep in the basement. I wasn't too excited about that proposal. The basement was unfinished and had a cold concrete floor.

There was an empty bedroom upstairs. Bart said that he wanted to keep it unoccupied because his fifteen year-old daughter would visit on occasion and needed that bedroom.

A woman with two children had previously lived with Bart for awhile. The kids had lived in the basement. So Bart had no qualms about sticking me down there. At the time I didn't have a whole lot of options so I reluctantly accepted the invitation.

At the time my priority was to just get away from Ethan. I moved in with Bart in early May. He helped me move, bringing a trailer from his job site. He also helped me move in and get situated.

I was very grateful that a friend would reach out to me in my time of need. I was pretty much in dire straits. I really needed someone to show me that they cared about my well-being.

I had known Bart for several years from our days on the rodeo circuit. He had helped Lorena and me move from Fort Collins to Northglenn in September 1998. We had kept in touch ever since and so he knew my harrowing personal story.

Bart worked a lot of hours for Fed-Ex so I would have the house to myself most of the time. Except for sleeping in the basement, I would be comfortable in his home.

Bart was up and gone every morning before I even got out of bed. Then he wouldn't come home until after 9:30 p.m. He never cooked and so I could load the refrigerator up with as much food as I wanted.

It was a very different living situation thanthe one in Northglenn. Although it still wasn't what I was looking for, it was a relief to be there. When Bart heard that I was writing a book about my rodeo career, he really encouraged me. That made me feel good, too.

Despite the more positive environment, about two weeks after I moved in we had a late spring snowstorm. When it melted it flooded the basement and many of my clothes and personal items were ruined. And there's no question that in my unsettled state I was hyper-sensitive. I almost laid down on the bed and burst into tears.

I had always been a decent human being. I was considered by many to be a good catch. I had been kicked out of my home again and beaten down. Now, what little I owned and had been able to salvage was ruined in a flooded basement. I just couldn't understand why my life was in such a state.

Bart and I were both out of the limelight as far as the rodeo world was concerned. He had become a World Champion in the Senior Pro Division. His World Championship was between a few older guys who were well past their prime. The real test of talent was to be able to prove yourself in the PRCA or the PBR (Professional Bull Riders).

Much to my surprise, I began to notice that the more media attention I received, the less encouragement flowed my way from Bart. The dynamic between us slowly began changing.

In June I was summoned to come back to New Jersey again. I had agreed to sign a Consent Order giving Lorena possession of the property, provided I was first allowed to get my personal things from the home.

I gathered a crew again and went to Rahway on Sunday afternoon June 22, 2003 when I took Justin home. I had to first stop at the police station because of the restraining order.

Lorena had all of the things that she wanted me to have outside in some boxes again. I was able to get my file cabinets and a few old dishes that she didn't want. She kept most of my dishes, all of my silverware, cups, glasses, pots, pans, kitchen utensils, and on and on. These were things that I'd had before we got married. The list was endless.

There were several items in the shed that I owned. When I tried to get my shovels, electric hedge trimmers, and my wheelbarrow Lorena came around to the back of the house out of view of the police officer and said, "Oh no you don't." She took everything that I had and put them back into the shed. Then she slammed and locked the door.

My attorney had told me to take a camera. Anything that was in dispute, I was supposed to take a picture of to present it to the court later. I had a camera. But because that stipulation wasn't listed on the paperwork and Lorena had a fit, the police officer wouldn't allow me to take any pictures.

The police officer had told me prior to going to the house that if Lorena and I argued, he would terminate the visit immediately. Lorena wouldn't allow any of us into the house. I insisted that I was supposed to be able to take an inventory of items in the house.

The police officer asked me, "Is your name still on the mortgage for this house?"

I replied, "Yes."

Then he told Lorena, "I'm going to allow him into the house."

Lorena asked the policeman to remove his shoes before he came in. He looked at her with a very surprised expression on his face and said, "I'm not taking my shoes off for you, ma'am."

Justin was up on the main floor. When he started to come downstairs, Lorena screamed at him, "Justin you get out of here and go back upstairs!"

First we went to the basement and Lorena watched me like a hawk. She acted as if I was going to steal something. I found the jewelry she had accused me of stealing hidden in some boxes.

I picked up a container of blue shoe polish that I had purchased for a pair of cowboy boots that I owned. I tried to take it with me. Lorena screamed out, "That's my polish." So the police officer made me put it back down.

Lorena tried to block me from going upstairs to the main floor. The officer let me proceed. When I tried to go upstairs to the bedrooms she objected again.

He stepped in again and told her for about the fourth time, "Look lady, I said that he could have a look in this house, you may not like it so I'm going to tell you again that you need to calm down. He is allowed to look in every room."

The whole time Lorena was throwing a fit. I was only allowed to write down things of mine that were still in the house that Lorena refused to let me take. Although there were several of my possessions in the house, I wasn't allowed to take any of them.

Back outside on the street the policeman asked me, "What in the world did you do to that woman? Did you ever cheat on her?"

When I told him, "No," he was shocked. He told me, "I've never seen a woman act so hateful toward her husband. Usually it's when they were cheated on. But, if you say you never cheated on her, there have to be some serious issues going on with her. I'm going to write up a police report."

And he did:

Case number 2003-013323

Incident Report
Rahway Police department

Detailed to 2303 Winfield Street to standby as a peace officer while Mr. Morris removed some articles that were specified in a court order dated 6-19-2003. As per the court order Mr. Morris was allowed to take an inventory of articles that were questionable as to ownership. During that time Ms. Morris was agitative towards Mr. Morris. I had asked Ms. Morris several times to read the court order which clearly specified the inventory of articles. After repeating my request several times Ms. Morris reluctantly agreed and continued to be antagonistic towards Mr. Morris. The articles were removed as per the order and the inventory was completed.

When we got back to my mom's house there were a lot of visitors. I unpacked the few things that I was able to salvage from Rahway. I wanted to go downstairs and keel over and cry. If Mom's house hadn't been full of so many people, I probably would have.

We stashed a bunch of my things in my mom's basement. It had been two and a half years before I had been legally allowed to return to my home to retrieve my things and had only been able to get a few of them.

As soon as I returned to Colorado, I informed my attorney that I wasn't willing to sign the Consent Order because Lorena hadn't allowed me to get my personal property as stated on the form.

By that time he was so frustrated that he wanted out of my

case. It was mutual. I sent him a letter dated July 16, 2003 expressing my dissatisfaction with his so-called professional representation and services. He had sent me a letter demanding payment for services which said, "In the event that payment is not received by that date, (July 7, 2003) I will file the Motion to be relieved as counsel as set forth above."

I asked him in my letter if it was another one of his bluffs. I wrote, "I accept your offer to resign as a legal counsel in behalf of my divorce case. Maybe this time you WILL file a motion that you have stated that you were going to on my behalf.

"I have been dissatisfied with your recommendations, hesitation and reluctance to pursue certain courses of action such as the subpoenaing of the phone records from Verizon, failure to file the Contempt of Court motions, pressure to sign a Quit Claim deed, and pressure to a accept a $5,000 cash settlement from Lorena in June 2002."

I had received several letters from him threatening to file motions against Lorena, and he had never filed a single one. Yet here he was sending me a letter telling me that he was finally going to file a motion. By this time I wasn't even sure that he knew what "file a motion" meant. He had never proved to me that he even knew how.

He sat down and wrote out motions and then charged me his legal fees of $240 per hour. All of those motions were still sitting in a file in his office, yet my legal fees were constantly going up.

I decided I wasn't going to be buffaloed anymore. I had already paid him enough money out of my pocket and was getting nowhere except frustrated in this case.

In August 2003, I received a two page letter from him dated July 21, 2003. The envelope was sent via regular mail and postmarked August 12, 2003. Since I had moved, the original overnight letter had been returned to New Jersey. His letter was very detailed stating:

"I am in receipt of your letter dated July 16, 2003. The motion to withdraw as your attorney was filed about a week and a half ago and you should have received a copy by now. You should be aware that in my nearly sixteen years of practice, this is the first occasion I have had to file a motion for leave to withdraw as a client's attorney."

The letter was pointless to me. I wasn't at all concerned about what this man had done in his sixteen years of practice. I was only concerned about what he had done for me as my legal representative. When he said "practice" in his letter I guess that's exactly what I had received was practice.

My case wasn't practice to me. It was the real deal. I didn't sign up for practice with him. For me this was the Sunday afternoon game day. He had left his 'A' game at home.

I was so sick and tired of Lorena sending me harassing e-mails and leaving me harassing voice messages on my work phone. My attorney had sent letters to her attorney dated March 5, April 19 and August 12 of 2002 asking and later demanding that she cease and desist from sending these e-mails to me at work.

The letters stated, "… a motion will be filed for an Order holding her in contempt for violating the restraining order."

He'd never filed any motion and thus Lorena continued to violate the court orders. Because he threatened her and didn't follow through, Lorena became more defiant. He'd made it obvious to her that there were not going to be any consequences for her behavior.

The other sad thing was he had sent me copies of the motions that he had charged me fees to write up and then had never bothered to file any of them.

One of the last straws before he decided to withdraw came when he called me at work one day and tried to convince me not to go to the police in New Jersey to file a complaint about Lorena's numerous restraining order violations.

Lorena had refused to allow me to pick Justin up on Thursdays even though I was already in New Jersey. I had constantly been trying to secure more time with Justin on each visit. Those airline tickets were expensive and I was trying to

maximize my time with my son.

My attorney called and spoke to me while I was at work. He asked me if he was able to get one extra day of visitation with Justin on my next trip to New Jersey, would I be willing to forego all of the prior restraining order violations by Lorena as if they'd never happened.

I thought the man must be crazy to make such a ridiculous offer. After a couple years worth of violations, he wanted me to forgive them in exchange for ONE extra day of being able to spend time with my son?

I told him absolutely not. Again I had to wonder just whose side was my attorney on. He certainly wasn't looking out for my best interests.

In April 2003, he called me at work and when I didn't answer the phone he left a message recommending that I ignore all of the restraining order violations and "... let her start over with a clean slate."

This is after writing and charging me fees for all of the "I'll huff and then I'll puff and then I'll blow your house down" threatening letters that he had sent to Lorena's attorney, Shelly Marti, over a period of about six months, all of which contained threats he'd never followed through on.

I finally took matters into my own hands and went to the police in Rahway, New Jersey on July 23, 2003 with the threatening e-mails and a cassette tape recording of some of Lorena's messages.

I spent about three hours filling out paperwork, playing the tape and then waiting for a response from the district attorney of Union County.

Finally, I was told that Lorena wouldn't be arrested for all of the violations and nothing was going to happen to her.

Had the shoe been on the other foot, and she had been the one to go to the police because I was violating the restraining order, I was convinced the police and district attorney would've wasted no time in issuing a warrant for my arrest.

So much for the common meaning of "justice" for fathers in these cases. Apparently it really meant "just us," in favor of the mothers, regardless of what they did.

After going through all the paperwork at the police station, I was late picking up Justin. He was a little upset because he had been expecting me much earlier. He asked me why I was so late. Of course I couldn't really tell him where I'd been for the past three hours. This was another reason for me to be upset. I could've been spending this time with him had I known nothing would come of my efforts to see the law enforced.

Lorena and her attorney had filed a motion with the Union County court system. This was because I had refused to sign the Consent Order after my visit to the home to get my things. The motion asked for several things.

Lorena had taken Justin to see a child psychologist and the bill was $500. The visit was covered by her insurance at work, yet, she had lied and gotten the psychologist to write her out a receipt and wanted me to pay for half of the costs.

The motion also would give her attorney power of attorney to sign the Quit Claim deed to give Lorena sole ownership of our property and home in Rahway. This struck me as very strange.

Lorena had falsely claimed that I was calling and harassing the staff members at the daycare center. This was ridiculous. The only way that I could have a connection with Justin was to call him at the daycare center. I wasn't allowed to call Lorena at home because of the restraining order. Also, she had finally gotten her own phone number at home after I was resurrected from the dead with Verizon. Her new phone number was unlisted and she hadn't given it to me.

There was no way that I would jeopardize my only channel of communication with Justin. I was always polite to the staff on each and every call. Lorena felt a need to control this, as usual. She had asked the judge to only allow me to speak to Justin on a cell phone that she purchased. I'd have to pay for half of the costs of the cell phone and new service.

The motion also requested that I pay for the costs for the filing of the motion and Lorena's legal fees.

My attorney had told me in a letter that until the court officially relieved him of his representation, he was legally bound and would have to respond and oppose the motion that had been filed.

The motion was going to be read and signed by the judge on August 1, 2003. In essence my attorney had violated the Code of Ethics of the Bar Association because he stood by and did nothing to oppose their motion.

I honestly don't believe the judge thoroughly read the motion. I believe he only skimmed it and then signed it into law right away.

As a result of that motion, I had to pay Lorena $720 more

dollars. This was also on top of the $360 per week that the system was gouging out of my paychecks at work.

I also lost my home. Lorena's attorney signed some refinance papers as the power of attorney on *my* behalf. How could her attorney represent me without my permission, nevermind the seeming conflict of interest by virtue of the fact that she was Lorena's attorney? As far as I am concerned they illegally took my home away from me.

The judge decided I was required to travel to New Jersey and attend family counseling sessions with a Dr. Davis. So according to this court order I was required to fork out travel expenses to fly to New Jersey. There was no consideration given on whether or not I could visit with Justin during those trips.

I had a restraining order in place that forbade me to be near Lorena, but yet now I had a court order in place saying that I was required to attend the sessions. So either I ignored the court order and was subject to be held in contempt of court for not coming to New Jersey, or I violated the restraining order and attended the counseling sessions with Lorena. Perhaps you can understand how frustrating and confusing I found this, along with the fact that no judge or attorney seemed interested in actually finding out what my concerns were.

The court order forced me to pay $90 for Lorena obtaining a cell phone for Justin and attached an additional $25 to my monthly obligation to cover the cost.

I found out the judge had ruled that I could only speak to Justin on a cell phone when I made my weekly call to the daycare center to speak to him. The staff refused to let me speak to Justin anymore because Lorena had promptly taken a copy of the court order and given it to them. I was dismayed.

I had no way to speak to Justin after calling every week for over two and a half years. Lorena didn't even provide me with the new cell phone number. I couldn't blame anyone at the daycare center. They were only doing their job, because of the court order.

My new task at hand was to find another attorney in Union County to represent me. I made a few calls to some attorneys in the area and told them my horror story.

I called and spoke to Joseph Martinez whose office was located in Clark, New Jersey. His exact words to me over the phone were, "Your case is so messed up that I don't think I'll ever be able to fully straighten it out."

He agreed to take over my case. I had to overnight him a retainer of $3,000. It was extremely frustrating to have to start over and bring my new attorney up to speed on my case. I felt as though I was spinning my wheels in sand. It was taking a huge toll on my patience, attitude and my bank account.

One of the first things that Joseph Martinez did was to calculate my child support. He said that it should've been $121 per week from day one. He couldn't figure out where in the world the judge had come up with those figures because they were outrageously skewed.

At that point I had been forced to live on about $867 a month. At the same time I was paying over $360 per week or $1,442 a month in child support, Lorena was depositing over $5,300 (after taxes) into her bank account every month between her salary and the money I was sending her.

My co-workers couldn't believe the stories I was telling them. They constantly asked about Justin and how was he doing. They were shocked to hear me tell them that I really didn't know because I hadn't spoken to him for a few weeks. It was crazy.

Joseph Martinez and I spent the next month or so getting to know each other and for him to catch up on the case. One of the first things that we discussed was filing a motion as soon as possible in order to get my child support payments adjusted.

Also, because Lorena had been reluctant to let me see Justin other than the third weekend of each month, we wanted to get my visitation schedule adjusted to every other weekend.

After he was onboard he contacted Lorena's attorney because it had now been a few weeks since I had last spoken with Justin. The weeks turned into months. Lorena finally gave my attorney the new cell phone number.

I started calling the number right away and it always went

straight to the voice mail. At first, I was under the impression that Lorena took that cell phone to the daycare center every day that Justin was in attendance, but I should've known better. The staff there said no, Lorena had never given them Justin's cell phone or the number.

After awhile, I started documenting every time I called that cell phone. I called that cell phone twenty-five times and Lorena refused to answer it. One time, I called it and she answered. It must have been by mistake. She said, "Hello," and then immediately hung up. When I called right back it went right to voice mail. It was a complete joke and a waste of my time, not to mention the fact I was paying for the phone and supposedly the privilege of talking to my son, which I wasn't even able to do.

Can you imagine a four-year child being subjected to only speaking to his father on a personal cell phone? Now keep in mind a Superior Court judge in the state of New Jersey signed that court order. One would think that adults usually make rational and logical decisions, especially a judge. I suppose Justin was supposed to carry that cell phone around with him on the playground when he was with the other little kids. I guess if the other little kids had asked him, he was going to tell them that he needed that cell phone just in case his Dad were to call and want to talk to him.

Imagine that I called and left him a message or asked him to call me back. How was a child going to retrieve the message or respond to it? It was a good thing that I didn't send him a text message, huh? At four he barely even knew his A,B, C's.

After awhile, I started documenting the date and time of my phone calls to Justin's cell phone. I was hoping to someday be able to use the evidence in court. I still couldn't understand why no one would listen to my side of this ridiculous story. Somehow, I still believed that Lorena would be forced to obey the court orders and the law.

Finally, in September we filed a motion asking for a lot of changes. Lorena's attorney had asked that Lorena be present when the judge made his decisions on the pending motion. I guess Lorena figured she would be able to influence some of the judge's decisions, and so she took off work and was present for the reading of the motion.

Finally something amazing happened. The judge signed a court order in October 2003 requiring Lorena to undergo an extensive psychiatric evaluation because of all of her bizarre behavior. He also required the child support department to do a thorough audit on the account because I had so grossly overpaid the system.

He also vacated his earlier decision about the cell phone. I would now be allowed to contact Justin at the daycare center again. He also required Lorena to pay all the costs incurred with that cell phone in the future.

My child support was supposed be reduced to $121 a week, the amount that it should have been set at from day one. Shelly and Lorena came up with some bogus calculation and an extra $15 per week was added to the figure. So in one swift move my child support obligation was reduced from $360 a week to $136.

My visitation schedule was changed to twice a month instead of the once a month deprivation that I had endured for almost three years. The judge also ruled that I'd be allowed to go back to the home to retrieve my personal property as long as a police officer and one of the attorneys was present.

The judge rescinded his earlier ruling and decided I wouldn't be required to travel to New Jersey to have family counseling sessions with Lorena and Dr. Davis. This is another reason I seriously don't believe he thoroughly read the motion on August 1. Why would he court order me to fly to New Jersey without any consideration of the time and costs involved with that decision?

Joseph Martinez called me at my work phone number to tell me that the judge had ruled in my favor. He also said that during the court appearance Lorena had gotten very upset and seemed to blame the outcome on her attorney. Her body language had done all of the talking and she wasn't very happy.

Afterward, I calling the daycare center to speak to Justin. Despite the court order, the staff still refused to allow me to speak with him. I told them that there was a new court order in place regarding that cell phone.

I had to get my attorney involved with the legal department at Kindercare. Lorena had lied to the staff saying that the judge had vacated the previous court order and that she would have to pay for all of the costs involved with the cell phone for Justin. Lorena told them that I was still required to use it to contact Justin.

It was only after Joseph Martinez wrote a letter to Kindercare explaining to them that Lorena had lied to them about the new court order that I was finally able to speak to Justin again. Of course that cost me more legal fees to have him draft and send that letter. It had been about four months since I had even heard Justin's voice. It was such a shame.

I wrote letters to my previous attorney and each partner in his firm asking them to return some of my legal fees. In October or November 2003 I received a notice from the Union County Court system that a civil lawsuit had been filed against me by my previous attorney and his law firm.

They were asking for $8,632.89 in unpaid legal fees plus court costs of $54.00. The total amount of the civil lawsuit amounted to $8,686.89.

This is breakdown of the lawsuit: I had previously paid my attorney $12,052.40 out of pocket costs to represent me. The lawsuit claimed I still owed him an additional $8,244.18 for services rendered. The accrued interest on this account was $388.18. So as of July 31, 2003 his law firm claimed I owed them another $8,632.89. This made his total bill for services $20,685.29.

Then to intimidate me, they court ordered and required that I show up in Scotch Plains, New Jersey in person to answer a serious set of interrogation questions.

Not one to back down from a challenge, I immediately got busy. I'm sure I got my tenacity from all those days of riding bulls and the mindset of a professional bull rider. I wasn't going to sit around, be upset and not do anything about it. I called a few attorneys in New Jersey asking for advice and wanting to know if they would be interested in representing me if I filed a lawsuit against Mark Schmidt and his law firm.

Although a few were willing to listen to me, I found out that they weren't willing to go up against one of their own. It was kind of like an unwritten code in a fraternity. They all pretty much stuck together. I did find one attorney who sympathized with me and my dilemma. He gave me some advice but told me that he would need to think about it as far as taking my case.

At least that was a brief breath of fresh air. When I told him that I was planning to counter sue, he told me the exact terminology to use in my letter when I filed the paperwork. By using that terminology their law firm was going to know that I had been doing some homework, and had been speaking with another attorney. This would keep them in the dark, so they didn't know exactly what they were up against.

Financially, I was in a funk. With so much going on around me it was like my head was spinning. I didn't have a girlfriend, mostly because I couldn't afford one. And I certainly wasn't comfortable with the prospect of bringing a viable candidate home to let them see my little bed parked in the concrete jungle of Bart's basement.

I was only bringing home about $867 per month and was forking out over $1,442 in child support payments. I approached Bart and asked him to lower my rent because I was struggling. He refused and wouldn't even consider lowering my rent payments to help another so-called "brother" out.

I was behind on my rent. I didn't even pay October. Around the third of November Bart left a note for me on the kitchen counter. It had broken down the rent payments month by month. There was no reduction in the monthly payments. So there was his decision. Despite my struggles, he wasn't going to give me a break on my rent.

At the bottom of the note it said balance due $1,000. Then the note said, "Abe, No pay—No Stay. You have 30 days to move. Thanks."

I had no option but to catch up on my rent payments and just endure the pain and suffering. What bothered me most of all was that Bart didn't even have the decency to tell me, one on one like a man. He had to take the cowardly approach and left me a note on the kitchen counter. It was obvious that our relationship had deteriorated, and in no small part, I'm sure, due to my situation with Lorena.

In 2002 I'd sat down and written a long letter to Lorena's ex-husband. I'd sent the letter to his parents' address and they'd forwarded it on to him. We'd kept in touch and in November 2003 he agreed to meet me in Denver.

Samuel was a traveling salesman and he still held the same job he'd had when he was married to Lorena. They'd endured a very tumultuous marriage, which was no surprise to me. They were separated for a few years and Lorena wanted to get back together. Samuel had refused. After awhile Lorena had filed for divorce.

When Samuel was served with his divorce papers, he in turn filed for divorce citing the reason was because "she was crazy." Lorena finally was able to convince him to change the verbiage to "irreconcilable differences." Altogether they were married for a total of eight years, they'd only lived together for the first three.

Samuel came to Denver approximately twice a year. We met in the lobby of his hotel and compared notes on Lorena for about an hour. We both agreed that she must be bipolar and had some kind of a chemical imbalance. Samuel also told me that Lorena was taking medication and seeing a psychiatrist during their marriage.

"Is Lorena taking medication now? I can't believe she's not

on some kind of medication."

Samuel confirmed that they had had multiple arguments and disagreements throughout their marriage. It had been very volatile for him, as well. He also told me that the police had been called to their home in Barlett, Illinois on a few occasions because of domestic disputes. He and Lorena had filed domestic violence charges against each other, but they were later dropped.

Lorena—no surprise—had continually lied to me saying that the police were never involved in any disputes in her first marriage. Lorena constantly told me, "Whenever Samuel and I had problems, we worked them out ourselves. We never got the police involved. You don't know how to be in a marriage."

Lorena many times had said to me, "I never loved you. I loved Samuel. I hate you. The only reason that I married you was because I was lonely."

My short meeting with Samuel sure shed a lot of light on some of the things that I had encountered with Lorena. After listening to some of his horror stories at least I knew that it wasn't just me. Lorena obviously had some serious deep-rooted problems that she'd never dealt with.

In December I went to the Wrangler National Finals Rodeo with another friend named Stewart. We were friends at the time, but since then we've gone our separate ways.

On the drive out to Las Vegas I told him in detail about my legal problems and woes. As a friend he strongly recommended that I just give in and pay the attorney the $8,600 and get it over with. He told me there was no way that I could win.

Stewart had had some problems of his own dealing with the legal system. I thought he'd encourage me to fight them, being a former bull rider himself. Instead he was telling me to "just cut and run." I certainly didn't appreciate his advice.

After I came back from Las Vegas I received another bombshell from Bart. He'd been around the house all weekend, doing some house cleaning. He said very little to me. He had hired a lady to come in and spruce up the place a bit.

On Monday morning I got out of bed and came upstairs to go to the bathroom. On the kitchen counter was a note that said, "Abe, you have till Sunday to move all your stuff out. Locks will be change (sic) on Monday. Thank. (sic)"

I was baffled. I was current on my rent and didn't owe Bart a single penny. I had paid him all the money that I owed him, even though he'd refused to lower my monthly rent. I read the note and walked into the bathroom and started shaking uncontrollably. I tried to stop but couldn't. It was the first time in my life that I can honestly remember shaking like that. I knew it had gotten to me. Emotionally, I was a wreck.

I didn't speak to Bart about kicking me out until Wednesday evening. He scolded me about not vacuuming the place and a few other minor details. I didn't feel like I had any real ownership in his townhome when I was sleeping in the dungeon basement. He agreed to allow me to stay and decided not to change the locks afterall.

When Christmas rolled around I had been sending e-mails to Lorena for a few weeks, asking if she would allow me to see Justin. As usual she refused to respond.

Since I wasn't going to be able to see Justin, I opted not to go back to New Jersey for Christmas. I couldn't afford to go anyway. I figured it was best for me to stay in Colorado.

I had told myself that every day I got up, it was because I was doing it for Justin. He was the one spark in my life that kept me going. Each morning when my feet touched that cold miserable concrete floor it was a reality check, but I was determined that despite the hardship, I was going to endure and wasn't going to give up.

My legal battle in New Jersey raged on. I had to write a letter and submit documentation to an attorney's arbitration committee concerning my unpaid legal fees. I missed the deadline by a few days and they refused to consider my case.

By the time the New Year rolled around I was getting beat up every which way but loose. It was tough. I was determined to hang in there.

I had also contacted the New Jersey State Bar Association and filed a grievance against mt former attorney and his law firm. I even included the tape recorded message of him recommending that I waive all of the restraining order violations by Lorena and let her start over with a clean slate.

A few months later the committee ruled in his favor. A few people had told me that they weren't going to do anything to him to start with. They said it was a "good ol' boys network" and they looked out for their own.

I had the option to file an appeal in thirty days and so I did. The bar association board again found no wrongdoing on the part of my former attorney. It turned out to be another waste of my time and efforts. But I continued to forge ahead.

The Union County Court sent notification that I was to appear in court in February 2, 2004 for the lawsuit hearing. One of their attorneys had approached my new attorney, Joseph Martinez, at a function and wanted to discuss the case.

I called the man on the telephone. He refused to talk to me. He only wanted to talk to my current attorney.

After I flew back to New Jersey, my attorney called me on a Friday morning and said they wanted to make me a deal. It had to be done and submitted to the court by 4:00 p.m. because the hearing was on Monday morning at 8:00 a.m.

They agreed to drop their lawsuit against me if I agreed to drop the sixty thousand dollar counter suit against them. My attorney had previously told me that even if I could prove that I was right, the judge would rule in their favor and require me to pay them the outstanding balance of $8,600.

He urged me not to fight them, because I was going to lose. Again, they were all going to stick together. What I mostly wanted was to not have to pay that additional $8,600 for all of my former attorney's shoddy and unprofessional work. I had already forked out over $12,000 of my hard earned money and had gotten absolutely nowhere with him. In fact I was worse off than before I had hired him.

Even after he had made a decision that he was no longer willing to represent me, my former attorney had charged me $516 for the time that he spent drawing up his motion for withdrawal for the court. He sure had a lot of nerve. I wasn't even considered to be on his clock anymore and yet he wanted to charge me more fees.

Reluctantly, I agreed to their concessions. Later on, I found out that the reason they were so eager to settle with me out of court was because if my malpractice lawsuit went to court, they would have to report that to their insurance carrier. Even if they beat me for the $8,600, their premiums would automatically go sky high because the firm had been sued. Moving forward the firm didn't want a black mark on their record so they let me off.

In a sense it was a moral victory for me. I had stood up to the big bad wolf who had huffed and puffed. What irritated me most was that we could have settled this before I even flew to New Jersey. I think they wanted to make sure that I was going to show up in court before they made their move. Otherwise, I would have lost by default.

My former attorney had allowed me to suffer for over two years with my child support payments. From day one he told me, "You are paying a lot more for child support than you are obligated to pay." He could have filed a motion right away to get that rectified. He never did.

I was down, but far from being out in January 2004. One of the big breaks in my life was when FOX 31 News in Denver decided to do an in depth story on my rodeo career and book. It couldn't have come at a better time. I needed something to start feeling really, really good about myself again. It was the perfect shot in the arm.

On Monday, January 19th the television station aired a segment on me that lasted for almost three minutes. It was also done to coincide with Martin Luther King's Holiday. I sat there in awe of the story. I was very impressed and amazed at how well it turned out. I give all the credit to Shaul Turner. She was the one who approached and then produced the story for FOX 31 News.

The segment was aired twice that evening. I stayed up late to watch it both times. There were a lot of things that I picked up on that I'd missed the first time it was on the air.

I went back to New Jersey to see Justin in late February 2004. During my other visits I was able to show Justin some footage of me riding bulls. He loved to watch the VHS tapes.

There were so many times that I'd pick him up and he would hardly say a word to me on the drive back to Mom's house. I had to really work just to get him to talk. I would focus my rearview mirror on him and watch him as I drove.

It seemed like most of the time Justin was sizing me up. It was as if he had to get to know me all over again. I was like a stranger to him. By the time we finally arrived in Woodstown he would say, "I want to watch Daddy ride bull on T.V."

I'd let him wear one of my old cowboy hats around the house. He wanted to wear it while he was watching my tapes. Then Justin would ride imaginary bulls while standing in front of the television set.

Sometimes, watching a tape he would say, "Slow Daddy, slow." That meant he wanted me to switch to slow motion. "I like to watch Daddy on slow."

Then Justin would stomp on the floor. This of course would make me laugh my head off. I'd ask, "What are you doing?"

"I'm spurring. I'm spurring like Daddy."

In one of my tapes I made a great ride and dismounted and tossed my cowboy hat into the air. Justin would mimic me and throw his cowboy hat across the living room.

That would get him warmed up. After that he would talk

and be comfortable the rest of the visit. The sad thing was by the time he would really warm up and be at ease, it would be Sunday afternoon and time to go back to his mom in Rahway.

I also sat down and showed Justin my photo albums of me riding bulls. He loved it. We would go through an entire album and look at all the pictures. He would ask me the name of each bull and I'd respond. Then at the end I'd say, "All done," and close the book. Justin would immediately open it back up and want to start the process all over again.

Sometimes Justin would just sit on the living room floor and pretend he was riding bulls. He would pretend he was taking a wrap with his imaginary bull rope. Then he would pound on the floor like some of the bull riders did on television. They were actually pounding their hands down tight before they nodded for the chute to open. Then he would stand up, nod his head and pretend he was riding, all the while waving his free arm in the air. Then he would throw his cowboy hat after the eight seconds whistle and hold both arms high in the air. Justin would go and retrieve his cowboy hat and repeat the entire process all over again.

Once, when we were walking across the parking lot going into the Acme grocery store, all of a sudden Justin fell to the ground and got up holding his shoulder. He exclaimed, "Ow big mean bull get off of me! Daddy, big mean bull stepped on my shoulder." Justin knew several years before a bull stepped on me and separated my shoulder. He was also aware of the scar in the middle of my back where a bull had stepped on me.

I picked Justin up at Kindercare on Friday morning February 27, 2004 and told him I had a big surprise for him. I was going to wait until the next day to tell him but he couldn't wait.

I told him I had tickets to the PBR. He didn't even know what PBR stood for. I explained it meant Professional Bull Riders. I had him say it over and over until he got it right.

The next evening we attended the PBR event in

Philadelphia, Pennsylvania. Justin was so excited to go. He had longed to meet some of his heroes such as Adriano Moraes and Justin McBride. Justin McBride was a superstar and a fan favorite in the PBR. My son also liked him because they both had the same first name.

We arrived at the event early and I introduced Justin to Justin. Justin McBride gave Justin Morris an autograph. My son thoroughly enjoyed the event and afterward we went down to the locker room to personally meet some of the other bull riders.

I took a few pictures. When we were leaving I asked Justin, "So did you have a good time?"

"Yea Daddy, the only problem was I didn't get to ride."

I could only laugh. I finally knew the feeling of taking my son to a major athletic event and watching the gleam in his little eyes. It was truly priceless.

Since my demotion at work, I had longed for another opportunity to move back into the telephone counseling center. Openings became available and an e-mail was sent out to people in our department.

I was eligible. It was considered a unilateral move so there wouldn't be a salary increase. Funny thing was, only a select few in my department were notified that there were openings in the counseling department.

I didn't receive the e-mail notification and only found out through the grapevine. I wasn't happy that my supervisors were trying to be so sneaky about the opening.

I went online through the company website and posted for a new position. I then received a call from Human Resources telling me that if I wanted to be considered for the new positions, I would only need to give a resume to my supervisor.

I approached Agatha, knowing that she wouldn't be very receptive to my interest. Agatha had purposely left me off of that e-mail distribution list. The other two women supervisors had gone along with her, even though they knew what they were doing was wrong.

I told her what I'd been told by human resources and Agatha said that wasn't the way it was supposed to happen. She said, "Let me call HR and I'll get back to you." Agatha wasn't supposed to be doing her own underhanded screening process of who she wanted to be moved on to the next department.

Agatha came back and told me I would need to give her a copy of my resume. She reluctantly accepted it a few days later.

I was scheduled for an interview a couple of weeks later. There were eight of us altogether who would interview for five open positions in the next training class. I sweated through the interview, but thought I did a very good job.

One of my interviewers asked me a question about the famous bucking bull Bodacious. After that, I lit up and felt at ease discussing my rodeo career.

A few days later, I was told that I didn't make the cut. One of the reasons was because I had talked too much about my rodeo career. When I heard this, it infuriated me. I wasn't the one who started asking rodeo questions. Then in the end I got hammered for it.

The other feedback was I had been asked a question about something I had accomplished in my business career that really made me feel proud. I answered the question saying, "One year I finished third in the nation for the company I was with, based on sales volume."

I got hammered for this, as well. One of the interviewers later told me that she wanted me to answer the question based on something that I had done since I had been employed with TIARRA. The truth of the matter was I really hadn't done anything personally since I'd been there that made me feel good.

I also found out that five people were accepted into the next training class to start in May. Two were held back, but would automatically enter into the second class which would start in July. These two wouldn't have to go through the interview process again.

I was the only one who wasn't accepted that would have

to interview all over again in order to try to get into the July training class. Talk about a huge slap in the face. I told myself to keep my chin up, and that I would simply just try again at the appropriate time. I interviewed a few weeks later and was turned down again.

Then I was broken and humiliated.

When my direct supervisor, Leah, called me into her office to do my year-end appraisal, I wasn't interested in discussing anything with her. Leah told me that the reason I wasn't accepted was because I didn't interview well.

When I heard that I thought to myself, "Oh, I can a be a broadcast television commentator for Prime Sports and FOX Sports Networks for nine consecutive years and garner rave reviews. But yet you're going to sit here and have the audacity to tell me that I don't interview well?"

I tore into her and said, "When I go to my grave no one is even going to mention this company or anything that I did here. They will remember me as a professional bull rider, rodeo cowboy, motivational speaker and a writer. My legacy in life will have nothing to do with TIARRA."

I was putting on a show. I was so loud that Tomeka Muhammad, one of my co-workers on the telephones, got up from her desk and came over and asked, "May I please close this door?"

Then I stared out the window and paid no attention to anything that Leah had to say to me. Finally, sensing my consternation, Leah said, "I think it would be best if we terminate this discussion."

I needed to sign my appraisal. We didn't even go over it. I didn't even read it. I didn't care how I had been evaluated. It meant nothing to me. When I walked out of Leah's office I knew my time at TIARRA was limited. The writing was on the wall. All I needed was a good excuse to go. I no longer cared to work for a company that considered me inferior. I knew deep down inside that I could make a lot more money and enjoy my work life more elsewhere. It was just a matter of time before I would be gone.

It was kind of like a kid being left behind in elementary

school while all of his classmates were promoted to the next grade level. I had to learn to live up to the saying "when the going gets tough, the tough get going." I would stay at my job and position as long as I possibly could.

Although not totally devastated, I was very disappointed that I wasn't selected to go to the counseling phone center. I put the blame 100% on my direct supervisor. If she had said yes, I would've been selected.

Another supervisor named Jane came over to my desk a few months later and asked, "So Abe what are your plans for around here?"

The first thing out of my mouth was, "I know one thing, I'm not going to stay here. When my book is published I'll come back and sign a copy for you."

We had gone to lunch a few months before, and Jane had told me, "I'm really surprised that you're still working at this company. There's no doubt in my mind with all of your talents that you could make a lot more money working somewhere else."

I reminded her of that statement. Then I went off on her. Jane had been a vital part of the conspiracy that had kept me from being accepted into the counseling center, and then she was bold enough to waltz over to my desk and ask me questions about my future at TIARRA.

I tore her up so badly that the co-workers in the surrounding cubicles were sitting at their desks and cringing. After Jane finally left, Javaz, a co-worker, stood up and said, "Man you were so loud. I couldn't believe what you said to Jane."

I wasn't afraid because I knew that I had viable options. They all knew it, as well. All I cared about was doing just enough to keep my job and not a bit more.

Javaz said she went home and told her husband what I had said to Jane. Javaz came back and said that her husband was glad that I had stood up to them, and let them have a piece of my mind.

Management in corporate America has been known to put the pressure on their employees. That person usually has a spouse and children at home. Then the person being picked on goes home and complains to their spouse. The spouse is going to say, "I sympathize with your situation, but we have a mortgage and a family to support, so you need to get on back in there and just put up with the nonsense for now. We can't afford for you to be unemployed."

I wasn't in that situation. There was no one at home that would be hurt by my paychecks or lack thereof except myself. My biggest obligation at the moment was paying my weekly child support, and that was being garnished from my paychecks according to Lorena's wishes.

Putting that golden carrot out in front of me, and telling me that if I wanted to keep my job or even be eventually promoted, wasn't going to work in my case. I realized that I didn't fit the model that a good corporate company was looking for.

After I got cut for the second time, in my mind I completely gave up. I knew as long as I remained at that financial services company, I would never again try to be a part of the telephone counseling center.

John, one of the managers who interviewed me, gave me some good honest feedback on why I didn't make it. I always liked John and listened intently. He told me that I should really concentrate on certain areas and then give it another attempt.

I had submitted the completed manuscript of my first book to a few literary agents. They had all turned it down. Finally, in June of 2004 a publisher from Wyoming agreed to publish it.

By that time, I had been handing off segments of my book to another writer in Denver to edit who would then give it back to me to make corrections in my manuscript. I spent quite a bit of time working on the book. I was also writing a monthly column for *Humps N' Horns Bull Riding News*. Both projects occupied a lot of my spare time outside of work.

In late January, Bart notified me that he was putting his townhouse up for sale and that I might want to start looking for someplace else to live. This was probably the only time he told me a significant thing in person instead of writing me a note. I had already sensed that he was leaving because a real estate agent came to visit him on a Sunday afternoon.

One morning I got out of bed again and there was another note on the counter saying that his home had sold. We needed to be gone by February 24.

I wanted to stay close to the area because I had a health club membership at the local Bally's in Aurora. Also I was fairly familiar with the bus schedule for my downtown commute to work. I found an apartment complex which was located only about a mile away. I signed a six month lease.

Back in New Jersey, Lorena had been writing letters to the judge complaining that I was stalling and attempting to delay the divorce proceedings. All I was trying to do was reach a fair and equitable settlement.

The expensive negotiations continued between the two attorneys. We went back and forth and back and forth on several key issues. My new attorney was a lot better and seemed to have my long term interests in mind.

After moving into my one bedroom apartment, one of the first things I did was go out and buy a brand new bed. I had been sleeping on a little twin size bed since I'd returned to Colorado, and it was time for an upgrade.

I bought a queen size bed and promptly purchased some new flannel sheets to go along with it. I had had flannel sheets in the past. Lorena said she didn't like them, probably because she knew I loved them. When we had moved to New Jersey, she had maliciously cut up my flannel sheets and made cleaning rags out of them.

I didn't own any dishes or plates. I had to go to the store and buy plastic plates and bowls because I couldn't afford the good stuff. Again this was another reality check. It kept things in perspective for me. Another thing that kept me in check was riding the bus to work each day. The bus went right down East Colfax in Denver.

East Colfax was known for drugs and prostitutes. There were many people who were struggling and just barely able to make ends meet. There were also a lot of single teenage African-American mothers that were on that route.

Seeing those people every day was a reminder. It was probably one of the most undesirable bus routes in the city. Many of my co-workers couldn't believe that I rode that bus. They said they never would. They encouraged me to seek another means of transportation to and from work.

I continued to fork out money for airline tickets in order to try and maintain a relationship with Justin. I tried to see him at least every other month. Financially, I couldn't afford it, but I did it any away.

I had to go back to New Jersey for court in early spring. My attorney told me that Lorena owed her attorney thousands of dollars in unpaid fees, and that her attorney was sick and tired of dealing with her.

I had written a letter to Lorena's attorney threatening to go to human resources at TIARRA because Lorena continued to violate the restraining order. The attorney told the judge about the letter and he forbade me to do so.

Here the woman was in violation of a court order and this judge was telling me that I couldn't do anything about it because it might cost her her job. Lorena should've taken all of that into consideration when she was calling me at work, and sending me harassing e-mails.

Her attorney also made the court aware that TIARRA was closing their New York City phone center. The employees were going to be given the option of relocating to Charlotte, North Carolina, Denver, Colorado, or receiving a severance package.

The judge told Lorena that in light of everything that was going on, "I will probably court order you to move back to Denver.

You may not like it, but you will go."

During that hearing it was decided by both of our attorneys that we would meet with an outside mediator to see if we could resolve our differences and close out our case. If this wasn't successful, then our case would go to trial.

Lorena had always insisted that I not be allowed to see Justin unless it was the third weekend of the month. His birthday just happened to fall on the third weekend of 2004. Lorena wanted to have a birthday party for Justin on the Saturday and insisted that because of the party, I wouldn't be able to have one of my scheduled visitations.

Lorena approached her attorney and had her draft a letter that said I would have to rearrange my May visitation because it would conflict with her previous plans. It was just another case of Lorena re-interpreting and making up the legal rules as she saw fit for her own convenience.

The previous year I had mailed a birthday card for Justin and put a twenty dollar bill in it. The next time I saw Justin he said, "Daddy you didn't even send me anything for my birthday." I have no doubt that Lorena told Justin that I didn't love him because I hadn't sent him anything for his birthday.

I realized that Lorena had opened Justin's birthday card and thrown it away. She had pocketed his money.

As proof that I mailed the birthday card I took a snapshot of it with a camera before I put it into the mail. A few years later I showed the photo to Justin and he vouched that he never had seen that particular birthday card. I had even mailed it to the Kindercare daycare center in Clark, New Jersey hoping one of the staff members would open it. I called and confirmed that they had received it. But I was told, "We sent that card home with Lorena."

I had to come back for our meeting on a Friday afternoon in May. Lorena had refused to allow me to have a visit with Justin that would last until sometime on Monday evening instead of the usual Sunday evening. My argument was our conference was going to cut into my usual Friday visit, and so I should be allowed to bring Justin back on Monday afternoon instead.

I was going to pick him up on Friday afternoon instead of the usual Friday morning scenario. Lorena was adamant and refused to give in on any extra time.

Gary Filosa, my attorney in Colorado, had told me long before this that, "You cannot be rational with an irrational person." He knew exactly what he was talking about.

The conference was at the office of an attorney in West Springfield, New Jersey. When I arrived, Lorena was already there. There was a small lobby as I stepped off of the elevator. When Lorena saw me, she purposely turned her back and acted as if she was gazing out the window.

The three attorneys wanted to sit and talk with each of us seperately first and then together. As usual Lorena had to go first, so she could try and set the stage. They finished with her and then I was in the room with the three attorneys.

I was still sitting down when they asked Lorena to re-enter the room. We went over a lot of issues and Lorena balked at letting me keep Justin until Monday. Her attorney had already assured me that it would be okay. I was asked to leave the room while they talked about the visitation issue.

I waited outside for a spell. Later, when I peeked around the corner, I could see Lorena yelling and screaming at her attorney and flailing and waving her arms. She was having another one of her temper tantrums. Finally, she jumped up out of her chair and flew past me, headed for the elevator. She hit the button and was gone.

The attorneys said that I could keep Justin until Monday afternoon and to drop him off at the daycare center before 5:00 p.m.

The next time we had another court hearing in New Jersey, Lorena didn't even bother to show up. I asked the judge about saying that he would court order Lorena to move back to Colorado and he attempted to retract his statement.

To further add insult to injury, he didn't do a thing about Lorena not showing up for his court. It was the second time

Lorena had done this and then gotten away with it. It was okay for me to have to fork out money for airline tickets and fly back East, but Lorena couldn't even drive ten miles to court. As usual, she would receive no consequences.

It was also during this visit that I found out Lorena had gone to Charlotte in anticipation of relocating there. She still didn't have permission from the New Jersey court system to take my son and move to Charlotte, but she forged ahead. The system was making it clear that she could do anything she wanted.

She had flown from Philadelphia to Charlotte and had secretly contacted someone to watch Justin for the weekend who lived only about forty-five *feet* from my mom's home.

My niece and nephew Tannah and Coley Morris were good friends with the babysitter's children. They had gone over there to play and had discovered that Justin was there.They went back to my mom's house yelling and screaming, "Justin is here, Justin is here."

The sad thing is, Justin was there for the entire weekend and never even saw his grandmother. One has to wonder what kind of a mother would do that to their own child? Why would you treat a poor innocent little child like that, putting him close to a grandmother that he hardly ever saw, and then not allow him to go next door and spend some quality time with his relatives?

The next time I was in New Jersey, I walked over there and talked to them. I saw the husband, whom I knew, in the backyard.

"I didn't come over here to start anything, but I can't believe that you and and your wife would keep Justin for the whole weekend and not even allow him to go next door and see his own family."

The first thing that he said to me was, "That woman is emotionally unstable." He was referring to Lorena.

During one of my conversations with him a couple of years earlier he had encouraged me to quit fighting to save my son. He had gone through a lot of the same things in a prior divorce and custody battle with his ex-wife. He already knew what to expect from the legal system.

At my court appearance in May 2004 it was determined that there needed to be what is called a plenary hearing before a custodial parent is allowed to leave the state with a minor child. During this hearing my attorney questioned the fact that Lorena had never done the court ordered psychiatric evaluation that was required of her.

For some unknown reason, and without any explanation, the judge vacated the order. Lorena had shown her defiance by not adhering to his court order, and now he decided to just let her off the hook.

The plenary hearing was scheduled right after the Fourth of July break. Lorena was there looking all prim and proper, dressed professionally in one of her nice business suits. The judge had seen more than his share of African-American woman in his courtroom, and I'm sure he was impressed, seeing her sitting there with her briefcase.

There were only a few of us sitting in the courtroom that day. Lorena's new attorney had been out of town attending his mom's funeral. Lorena's previous attorney was not a trial attorney. For that reason she had to hire a new one to continue with the divorce proceedings. My attorney had called me to tell me that the hearing was postponed, but wasn't able to reach me. My attorney didn't show up for the hearing.

During a previous hearing in 2004, the courtroom was packed full. This time he scanned the audience and commented, "I see Mr. Morris is here all the way from Colorado."

This time, with only about five people present, the judge said to Lorena, "I don't believe that Mr. Morris is going to show up today. Mrs. Morris you may be dismissed."

Lorena stood up and said, "Thank you, your honor." She knew I was there and didn't even have the decency to tell the judge. She was leaving the courtroom, and had every intention of walking right past me.

I said to the judge, "I'm sitting right here."

I was the only black man there. I couldn't believe that the judge—who had previously picked me out of a crowded courtroom—now, found me invisible.

The judge asked us to come to the front of the courtroom.

We discussed a few things. He brought up the topic of the difficulties I had trying to spend time with Justin. Out of the blue Lorena suggested that I accompany the daycare center kids and staff the following day to the New York Jet's training camp.

I was dumbfounded. This woman had done everything imaginable and unimaginable to prevent me from spending any extra time with Justin. Yet, right here in front of the judge with her most deceitful and syrupy demeanor, she was proposing that I spend the day with Justin. She could've won an Oscar for her acting. Maybe she'd chosen the wrong career.

So with Lorena trying to be so convincing and nice in front of the judge, I couldn't step up to the plate and complain about her past behavior. He would've looked at me like I was crazy. Lorena was conceding and acted like she thought it would be such a nice idea for me to spend an extra day with Justin since I was already in New Jersey.

The judge dismissed us and I decided to go to the daycare center to tell them I would be going with them the next day. Lorena and I stood and waited for the elevator.

When the doors opened, I followed her into the elevator. She glared at me in her usual hateful, big-eyed gaze and said, "Get your own elevator." At the same time she pushed her briefcase in front of herself, and used it to try and push me out. I got onto the elevator. Realizing that she wasn't going to get her way, she got off. I told her that she needed some help for her emotional instability and rode the elevator down alone.

After I went to the daycare center and found out that the trip the next day had been cancelled I went to my attorney's office to get him to send Lorena an e-mail. He sent an e-mail to her home and work e-mail addresses. The e-mails said I would come back to North Jersey the next day and get Justin and return him when we were called back to court. Court had been postponed for a few days until Lorena's attorney returned.

Lorena never responded to the e-mails and so I remained at my mom's house. The next day she received a call from the daycare center and had to go and pick up Justin. Lorena played it off saying she thought Justin was with me.

As a result I had missed out again in spending some time with my son. I had stayed around Mom's house all day waiting for my attorney to call and say come and get Justin. Lorena had won again. Her scheme had worked to a tee. At least in the judge's eyes it would appear that she was doing all she could to cooperate with me.

A few days later when we were back in court, the judge wanted to know how the visitation went with Justin. I explained to him that it never happened. I hadn't been able to spend any time with Justin. The judge didn't sound too happy.

When he questioned Lorena about the e-mail, she lied and said she never saw the e-mail from my attorney because she hadn't returned to work. We told the judge that we sent e-mails to both her home and work addresses.

Although the judge wasn't happy with Lorena and wanted to discuss this situation a little more in depth, he never did. Lorena had gotten away with something, again. Big surprise.

This was another example of the restraining order being a complete hindrance to me and my visits with Justin. I could have called and spoken to Lorena directly and been able to spend a couple of days with Justin. But I was limited to trying to communicate via e-mails that she refused to answer. Later my attorney told me that Lorena had never even opened the e-mails he'd sent to her. She had simply deleted them.

My attorney had done a lot of background work in preparation for the plenary trial. I had also told him what the judge had said to us in court before. Outside the courtroom my attorney recommended I bypass the plenary hearing and not waste the money. He told me that despite anything we might do, he believed that the judge was still going to allow Lorena to move to Charlotte and take Justin with her.

Before we went to court, he also showed me a paper that supposedly documented all the financial institutions that Lorena had contacted in North Jersey and New York City for a job. According to her, not one of them replied. Of course it was another one of her lies.

The judge turned the tide on us and suggested that since all of the parties were present, we should try and close out the divorce case. I was shocked and it caught me off guard. He wanted to speak with Lorena and me separately in a small back room. He talked to Lorena first. Then he talked to me.

The judge told me, "I made a mistake when I signed the court order requiring you to speak to your son on a cell phone."

My thoughts were, okay, if you just admitted to me that it was your mistake, why don't you do something about it now? I had been court ordered to pay for his so-called mistake. Was he going to court order Lorena to give me the money back? I didn't say anything.

He also recommended that we drop the mutual restraining orders that were in place. He also told me that Lorena had told him earlier, "I honestly believe that Abe will want to reconcile with me in about two years."

I looked at him like he was crazy after he made that statement. How could that woman possibly think that I would want to reconcile with her after all of the things that she had done and said to me in the past five years?

Then he said, "Now I wish I had never told you what she said."

Afterward, Lorena, the two attorneys and I retreated to that same little room to hash over some issues. At the end of the day the judge checked in to see if we were making any progress in the negotiations.

I told Lorena that I was willing to drop my restraining order against her. She refused, saying she wanted to think about it, and would give us an answer the following day.

The attorneys suggested that Lorena could bring Justin to Colorado and that we could all attend a rodeo together.

I said, "Lorena hates rodeos."

She responded, "I don't even use the word hate. It's not a part of my vocabulary."

The woman had told me that she hated me at least fifty or more times. Now she had the nerve to sit there in that little room and claim that she never even used the word "hate."

I asked Lorena, again, for my life insurance policies that were still in the house. Lorena lied as usual saying that she didn't have them. I had been asking for them for months. She always adamantly insisted that she didn't have them.

About four months later they mysteriously showed up in my home mailbox. They had been mailed to my attorney and he in turn had mailed them to me. I had a life insurance policy on Justin as well. They were all together in a file. Lorena had kept that one, refusing to send it to me.

My attorney also had me obtain a copy of the transcript of the court hearing on December 15, 2000 when Lorena said that her jewelry box had been broken in the fight. Then later under oath she swore that I had stolen it in a motion submitted in 2002. It cost me over $300 for that transcript and then we didn't even use it. It was another waste of my hard earned money.

On day number two, Lorena refused to drop the restraining order against me. She had had her twenty four hours to consider it and still didn't change her mind. To this day both hers and mine remain in force. Lorena continues to violate it at will.

Lorena was insistent, "I don't hate you. Do you hate me?" After all of the things she had done to me, I was curious as to why she wanted to know this. At that stage of the game why would she even care if I hated her or not?

I just looked at her and refused to answer. Then she said, "If you do hate me, then you're not hurting me. You're only hurting yourself. As the son of a Baptist minister I'm surprised that you're acting this way. You're supposed to be a Christian."

In the back of my mind I was thinking, "Yes you are supposed to be a Christian, too, but you certainly haven't acted that way for the past five years."

All during the negotiations her attorney kept bearing down on me. I'm sure he had listened to all of the junk that Lorena had filled him up with. He did his best to push my buttons and try to make me go off, but it didn't work.

I know he was upset by the recent death of his mother but he didn't have to take it out on me. When I brought up some of my valued items that Lorena had destroyed or else thrown into the trash, I could tell by his expression that he was totally disengaged and not interested at all. He didn't give a hoot about me, Justin, my stuff or Lorena. All he really cared about was getting paid.

At one point he started yelling and pointing his finger at me across the table. My attorney had to intervene and tell him to calm down.

It happened more than once. As far as I was concerned he was a total jerk and just as unprofessional as an attorney could be. Never once did I raise my voice to the man, but he had no problem acting out and shouting at me in front of the group.

At one point I asked him, "Are you trying to intimidate me?" Then he really got upset and went off of the deep end. Toward the end of the negotiations he jumped up from the table and told Lorena, "Let's go Lorena. I've heard about enough of this. Why don't you go back to your bull. Lorena, I'll represent you in the future for free if I have to." It was all just a big show.

With that they both left the room and went back into the courtroom to wait for the judge. I wasn't interested in being married to Lorena any longer. I was ready to end this thing and move on. In the back of my mind, I also knew that my book was going to be published sometime in 2005. I didn't want Lorena to have a say in the profits or proceeds from my book. I figured I had a very good reason to cut my losses and move forward. I didn't want my book to hit the bookstores and bookshelves while we were still legally married.

I had gone through a lot, but once the book was published it would give me a major sense of accomplishment.

I passed Lorena's attorney a note. They both read it and

agreed to some of my demands. So by the time the judge came back into the court I was ready to end it all. We were divorced that day. I was ready to go and spend some time with Justin.

During all of the negotiations in that back room Lorena finally divulged the proceeds from the sale of the house in Northglenn. I'd never known until then. She also provided proof of the appraised value of the home in Rahway, New Jersey when I was court ordered to leave it.

They wanted to give me a settlement check for about $17,000 and I refused to accept that for payment. I insisted on about $27,000. When I passed them a note in court after we returned, they countered with an offer of $24,000. I agreed because I wanted out.

When I was leaving the courtroom Lorena's attorney said to me, "Mr. Morris I wish you the best and good luck." He approached me and stuck out his hand. As bad as I didn't want to, I shook it. After the way he had yelled and berated me in that back room, I wanted nothing to do with him. I guess I wanted to show him I was the better man.

Then I reached out and shook Lorena's hand and wished her, "Good luck."

One thing that bothered me was during the lunch break my attorney spent quite a bit of time calling other clients and chatting with them. I was the one he was billing for his time and yet he was spending some of it on his cell phone.

I also met another attorney while I was standing outside of the courtroom. He gave me a business card and a big "rah rah" speech about how if I really wanted to get some things done with my divorce and child custody case, to give him a call. He was like a politician and very convincing.

I picked up Justin and drove back to Mom's house in Woodstown. When Mom realized that the divorce was final she said, "You need to write a story about this case." My response was, "I'm not going to write a story. I'm going to write a whole book."

Lorena was to send me a settlement check within thirty days of our divorce being final. There were several concessions as well. As part of the settlement, she had agreed that Justin could come to Colorado to visit me in late July. I wanted to take him to experience Cheyenne Frontier Days.

When I sent her e-mails to set up the visitation she refused to respond. I got my attorney involved and he sent her e-mails as well. The July visit to Colorado never took place even though it was agreed to in writing and filed on paper with the Union County court.

I was extremely upset that Lorena could continue to violate my court ordered visitations and get away with it. When talking to my attorney on the telephone, he told me, "The e-mails that I sent to Lorena regarding the Colorado visitation with Justin, were all deleted by Lorena. She never opened any of them." He had been able to tag them so he would know if they'd been opened and read.

When we were negotiating the final settlement I'd asked Lorena's side to let me know the address where she would be living in Charlotte. Her attorney was taking notes. Each time, he wouldn't even look up from his paper and he'd say, "You're not getting that information."

My attorney, Joseph Martinez, wouldn't respond and simply let them get away with it. I was under the impression that because of the restraining order they weren't legally obligated to divulge Lorena's new mailing address. I've since learned that they had no right to move my son to another state and not tell me, as the father who had joint legal custody, exactly where he would be residing. They'd gotten away with another big fat one.

During the negotiations I'd also insisted, for Justin's safety and welfare, that the order for the psychiatric evaluation be put back in place. Her attorney kept insisting that it wasn't necessary. I refused to budge. They finally figured out that unless Lorena agreed to do it, there would be no divorce. So they reluctantly agreed and put it in the divorce decree. Of course it meant nothing to Lorena.

It was quite awhile before I was able to contact and speak to Justin on the telephone. Lorena had set up a separate phone line at her house in Charlotte so I could call him.

I asked Justin about a cowboy hat that I had given him while they lived in New Jersey. Lorena had told Justin that the movers had lost it during the move. I'm sure she'd thrown it into the trash long before that.

Now that Lorena and Justin had moved to Charlotte, North Carolina I knew it was going to be a major glitch for any future trips back East to visit him. I would no longer have the convenience of borrowing my mom's car and staying with her. That meant forking out extra money for a rental car, hotel and all our meals.

I know it really didn't matter to Lorena. All she really cared about was receiving her weekly child support payments. She had been trying for years to make me walk away and give up on my son. I'm sure Lorena hoped that her move would be the last straw for me and would make me give up the fight.

During the multiple trips to New Jersey, Justin and I had bonded pretty well. It had cost me an arm and a leg for all of the airline tickets for both court appearances and visitations since December of 2000. In our short time together I'd taught Justin as much as I possibly could about baseball, basketball, football, kick ball and soccer. We also went to the recreation park in Woodstown as often as we could and spent several hours there.

At first we'd go and Justin would play on the swing, slide, spring horse and other apparatus on the playground. As he grew, we concentrated on the athletic games. He loved every single second that he was able to spend with me. It was mutual. I love him dearly. I hated that I was placed in this predicament, but I was determined to maintain a lasting relationship with my one and only child.

Two different times we had attended the Woodstown High School football games on a Friday night. Both times the weather wasn't all that accommodating and it was a little cold and one time we sat in the drizzling rain. Both times I had asked Justin if he wanted to leave and it was always an unequivocal, "No." Despite the conditions, he wanted to stay and watch the entire game.

During the summer months, whenever I went to New Jersey we'd go to Cowtown Rodeo on Saturday nights. Justin became a big rodeo fan. He thought Cowtown was a big rodeo, until one night I told him that Cowtown was a little rodeo. Cheyenne, Wyoming was a big rodeo.

That was one of the reasons I couldn't wait for Justin to come to Colorado and visit me in July. I wanted him to see and experience the Cheyenne Frontier Days Rodeo. There were a lot of reasons it was referred to as "The Daddy of 'em All." Also, I had been a television commentator at that rodeo for nine consecutive years for Prime Sports and later FOX Sports Networks. It held a special place in my heart.

In September, I had my attorney file a motion in New Jersey concerning the visitation violation and the settlement check I had never received. I had also wanted Lorena to show proof of the savings account that we had started for Justin while we lived in Colorado. Lorena had lied saying I never put any money into that account, therefore I didn't need to know anything about it. During our mediator conference in May I had given both attorneys copies of a personal $150 deposit to that account in August 2000.

Apparently my attorney attended the reading of the motion and charged me for his time. Usually he would call me right away and notify me of the outcome, but this time he didn't. I later received a letter with the information. He knew I would be upset by the number of things that went Lorena's way.

The judge didn't find Lorena in contempt of court for violating my visitation with Justin, nor did he find her in violation of litigant's rights for sabotaging the visit. He also ruled that I would have to purchase a home computer and that I could no longer e-mail Lorena at her work address. He also said that Lorena would never have to divulge any information about Justin's savings account because I didn't bring it up during the divorce proceedings. This was an absolute lie.

Continuing to do as she pleased, when Lorena took Justin to Charlotte she had never notified me of the elementary school he would be attending. Nor did I know the daycare center where Justin would be staying during his after school programs. Justin was now starting kindergarten.

Justin had told me the name of the daycare center was the Sunshine House. He also told me the name of his school. It was a shame for a father to have to cross examine his own child to learn this important information.

When I first contacted the Sunshine House and identified myself, the staff let me talk to Justin. A few weeks later, when Lorena found out, she threw a fit after which the staff refused to let me speak to him again.

Once I faxed them the corresponding court order from New Jersey pertaining to Kindercare, they again allowed me to speak to Justin. Then when Lorena and her New Jersey attorney responded to the motion that was filed by my attorney in New Jersey, they attempted to keep me from calling the Sunshine House and talking to Justin.

Consequently the judge ruled that I would be allowed to call the daycare center and speak to either the staff or Justin.

The judge didn't penalize Lorena for not sending me the settlement check as was agreed on in the court order. He didn't even bother to address it. I eventually got it, but it was long after it was due and only because we had complained and applied pressure to her and her attorney to comply. Of course I had to pay my attorney to do this.

It seemed as if the judge was saying, "It's okay to violate my court orders because I'm not going to stand behind them and give you a consequence. And if it makes me look bad, then I'll just vacate the previous court order."

He also ruled that Lorena's psych evaluation needed to be submitted to his office by December 15, 2004.

After I returned to Colorado, I began to think about my living situation. My apartment lease would expire at the end of August. With Lorena off of my back, I looked into the possibility of buying a home. The market couldn't have been more favorable for me at the time and I had an excellent credit rating. The real estate agent sent several pictures of available homes via e-mail.

I narrowed my search to about ten to fifteen homes. On a Sunday afternoon in early August we met and went to see several in the Aurora area. Most of them were still occupied. Only a couple were vacant.

I really liked one home in the Toll Gate residential area. It was empty and was a bank foreclosure. It had four bedrooms, four bathrooms, a family room, a dishwasher, a fireplace, two outside decks, and a fireplace. The master bedroom was huge and the basement downstairs was fully carpeted. It had a lot of trees, and the front and back yards were nice and big. It was my number one choice.

At the end of the day, we went back to that house and I made an offer on it. There were already other offers out there. My agent recommended that I go one dollar higher than the highest. I'm sure the bank wanted to get it off of their hands because it was costing them money while it sat unoccupied.

I honestly didn't believe that I'd get that house. I didn't want to be disappointed again. I'd had enough disappointments in the past few years. Not all of them had to do with my divorce, either. There were disappointments with my job, attorneys, judges, friends, roommates, and women that I thought I liked. But I chose to push forward and tried not to look back.

By the grace of God, I was able to get the home. I couldn't believe that I could be so blessed after going through so much emotional trauma.

Because the home was empty, I was allowed to start moving my things in the weekend before I closed on it. I worked feverishly on Saturday and Sunday. I closed on a Thursday morning. Then that weekend I borrowed a pickup truck from a friend and asked a co-worker to help me. He brought his son along and we moved all of the big items on Saturday afternoon.

I still couldn't believe that this was happening to me. I felt extremely blessed to be a homeowner again. I was living proof that a person could rise from the ashes. It had been a long and arduous struggle.

This is one of the big ducks that I had in mind when I snarled at my supervisor and told her, "When I get all of my ducks in a row, I will be gone." Getting a new home was right at the tip top of my list. I knew if I left my job before buying a house, I wouldn't be able to qualify for a mortgage. So I'd toughed it out and stayed.

When the director of the Sunshine House in Charlotte found out who I was and that I had written a book, she asked me to send some pictures of myself.

"We'll be happy to post the pictures of Justin's dad on our bulletin board."

I made it very clear that if I sent some pictures, I didn't want her to give them to Lorena because she would dispose of them.

"Oh no, we won't give them to Lorena," she promised.

I took some of my best photographs and had them professionally copied. I mailed them in and called back about a week later to see if the Sunshine House had received them.

Her response was, "Oh we gave those pictures to Ms.

Morris. She said she was going to put them in Justin's bedroom for him to enjoy."

The next time I talked to Justin on the telephone, I asked him if he had seen the pictures. He said no. So I knew Lorena had thrown them away.

The next time I called the daycare center I chastised the director for giving them to Lorena.

"You told me you were going to post the pictures at school. Lorena lied to you, saying she would hang them up in Justin's bedroom but Justin hasn't seen the photographs. That means that she promptly threw them away, just like I said she would."

I called a different attorney back East and agreed to have him represent my case moving forward. He had convinced me that Lorena had no right to keep her address and the whereabouts of my son from me and he made me believe that he would get aggressive and address some of these things that had been sliding for far too long.

I called Joseph Martinez and told him that I would no longer need his services and to forward my file to the new guy. Sadly, the new attorney fit right into the same mold as my first attorney. He was totally worthless and incompetent but that was something I would have to pay to learn.

I was determined to fight for my son no matter what the cost. I didn't want to have something happen to him. I didn't want to have any regrets. This new attorney knew I was emotionally spent and vulnerable and promised to step up to the plate on my behalf.

I sent him a check for $2,850 for a retainer. His firm and attorneys proved to be a total waste of my time and money. Harry was supposed to file an appeal within thirty days from when the judge ruled on this latest motion. He didn't. His receptionist claimed that he'd come down with pneumonia.

One of the reasons I had gone with this attorney was because I had explained to him there were times when I had contacted my previous attorneys and they wouldn't return my phone calls for days.

Harry promised, "You'll never have to worry about that from my firm. You call us and someone will return your phone call within twenty four hours, max. There won't be any of this bullshit about returning your calls. Listen Abe, you're an athlete. I'm an athlete. I used to be wrestler. I hate to lose. But even if I lost, just as long as I knew that I got in there and gave it my best, I was okay with the result. I can't guarantee that you're going to win this thing with your son, but I promise you that I'll get in there and fight for you."

I thought finally I'd found someone who would step up to the plate on my behalf. It just turned out to be a lot of rhetoric. Harry never filed the appeal. His next move was to hand me off to one of his associates. Harry was the lead attorney in his firm. The name of the firm should have been Houdini and Associates.

Harry knew I'd written a book, but it hadn't been published yet. He told me that he was proud of the clients he represented. Harry also wanted his son and daughter to know who he was associated with. He asked me to autograph and mail him an action photo on a bucking bull. He wanted to show it to his children. I thought about it. At first, I was going to do it right away. Now, I'm glad that I never did. I wasn't inclined to send him anything after he jerked me around for the next three years.

Donald Black, Harry's associate, assured me that this time we were going to get some things done. One of the first things I was going to do myself was file a lawsuit against Lorena for $10,000 for disposing of my personal property in violation of a court order.

I had the lawsuit all written out and ready to mail the following day. Donald talked me out of mailing it in saying, "Let me file the lawsuit. Why file it for $10,000? Let's file it for a lot more than $10,000."

One thing that he told me over and over again was, "We're going to jam her up." Just like with his boss, it only turned out to be rhetoric.

One of the first things I asked Donald to do was get my child support straightened out. It had been over a year since the judge had court ordered that an audit be done on my account, and it still hadn't been done.

He said, "I'll get this thing straightened out even if I have to personally go to the Union County courthouse to get it done!" More empty words.

While all these things were going on back East, I was trying to get settled into my home. The place needed a little fixing up—just a little, though. The grass hadn't been mowed for weeks and there were weeds everywhere. I set about pulling the weeds and mowing the lawn.

I had an old college roommate who was living in California. He was coming back to Colorado frequently to spend time with his twin girls. Stuart asked me if he could stay at my place and that way he would have somewhere to bring his girls on his visitations.

Stuart was a retired bull rider like me and so I consented. He said he would only be there approximately one weekend a month, and otherwise I'd have the house to myself. I figured that couldn't be a bad deal at all. Wrong. It turned out to be a huge mess.

I had known Stuart ever since my days at the University of Wyoming. He had been extremely successful in business and the financial services industry. He was very intelligent and a shrewd and savvy businessman. He ran a brokerage firm in the 1990s and had had a securities license but somehow lost it. I never knew the whole story. But Stuart had run into some tough times financially in the past few years and had to file for bankruptcy.

Stuart had aspirations of getting into the movie and entertainment industry in Hollywood someday. That's the reason he lived in California.

So he moved in and ended up being there all the time. He was broke and taking advantage of me and, while I was very uncomfortable with the situation, I didn't throw him out.

JUSTIN

The weekend before and after Thanksgiving 2004 I was the victim of identity theft. It was very devastating. Someone back in the state of New York had gotten hold of my social security number and other pertinent information and lit me up.

I had recently opened a Sears account in order to purchase a few items for my home like a washer and dryer, freezer and an oven. Somehow someone had gotten my account number and charged some power tools and other items to the account.

Someone from a fraud agency in Maryland had called me at work to alert me of the theft. I called Sears and they cancelled the card account and issued me another account number. Ironically, before I even received that new account number in the mail, it was intercepted, and more items were charged to my name.

About a week after the first phone call, I received a call from the fraud alert division to call a special phone number for Macy's in New York City. When I called and gave my name the lady asked me for my social security number.

I was reluctant to give it out over the phone because of all of the recent activity on my accounts. I gave her some other information. Finally, I gave her my social security number. The first thing out of her mouth was, "Oh no!"

I instantly knew the information wasn't very good. Some culprit had opened an account at Macy's and maxed it out. My credit rating score was very good because I had just recently qualified to buy my home. My realtor said my credit score had been the highest of all of her 2004 clients.

I was told the thief had purchased a $1,100 watch, Sean John leather coat and a few other clothing items. Then a few days later had opened another account in my name and had purchased an $800 watch and another Sean John leather coat.

These are all items that could easily be discounted and sold very quickly on the street. Altogether, they made off with over $4,600 in merchandise and apparel from Macy's using my name and information.

The people or persons using my information had struck very hard and very quickly. They had opened accounts at Sears, Macy's, Home Depot, JC Penney's, and T-Mobile. At T-Mobile they had purchased two cell phones and run up charges of over $200 before the service was disconnected. Altogether, they had hit me for about $8,600 in fraudulent charges. A nationwide alert was placed on my name and social security number. It was a lot of frustration on my part and a huge mess.

I was told that I needed to file a police report. When I went to the Aurora police station they wouldn't take my report because the criminal activity had taken place in New York and not Colorado.

It took me a couple of months to clear up the mess. I had to sign an affidavit stating that I wasn't in the state of New York during the last two weeks of November 2004. I hadn't been back to New York since December 2000.

Still dealing with Lorena and the New Jersey court system was no picnic. The date for her psychological evaluation had come and gone with her not complying and no consequences for her.

It had now been over a year since the audit was court ordered on my child support account and it was nowhere near completion. I had already paid my previous attorney over $11,000 to fight my divorce case. Add this to the $12,000 I paid my first attorney. Plus I had paid a Colorado attorney more than $2,300 for the divorce case while still in Colorado. Obviously I had spent a great deal of money with no resolutions or enforcement of the various orders Lorena so often violated.

In October 2004, to add insult to injury, the child support system intercepted my IRS refund check for $2,699 claiming that I owed back child support. I had overpaid Lorena about $24,000 in child support payments and in a year they had not gotten around to checking the account and straightening it out but now they had the nerve to do this.

I kept after my attorney, asking when was he going to take the actions he'd promised. One day he called and left me a voice mail message at home while I was at work.

I tore into him. "Why would you call me at home and leave me a message when you know darn well I'm at work? You have my work phone number. " I kept asking him when he was going to file the lawsuit against Lorena for throwing away my property. He kept putting me off saying that he didn't want to file several lawsuits or motions. He wanted to get everything together and then file all at once.

One of his favorite lines was, "We want to 'posture you' before the judge. Look, Abe you're the good guy in this case. We want him to totally forget about all of his other decisions regarding this case. We want him to totally forget who he thought you were and not recall his rulings in the past against you."

I got sick and tired of hearing the term "posture yourself." Every couple of months it was the same old thing. Finally, I said, "Just how many black professional rodeo cowboys do you think that judge has seen in his courtroom? He's never going to forget about me. You know that and I know that."

When Christmas came around I went back to New Jersey to see Justin and my family. Stuart gave me a ride to the airport and was to pick me up when I returned.

Per the court order, Lorena brought Justin over to Mom's house. She brought her nephew along to take Justin into my mom's house, while she sat outside in the car.

This was the first time I'd spent the entire day of Christmas with Justin since 1999 when he wasn't even a year old.

As usual we had a good time together. It was bitter cold that year. Justin loved to play sports outside. We weren't able to spend much time outside. The ground was extremely cold and hard.

We were able to go bowling as a family, though. I let Justin take a few of my turns. I could tell he wasn't enjoying sitting there and not participating in the fun. Some strangers got a kick out of Justin's antics and gave him a dollar.

One night we watched movies at my brother David's home in Salem. Justin would always either sit right next to me or else in my lap. One night he couldn't figure out how to get to me because I was sitting on the other side of the kitchen table. He bumped his head trying to go underneath the table. Overall the trip and time together was good. It was hard to leave him again.

The day that I flew back from Philadelphia, I called Stuart on my way to the airport. He didn't answer his cell phone and so I left a message telling him what time my flight was arriving in Denver.

When I got off the plane, Stuart had left me a message on my cell phone saying that he was in California, and I would need to catch a taxi cab home. I wasn't a happy camper. I knew it would cost me about fifty dollars to take a taxi cab to Aurora. When I got home there were newspapers laying in my driveway. I had told Stuart that I was going to suspend the delivery while I was out of town but he'd asked me not to, saying that he would read them.

When I entered the house Stuart had left the television and the lamp on in his bedroom. When he finally returned our relationship deteriorated even more.

My book was about to go to the printer. I was spending all of my spare time proofreading the final manuscript. It was extremely exciting to know that I would be a published author in another month or so. That is the spark that kept me going. It was so exhilarating to see what I had written a couple of years before laid out into a book format. It was kind of like becoming a father all over again, because this was something very profound to me. I could have cried the day that I received my proof copy in the mail.

A few days later, I went to Fort Collins for the Sunday Easter service. I was driving down a four lane road and noticed that a white SUV was driving along beside me. I was listening to my music pretty loudly so at first I didn't notice it.

Finally, I recognized the driver and his wife. It was Brent Meyer and his now ex-wife Jamie. We started talking back and forth. I told him that I had my new books in the trunk of my car.

Brent yelled back at me, "I know, I want one."

So I pulled over and sold him one right there on the spot. I guess you could say I hurriedly set up my roadside stand and made a quick sale.

The reason Brent knew about the book was because the Fort Collins *Coloradoan* paper did a big story on me and my new book in the Sunday edition in February of 2005 as part of Black History month.

I had several people contact me after that story was published. In fact, I had checks from people in my possession before the books were even published. They wanted one fresh off of the press. The advance sales sure made me feel good.

I did my first official book signing at the American Heritage Center on the University of Wyoming campus in Laramie. It was Friday, April 8, 2005. It was a busy day for me. I stopped in Loveland, Colorado and spoke to a group of school children at an elementary school. Then, I stopped in Fort Collins and picked up the Rev. David Williams from the Abyssinian Christian Church and we drove to Laramie.

I spoke to an African-American studies class taught by Professor Keith Armstrong in the Classroom Building at the University of Wyoming. Next, I had a speech and book signing at the museum. The hot question that I was asked at both venues was if my book ever became a movie, what actor did I want to play me? I was flattered!

The next day, I did a book signing at the re-opening ceremony at the PRCA Hall of Fame in Colorado Springs, Colorado. On Thursday morning of the following week I did a live interview at a Colorado Springs television station. Then on Saturday I had another book signing at the PRCA Hall of Fame.

I was wearing myself out. I was still holding down my full-time job but it was a very exciting time.

A few days later, I traveled to Fort Worth for more book signings. I did one at the Cowboys of Color Hall of Fame and Museum in Fort Worth. Then I did one at the Mesquite Championship Rodeo in Mesquite, Texas. I was also able to watch my nephew Randall Hairston compete in a track meet. I stayed with my sister and brother-in-law Roy and Rosalyn Hairston for the weekend.

My co-workers started whispering and asking how much longer I was going to stay at TIARRA. I told them that I wasn't a fool. I would eventually leave, but only when the timing was right. Even people that called in to the phone center asked, "What in the world are you doing working there? You should be out there traveling and promoting your book."

I knew I couldn't survive on just one published book. I also really needed to get my motivational speaking career up and running.

People often talk about how they can't afford to leave their place of employment. They want to leave but know that it would put them in a financial bind, so they stay put. I began to tell myself that I would leave my place of employment when I could no longer afford to stay.

I had had write ups in the *Denver Post, Fence Post, Rodeo News,* the *Today's Sunbeam, The Coloradoan,* plus my monthly column in the *Humps N' Horns Bull Riding News.*

I had also done radio interviews and had a news story broadcast about me, my rodeo career and my book on FOX 31 News in Denver and CBS Channel 5 in Cheyenne.

I sent about fifty books home to my brother David for friends and family.

Things became more difficult at my house. I had reason to believe Stuart had taken some things, including money. Finally it came to a head and I told him he had to leave. A couple of weeks later, he said he was going and offered to sell me a lot of his furniture to help pay off his outstanding rent and utilities. I took some of his furniture for two reasons: I needed some of the things he had, and I also figured that was the only way for me to get paid.

In late June, I flew back East to spend some time with Justin. I didn't tell Stuart I was leaving or when I would return. My flight was delayed and I was late arriving in Philadelphia. As a result I wasn't at Justin's gate when he arrived from Charlotte, North Carolina. When I inquired if his plane had arrived, I was told that it was delayed. The truth was Justin was already in Philadelphia, and I was given the incorrect information.

After getting the runaround, I finally found him. Justin had arrived at a different terminal even though we were traveling on the same carrier. Then, because I wasn't at the gate to greet him, he was moved to a different terminal.

The airline had called Lorena and she was in panic mode. She had called my cell phone several times, but never left a message. When we got to New Jersey, I had Justin call her and tell her he was with me. She certainly would have never extended me the same courtesy.

I was truly amazed at Justin's athletic talent. He loved sports just as I had always loved sports. Even at six years old he was far more talented than me. I'm not saying this just because he's my son. I was proud of him no matter what, but judging from his talent even as a little kid, I felt he could be a professional athlete someday if he wanted to. He was that good.

We were playing kickball in the backyard with the kids. Someone kicked the ball onto the roof of my mom's house. Justin ran along as it bounced a few times and then easily caught it with both hands for the out. Another time he was playing basketball at the neighbor's house and Justin made about ten shots in a row.

I had never seen a young kid with that much natural talent. Justin could hit, throw and catch baseballs with power. He could throw and catch a football like you wouldn't believe. And Justin could shoot and dribble a basketball with precision. We had a great time together and a lot of fun.

While I was in New Jersey, I did book signing on two consecutive weekends at Cowtown Rodeo. I sold a book to a rodeo fan named Warren Morphew from Bear, Delaware. The next Saturday he told me that he had read it twice in one week. Warren enjoyed it that much.

While I was in New Jersey I also did a telephone interview with a newspaper from Cheyenne. That story was later published in a July issue.

I was busy the entire time I was home. I celebrated a birthday and Justin made and gave me a special card. I can't tell you how moved I was. I always had a good visit when I spent time with my son and with my family and it did a lot to boost my spirits after the trouble with Stuart.

Coming back, though, was a fiasco. I missed my flight and then had to try and go standby on the next flight to Denver. By the time I made it through the ticketing line, it was too late to board that flight. I called my brother David on my cell phone and had him return to the airport to pick me up.

I was re-scheduled for an early flight the next morning. After I arrived at the Philadelphia airport, I found out that the flight had been cancelled. I was at the airport all day long getting bumped from one flight after another.

Every time I got bumped I had to go back to the ticket counter and through security again. The second day, I sent my luggage and was told that if I didn't make the flight that my luggage would be pulled off of the flight because of security reasons. My luggage wasn't pulled. I called David again and went back to Mom's house with only the clothes on my back.

The next morning, I had David take me back to the airport and started the same process over again.

I got bumped off of two earlier flights and the agent at the counter assured me that I would probably make it this time but my name was never called, and I got bumped again. Before the next flight a couple of hours later, I approached the ticket agent and gave him my long and sad sob story.

He made a few calls and the next thing I knew it was like

magic. He pulled a first class ticket out of the machine and gave it to me. I had spent over twenty hours in the airport over a period of three different days. I was finally going home to Colorado.

When I got back home, Stuart was gone for good. He had left me a check for so-called miscellaneous expenses. He never paid for his last month's rent and I figured that he still owed me about $800, but I knew I'd never see it.

At least he was gone. There would be less stress in my life. I had let him stay with me to help offset my mortgage payment, but in the end, I discovered it wasn't worth it to have a roommate.

I was really looking forward to having Justin come out to visit me in the summer. I could show him a good time and share my home with him for about ten days. I could hardly wait to take him to the Cheyenne Frontier Days Rodeo. It was a scheduled and court ordered visitation for the last two weeks of July.

I was especially excited since Lorena had violated our divorce decree and court order and not allowed Justin to come to Colorado and visit me in July 2004.

I had been back and forth on the telephone with my attorney in New Jersey concerning the upcoming visit. He had been communicating with Lorena through e-mails and phone calls. He assured me that this time the visit would take place per the court order.

I had already purchased the round trip airline tickets for Justin's visit. I had taken all of the necessary vacation days off from work. I had spoken to Justin on the telephone a few times at the daycare center and at home.

When I called Justin at home, he got off of the phone a few times to ask his mom if he could bring certain items to show me. She told him yes. Justin sounded excited to come out. The day before he was to leave, I called him at the daycare center again to see if he was excited about the upcoming trip.

Justin said, "I'm not coming."

I immediately called my attorney to tell him that Lorena wasn't going to put Justin on the airplane. He called Lorena at work and left her a message.

I called my mom that night because I was so upset that Lorena was going to pull of one of her shenanigans for the second consecutive summer. I didn't sleep very well that night.

The next morning, Thursday July 21, I called US Airways to see if Justin was on the flight. The agent that I spoke to assured me that Justin had checked in and was on the flight from Charlotte to Denver.

I was relieved. On my way to the airport, my attorney called me on my cell phone and said that Lorena hadn't put Justin on the flight. Not only did she not put Justin on the flight, she didn't even have the decency to call and tell me so. She could care less that I was running around the Denver airport in a panic trying to locate my son, when she knew he was still in Charlotte.

That day my attorney spoke to her on the phone at work. Lorena lied saying that she never agreed to put Justin on that flight. She also argued with Donald Black that it wasn't within the time frame of the last two weeks in July.

If any rational human being were to look at a calendar, they would see that any time after July 16 is considered as part of the last two weeks of the month. Lorena went as far as arguing that this visit wasn't during the last two weeks of July.

My attorney threatened that he was going to sue her in court for violating yet another court order. According to him, Lorena begged and pleaded with him not to file the suit.

I took a couple of days off from work. When I showed up again, my co-workers were wondering what happened. I told them that Lorena had done it again. One co-worker said if you were to send the sheriff over and get her picked up she wouldn't continue to do this stuff.

I sat down and wrote the judge a long letter and complained about Lorena continuing to violate his court orders. He again proved to me that he really didn't care, because he never responded to my letter.

I wrote letters to several people including congressmen in Colorado and New Jersey. I also wrote letters to television and radio personalities. I even wrote a letter to NBC Dateline.

I let Mike Bond read the letter that I sent to Dateline. We met and played racquetball and then went out to lunch. He read the letter during lunch. Afterwards, Mike told me, "If I didn't personally know you, I wouldn't have believed one single thing in that letter." It was so bizarre.

I was still fighting with the child support system to complete the audit in my overpayments. They had sent me notification in April 2005 that my child support obligations were going to be increased to $380 from the previous amount of $360 per week.

I was livid. My child support obligation was reduced by a court order in October 2003 to $136 per week. Now, they were going to go back to an old figure that was supposed to have been abolished, reinstate it again and then add a cost of living increase to it. They not only couldn't get my audit done, but they were going to make another gross mistake as well.

I suspected that the computer systems were so antiquated and the people running them were so incompetent that they couldn't get it right. It just caused me more stress and frustration.

Monte Jones was supposed to be my contact person for my child support payments. For more than two years I had called him multiple times and left him unpleasant messages, and he had never returned my calls. I had also written him complaint letters, and he'd responded by sending me a computer printout of my account. None of the printouts were even close to being correct. The only relief I got was when I spoke to his supervisor. She was extremely pleasant and caring.

The supervisor admitted to me a lot of the figures that they were going to use in my calculation were from the payment history that I had supplied. I thought this was a horrible thing for her to admit. How in the world was the child support department going to conduct a court ordered audit on my account when they didn't even have the correct dollar figures and dates to work with?

Their whole program was apparently so outdated that they were never going to even come close to a figure of how much I had overpaid their system. Lorena certainly didn't care. She was socking away all of the extra money in preparation for her retirement.

In August, I pestered my attorney about when he was going to file the lawsuit against Lorena that he had threatened her with. As usual he continued to put me off. He still hadn't done anything to get my child support straightened out as promised, either. And of course, nothing about the fact that, once again, I did not have Justin for a summer visit.

"You told Lorena over the telephone that you were going to file a lawsuit against her and yet you still haven't done it. Just what are you waiting for?"

As far as I was concerned I hadn't received much for my $2,800 retainer. I wasn't about to send them any more money.

In September 2005, I bought a one-way ticket and flew back East for the 50th Anniversary and Reunion of the Cowtown Rodeo.

The reunion was on Friday evening September 23. I arrived in New Jersey on Thursday afternoon. That night I picked up my cousin Jimmy Lee Walker, and we went to a motel where some of our friends from the bygone era were staying.

They were delighted to hear that I had written a book. Byron Reid, who was raised in Cowtown, asked me if I had included the story in my book about when the horse Prairie Creek had run me over in North Washington, Pennsylvania one year.

I grabbed a copy of my book and turned to page seventy-one. He laughed his head off after he read my version of it in my book.

Byron said, "You got the story wrong though for two

reasons. First of all, we laughed right away after you got knocked down. And second, Prairie Creek was a mare not a gelding."

I said, "I was just trying to be nice and civil to you guys when I said after you all found out that I was okay, then you burst out laughing."

We had a great time laughing and talking about the good ol' days growing up and hanging out at Cowtown and the rodeo. I really helped get my mind off the sadness and frustration of not being able to see Justin.

The next day, I was on the go all day long. First, I stopped at Mary S. Shoemaker Elementary school to visit some of the women who were now teachers there. I had gone to high school with a few of them.

Next, I went to the John C. Fenwick Elementary school in Salem, New Jersey where my brother David was a teacher. Several of those teachers had bought a copy of my book and wanted me to sign them the next time I was in New Jersey for a visit. I promised David that I would stop by and sign their books.

Then I went to Pennsgrove, New Jersey where my sister Patricia had set up a book signing at a delicatessen and popular convenience store. I was there for about two hours. Many local people stopped there for their lunch break.

Then I rushed home and took another shower and headed out to Cowtown for the Rodeo Reunion. I wanted to get there early and set up so I could sell some more books. I saw some people that I hadn't seen in years.

The next night I went to Cowtown Rodeo. I had a great weekend overall. The highlights were visiting and seeing a lot of familiar people. Following the rodeo there was a spectacular fireworks display. It made for a grand weekend. If only I culd have shared it with my son.

On Sunday afternoon I packed a rental truck with the few things that I had been able to save from Hurricane Lorena and started back to Colorado. I wasn't looking forward to that long drive, especially alone. I knew the gas prices and roadway tolls were going to put a huge dent in my pocket.

I made good time though. On Tuesday night I pulled into my driveway. I was glad to be home again and off the road.

In October, I was on my way to a speaking engagement at an elementary school in Galeton, Colorado. I had a very long conversation with my attorney and again told him that he needed to take some action.

I had a scheduled court ordered visitation in which Lorena had agreed to bring Justin to my mom's house in New Jersey for Christmas that year as per the divorce decree.

I told my attorney that because he hadn't done anything to Lorena for violating my July visit, that she was likely to violate the Christmas visit as well. Donald checked with his boss Harry and told me that I would need to make a $1,000 payment against my outstanding bill before he did anything. I refused.

A couple of weeks later, he suggested making a call to the judge to see what steps he could take to help resolve my case. When he got back to me, he told me the judge said that because Lorena had lived out of state for more than a year the case was no longer within his jurisdiction. I can't help but suspect that that was the real reason that my attorney had done so little. He must have known that the jurisdiction had passed to North Carolina and was just stringing me along.

The only way that I was going to get anything resolved was to find a North Carolina attorney to take over my case. At that point I was extremely upset again. Donald Black had talked me into not filing the lawsuit against Lorena for destroying my personal property, claiming he'd do it. He never did and now it was too late. Nevermind all the other issues he had never taken any action on.

In December, I flew out to Las Vegas for the Wrangler National Finals Rodeo. I was invited and did a book signing at the PRCA Hall of Fame booth as part of Cowboy Christmas at the convention center. One night after the rodeo, I was standing in the taxi line outside the Thomas & Mack Arena. Some people behind me were engaged in a conversation and I overheard they were from Riverton, Wyoming. I didn't want to be rude and interrupt them, but they kept on talking. Finally, they paused for a breath and I turned around and asked if they knew Charlie Needham.

"Yes. How do you know Charlie Needham?"

"I used to rodeo with him."

"So what's your name?"

"Abe Morris."

"Abe Morris. Abe Morris. You're Abe Morris? I thought that's who you were. My name is Jesse Moss and this is my wife Renée. Man, I used to watch you announcing Cheyenne Frontier Days Rodeo on television when I was a kid. You're one of my heroes. Can I get your autograph?"

Then Jesse started looking for a piece of paper for me to sign. So I reached into my bag and showed him one of my books.

"You wrote a book? How much are you selling them for?"

Then the people they were talking with also wanted to buy one. So as I was moving forward in line, I quickly sold and autographed two books just before I jumped into a taxi. If I had known I would get that kind of a response in a taxi line, I would have tried selling there a lot sooner!

I stayed with Charles Sampson at the Mirage motel and casino in Las Vegas. Sampson was the 1982 PRCA World Champion bull rider. One night I was out of my rodeo attire when I saw Don Gay, the eight-time PRCA World Champion bull rider, in the lobby. Since I was incognito, I knew he wouldn't recognize me. Don Gay barely knew me with my full rodeo regalia on. I decided to have a little fun with him.

Don was a television commentator for the Wrangler

National Finals Rodeo with ESPN. I walked up to him and said, "You look familiar."

He stuck out his hand and said, "I'm Don Gay, eight-time World Champion. Who are you?"

By asking me who I was, he had ruined all of my plans.

"Abe Morris."

"Gosh Abe, I didn't even recognize you without your cowboy hat on. I guess your cowboy hat doesn't fit anymore." He laughed, referring to the title of my book.

I flew back to Colorado early on Sunday morning. I wanted to get back in time to watch the final go 'round on television. I also knew I had some more personal business to take care of in the form of one Justin Abraham Morris.

I sent e-mails to Lorena asking her if she was going to bring Justin to New Jersey for Christmas. She was extremely nasty, as usual. I had learned not to trust the woman. Sure enough, Lorena didn't bring Justin to Mom's home per the court order.

I stood up as a visitor when I was attending church at Morning Star Baptist in Woodstown. I was starting to become very vocal. I told those in attendance that I was supposed to have a court ordered visit with my son for Christmas that didn't happen. I blamed the judge because he had allowed Lorena to get away with one violation after another. I told the congregation that I was going to file for sole custody of my son.

When I sat down, Lorena's aunt was sitting right behind me. She tapped me on the shoulder and said, "I'll back you 100% on trying to get your son. You go and get him. Lorena doesn't deserve to have custody."

My attorney never called me again. The attorney that they put me in contact with in North Carolina wanted $4,000 as a retainer. I turned him down.

TIARRA had a big business conference in Denver and in Charlotte. Lorena was put in charge as one of the coordinators of both conferences. When I found out that she was going to come back to Colorado, I high-tailed it down to the Denver police station to try to get her in trouble for constantly violating my restraining order.

I had every intention of having her show up with her high and mighty self and getting arrested right in front of her business associates. I took all of the necessary paperwork and a cassette tape recording as evidence of the violations down to the Denver police station.

I filled out all of the necessary paperwork and forms. A few days later I was told that the district attorney wasn't going to do a darn thing about the violations. It figured.

The business conference was mandatory for all employees. I refused to go. Leah, one of my former supervisors, told me that I didn't have a choice. I had to attend. I told her that I wasn't going, because of the restraining order of which she was aware.

I didn't trust Lorena at all. No one in their right mind would. I wasn't about to put myself in jeopardy of being arrested for being anywhere near her. I have no doubt that she had brought her restraining order paperwork along and would have come up with a story that I had threatened her in front of her business associates.

According to the divorce decree, whenever Justin was away from home for more than forty-eight hours Lorena was supposed to give me a contact phone number of where he could be reached. Lorena left him at a man's house that I didn't know and never told me where Justin was or provided me with a phone number. Again she continued to act as she pleased, never afraid that there would be any consequences.

A few weeks after the business conference in Denver, I ran into Harold Carter. At one time he had been one of my supervisors in the ATS Unit. He wanted to discuss Lorena with me. I had told him a lot about her bizarre escapades.

Harold had worked with Lorena for a few weeks before

she came to Denver. He said, "Now, I can see how some of those weird stories that you me told were true."

Harold found Lorena to be extremely volatile and difficult to work with. She had thrown a few fits with him over the telephone. He said he could see why I was so concerned about the safety and welfare of my son. He could also understand why I believed Lorena was very capable of flipping out and injuring Justin. Harold told me that just from working with Lorena, he could tell that she was very emotionally unstable.

Harold also said, "I really feel sorry for you and your son. I hope and pray that your case doesn't become a national news headline because Lorena hurts your son."

During this time I was on an emotional rollercoaster that took me from extreme lows over my frustration with the legal system and not being able to see Justin, to the highs of my book's success. I tried to focus on the "ups" and prayed that somehow resolution would come in my case. I figured prayer would probably be more effective than any of my attorneys had proved to be.

I had mailed a copy of my book to my aunt and uncle Pearlie May and R.C. Thompson in New Smyrna Beach, Florida where I was born. They had showed the book to Mary Harrell who was in charge of the Black Heritage Festival there.

Mary contacted me and asked if I would be willing to come down to New Smyrna for the event. She asked, "What would it take to get you to come down to our festival?"

I said, "If you pay for my airline ticket, I'll call it good."

"We're going to want you to give a speech to the crowd. What about a speaker's fee?"

"If you agree to pay for my airline ticket, that will be good enough for me. This will be an opportunity for me to visit with my relatives that I haven't seen for a few years."

The first weekend in February I flew to Daytona Beach, Florida. My cousin, Chris Thompson, came over and met me at the airport. Later his brother Paul picked me up and took me to New Smyrna Beach to his mom and dad's home.

It was indeed an honor to be asked to go back to Florida as a special and invited guest. The local newspaper had interviewed me prior to my visit and then ran a front page story while I was in town.

I saw people that I hadn't seen for several years. I tried to get out and about and see as many of my relatives as possible. I had lived in New Smyrna Beach where I was born for three years before moving to New Jersey.

It rained on Friday and part of the day on Saturday. It finally cleared up that afternoon and the people came out to celebrate. On Sunday morning, I went to the Pleasant Grove Baptist Church. It was the same church that I had attended as a young child. Then I went back to the festival and gave a speech.

Afterward, I went to my cousin Paul Thompson's home in Deltona to watch the Super Bowl and spend the night. Then I flew back to Colorado the next morning.

The third weekend in February, I was the keynote speaker at the Colorado Professional Rodeo Association's convention in Cripple Creek, Colorado.

The last weekend in February, I was back in New Jersey for Black History Month. I did a speech and presentation at Salem High School on a Friday, and then another speech and presentation at Woodstown's Mary S. Shoemaker Elementary school on Monday morning. How could I not wish Justin had been there?

I also signed a few books for teachers. Afterward, one of the students asked me to sign their hand. Then, I was mobbed by many of the students wanting to get my autograph.

They treated me like some kind of a Hollywood star. As I was walking down the hallway, some of them were calling me "Mr. Cowboy." A couple of the students approached me and asked if they could touch me. Of course, I obliged them all. It sure made me feel good. I never expected that kind of a reception from the little kids.

In order to give me some relief, the principal told the students that I had to go to the airport to catch a plane. I did, but my flight wasn't scheduled to leave for another five hours and it was only thirty minutes to the airport. That afternoon I flew home.

The next morning the *Today's Sunbeam*, a local newspaper, put a color picture on the front page of me signing autographs for the elementary students. As they say, a picture is worth a thousand words. You could see the gleam in the eyes of the kids in line waiting for an autograph.

Back at home I got back to the business of working on my legal issues. I was still spinning my wheels trying to get my child support fiasco straightened out. The supervisor in New Jersey continued to be cooperative with me but the lack of forward movement was still very frustrating.

My former attorney's boss had called me while I was in Florida and said they agreed to pay back part of my retainer. A few months later they sent me a legal document that needed to be signed and notarized saying that I wasn't to divulge their names in a book, etc.

He told me that their firm didn't want negative publicity which he knew my book would generate. Included in that package was a photocopy of the $1,000 check made out to me that I would receive as soon as I sent back the signed document.

I wasn't hurting for money financially, so after I had the form signed and notarized I sat on it for awhile. That proved to be a mistake.

Instead of sending me the $1,000 check that I was promised, I received one for $500 in January 2007.

I was told that I would receive the second check for $500 the following month. Instead of sending the second check for $500,

I was sent a check for $250.

I was under the impression that I would be receiving another check for $250 the following month. A few months later, I received a check for $150. Each time they would give a lame duck excuse about their cash flow. I could care less about his firm's cash flow. I just wanted the $1,000 they had agreed to return to me.

Each time a lesser amount check arrived I would call and chastise his firm. One time the boss, Harry Houdini, tried to calm me down by saying, "Abe, you know you're a hell of a nice guy." Then he had the nerve to ask me to sign and send him a copy of my book.

I told him if he wanted one of my books, then he could send me a check just like everyone else. I certainly wasn't going to give him a free copy of my book after all of the crap that he and his associates had put me through. There was complete silence on the other end of the phone.

It wasn't until August 2007 that I finally received the last installment ($100) on the $1,000 that he'd had agreed to pay back to me in February 2006. This was only after constantly bugging them to send my money. I guess you can see why I don't have a lot of faith in attorneys and their promises.

At work, I could sense I was giving my supervisor fits. One day he saw me with a baseball cap on the floor. He told me that the building supervisors didn't want us to be wearing baseball caps while on the premises. He had no right to ask me not to wear a baseball cap to and from my desk whenever I was going outside on a break. I wasn't violating any policies. I could understand if I wore it around the floor or while sitting at my desk, but I didn't. I only wore it when I went outside in the summer, when it was sunny and hot.

I was starting to get a little heat from my supervisor. I was asked to move to another department. I was told that I no longer was required to interview to go to the Core unit. All I had to do was agree to go, and I would automatically be moved.

I refused, saying, "I interviewed twice and was told no twice. Now it's personal. I have absolutely NO desire to move."

My supervisor, Mickey Safeway, came to my desk one day. He told me, "You'll be given a notice. After your official notification, you'll have eight months in which to make a decision. At the end of the eight months, if you don't move, then you'll be terminated."

I sounded off on him. "Look Mickey, you don't scare me. I didn't lose any sleep over this job last week. I didn't lose any sleep over this job last night. I don't plan on losing any sleep over this job tonight. So, you go ahead and do what you think you need to do."

I know that he wasn't expecting that kind of a reaction from me.

After Mickey left my desk that day, he knew better than to ever come back. He realized that I would open up and get loud on him, just like any other supervisor that came over to my desk to confront me.

As soon as he left, Ken Marquez, who sat right next to me, jumped up and did the Muhammad Ali shuffle and then did a left-right, left-right combination into the thin air on the nineteenth floor. I laughed at Ken's antics. I had made it very clear to Mickey that I wasn't going to leave without putting up a good fight.

Mickey came over to my desk again around May 1, 2006, and told me that my eight month clock had just started. Soon after, I was in his office and told him, "Go right ahead and terminate me. I guarantee you that your name and this company's name will be in my next book."

"The shelf life of a newspaper article is only about six weeks," he replied.

"I'll assure you that the shelf life of my book will be a lot longer than six weeks."

Outside the company's walls, I was having success with my book. It was garnering a lot of media attention. In March 2006, I was recognized by the *Urban Spectrum* newspaper as an outstanding African-American who was making a difference in Colorado history.

A review of my book was included in the March 2006 issue of *Western Horseman* magazine. I did an interview in April for (NPR) National Public Radio. These things contiinued to reinforce my belief that I could soon leave TIARRA and do just fine on my own.

After Justin moved to Charlotte I made it a point to call and talk to him at least twice a week. I would usually call him midweek and every Sunday evening. I tried to be consistent and call him on Sunday at about 7:00 p.m. (EST)

I wasn't too keen on flying to Charlotte for a so-called "scheduled visit" and having Lorena pull another one of her shenanigans. I could see myself going there and after I landed, her refusing to let me see Justin. I couldn't risk getting upset and playing right into her hands to get arrested and lessen my chances of obtaining custody, for that is what I knew she was determned to do.

In late April I was on a flight to Denver from back East.

It was late in the day but there was still plenty of daylight. The entire flight had been smooth except for a little turbulence.

As we were descending into DIA we hit a very vicious hail storm. There were periodic flashes of lightning. I had my usual window seat and could see the hail as it pummeled our airplane.

The captain said, "Flight attendants, please prepare for landing."

Our descent was normal and nothing was unusual or out of the ordinary. All of a sudden our plane dipped at a forty-five degree angle, sideways. The left wing went up and the right wing down. Simultaneously we dropped down and to the right. We felt the sudden change in altitude. It was a definitely an "allemande right."

A woman, who I guessed to be about twenty years old, cut loose with a bone chilling and murderous scream. There was no doubt that the pilot had temporarily lost control of our plane. As he regained it, we teeter-tottered back and forth until we leveled out again.

It scared the heck out of me. I reached down and tightened my seatbelt as much as possible as if that was going to do me any good. All I could do was sweat and pray that we would land safely. My hands were wringing wet.

Then about forty seconds later and without warning, we did the exact same thing. An abrupt forty-five degree angle change and drop to the right.

The same woman cut loose again. But this time around she had already riled up the other passengers. There was a chorus of screams and I believe every woman on that flight joined in. I was terrified, too, to say the least.

Again we teeter-tottered until the pilot regained control. I just knew we were going to crash. I was scared to death. It was the first time in my thirty plus years of flying that I was sure we were doomed.

All of a sudden and without warning the pilot gunned the engines and we climbed back up. He never said a word of reassurance to the passengers. He must have had his hands full.

Finally, he came back on and said, "The conditions were just too bad. I decided to go back up and we'll try it again."

There was complete silence on our flight as we circled the airport. All the while, we still had a very clear shot of DIA but we could still see the lightning flashes and the hail.

A few minutes later we safely landed and you could hear a pin drop. No one on our flight uttered a single word. After all we'd just gone through I'm surprised that everyone was still so quiet.

Finally a flight attendant came on and said, "Ladies and gentlemen, welcome to Denver. All of sudden there was a cacophony of cheers and "amens." The young woman who had initiated the entire escalation of screams was sincerely apologizing to everyone on board.

"I'm sorry. I'm sorry," she said. "I have a connecting flight to San Francisco in an hour and there is no way in hell that I'm getting on that airplane!"

When I got home, I contacted an attorney in Charlotte who agreed to take my case. He asked me to send him a $1,000 retainer fee. I told him to get my file from the attorneys in New Jersey. I was concerned about Lorena violating my court ordered visitations in the summer of 2006 as she'd done in 2004 and 2005.

I dealt with that attorney for about two months. I had very little patience at the time. It didn't seem like he was going to work out for me. Meanwhile, I did an Internet search and contacted another attorney in the Charlotte area. I was actually talking to two different attorneys at the same time.

The first one balked at a few things that I asked him to do, so in disgust, I decided to call him up and give him the third degree. He wasn't available. Although he had already done a couple of things and could have charged me, I demanded my entire $1,000 back.

The summer was fast approaching and I didn't have time to dink around with him. His receptionist said, "Mr. Peyton is a very good attorney." I didn't care how good he was, he wasn't good for me. He seemed tentative and he hadn't done anything to impress me. Sure his website and resume were very impressive.

About ten days later, I received a $1,000 check in the mail with no questions asked. The letter said that he would call and speak to me at a later date, but he never did. I really didn't care. He had already wasted enough of my precious time.

My primary goal for the summer was for Justin for a long overdue visit. My newest attorney told me that we wouldn't have time to legally do anything about it.

Lorena came up with a scheme that the only way that she would allow me to have Justin come to Colorado was for me to fly to Charlotte and pick him up personally. In June 2005 she had sent him alone on a flight to Philadelphia. The only reason she did that was because she was scheduled to go to Philadelphia about a week later to do some company training in there.

Lorena continued to use the ludicrous excuse that Justin might have an asthma attack while on the flight. The only reason that she insisted that I come and get him, was because she was so sure that I would refuse to buy three round trip airline tickets just to see my son. But once I did, she realized that she couldn't back out. It would have only cost me an extra forty dollars for the usual airline escort fee for Justin to fly as an unaccompanied minor. It was just down right hateful on her part to insist that I purchase two additional airline tickets for myself.

It ended up costing me $2,400 for the three airline tickets because I got them at the last minute. In order to accommodate her schedule I'd have to catch a late night flight to Las Vegas, then get on a red-eye from Las Vegas to Charlotte. I would be in the airport in Charlotte for about an hour and a half, before I would board a flight back to Denver with Justin.

When I arrived at DIA, I found out that my plane to Las Vegas was running late. When I told them I had a connecting flight to Charlotte, they said I would still be able to make it. So I didn't panic.

Because we were so late arriving in Las Vegas, our gate was occupied. We sat on the runway for about twenty minutes after we landed. It seemed like forever. I was a nervous wreck. I knew if I missed my flight, I probably wouldn't be able to pick up Justin after forking out all of that money.

I didn't have a cell phone number for Lorena. She'd refused to give me one. I had no way to contact her. Yet she had insisted that I sign a statement that said at the end of the visit, I'd send Justin back to North Carolina and not try to keep him in Colorado.

When we finally pulled up to the gate, I jumped up and moved toward the front as far as I could. There was no time to explain myself or be courteous to the other passengers. I had to go.

It was extremely hot in Las Vegas in July. I bet it was still ninety degrees outside. My connecting flight was on another concourse. And it was almost time for it to depart. I ran like a madman through the airport. I was so out of breath at times I felt like I was going to have a heart attack.

I was sweating profusely, but would only slow down long enough to catch my breath and then I'd run again. I knew I would be heartbroken if I missed my flight. I felt horrible, but somehow kept pushing myself onward. I hadn't seen Justin for over a year because of all of Lorena's visitation violations. I was a nervous wreck.

Only through the grace of God did I make it. I just knew I would collapse in the airport from exhaustion. I collapsed instead in my seat on the plane and didn't care to talk to anyone until I'd caught my breath. I knew I looked like I'd just been in a fight or something. I felt like it, too.

Crazy, ridiculous, unnecessary—I could go on and on and on. It was such a shame. Lorena continued doing everything and anything that she could think of to cause me trouble and to keep me and Justin apart and was allowed to get away with it through the court system. I suffered so much just trying to maintain contact with my son.

Friends and family had often told me that someday God was going to properly deal with Lorena for all of her evil ways. "You just keep doing the right thing and someday you'll be blessed for it. Justin will see through all of this someday. He'll find out the truth. Justin is going to grow up to realize what his mother has done."

Others believed in Karma. "What goes around comes around. Someday Lorena will get just what she has coming to her. Just wait and see."

Lorena brought her fiancé, (I learned this later) Lucius Brown, along to the airport. I saw the three of them come through the main door and then lost sight of him. I did see him give Justin a goodbye hug. I'm sure Lucius ducked behind a pole or something so he could get a good look at me. All Lorena did was lie about me and I'm sure he wanted to see if I actually looked like a real live monster.

Lucius stayed out of sight while Lorena brought Justin up to the line I was standing in. When I was going through the security line, one of the workers noticed the T-shirt I was wearing and the buckle that I was wearing. He asked me if I competed in the bull riding event. I told him yes.

Then he asked me in a very sarcastic tone, "Were you any good?"

I replied in the same tone, "No, they gave me the buckle because they felt sorry for me." Then I told him to go online and look at my website and book. "You figure it out for yourself if I was any good."

I always hated for someone to look down on me and ask if I was any good. Common sense tells you that anyone that wears a nice trophy belt buckle had to have some talent. They don't just give those away. You have to go out the old-fashioned way and earn them.

I could see how much Justin had grown since I hadn't seen him since June 2005. He was much taller. On the flight back to Colorado I was dog tired and wanted to sleep, but Justin was wound up and kept me awake. He wanted to talk.

DIA is located out in the middle of nowhere. When we landed Justin said, "Daddy this looks like a desert."

The passengers sitting around us kind of laughed. I know they were paying attention to us because Justin wanted to read my book on the flight coming back. Justin read the parts that I had written about him out loud. So I know they were curious as to who we were.

While we were outside waiting for the bus to take us to the RTD Park N' Ride Justin told me that Lorena had said, "The judge in New Jersey had court ordered her to move to Charlotte."

It upset me that she could lie like that to Justin.

On the way Justin said, "Mommy said you probably live in an apartment." I told Justin that I lived in a nice house.

Before I opened the door he said, "I'm going to close my eyes." When we were inside and he opened them, Justin's reaction was, "Daddy, this is nice!"

Although I was tired, I still went to practice for our co-ed softball church league. The next morning, I slept in and Justin came into my bedroom and said, "Daddy, I want you to get up."

A couple of days later we had a softball game and Justin asked me to hit a home run for him. I hit an inside the park homerun. Justin was sitting in the grandstand watching the game. After I crossed home plate, I yelled to Justin that there was his home run that he requested. He was awfully proud of his father.

On Sunday morning, we drove up to Cheyenne Frontier Days. In the parking lot I met a friend with a horse and asked him to give Justin a ride. I took his picture. Justin had a blast. I was glad that he could finally make it to Cheyenne. Justin was supposed to have been there both of the past two years, but his mother had sabotaged those trips.

Justin needed some new cowboy boots. He had outgrown his black boots. Justin bugged me because he didn't want to go to the rodeo in tennis shoes. So on Monday afternoon we stopped at a western wear store and bought a new pair.

We returned to Cheyenne again on Monday night for the PBR event. Justin had a blast again. He kept dancing in between the bull rides. He caught the eyes and attention of some young teenage girls. They kept watching him, and wanted to know if he was going to be there the next night, too.

We spent the night with Jeff Cathcart and his family on Monday. We skipped the rodeo the next day and went to the PBR on Tuesday night. Justin kept asking me if he could participate in the mutton bustin' where the little kids are put on a sheep and try to ride them. I didn't have a problem letting him get on, but I knew Lorena would throw a fit when she found out, and try to take some kind of legal action against me, so we had to pass.

Lorena called to speak to Justin. During one conversation she asked him if he missed her and he said, "No." Then Lorena got

upset. She got Justin upset and he went upstairs and slammed his bedroom door.

Later she called to speak to Justin and wanted to talk to me. I was very hesitant because of the mutual restraining orders. I decided to listen to what she had to say.

Lorena talked about trying to be civil in the future and not wanting to continue fighting with me in the court system. She also offered to pay me $20,000 for my property that she had destroyed. Lorena wanted to know if this would help to mend our relationship. She asked several times if I hated her but I refused to give her an answer.

Lorena tried to sound like it would be in Justin's best interests if we were to start getting along. It was true, of course, but from past experience I knew she was up to something. After all she had done to me, there was absolutely nothing she could do to ever gain my trust again.

All week long Justin and I did a lot of talking and bonding. We also spent time in the park which was only a block from my house. We played baseball, basketball and football. I helped Justin work on his fundamentals.

For baseball I pitched him a lot of balls and let him swing away. Justin has great hand to eye coordination, and could hit the ball extremely well. At times we switched to wiffle ball. He'd hit those plastic balls and launch them into the outfield. People walking around the park watched, and commented on how well Justin could hit.

I threw long passes to him and he caught most of them. I was amazed at how well he could throw and catch a football. When we played basketball, I mostly let him shoot over and over again. I wanted him to work on his shooting skills.

I told Justin that he would be good. Justin replied that he wanted to be great. He also said he wanted to come and live with me. He kept telling me that he wanted to stay with me for more than ten days.

One time he said, "Daddy, I want you to get me out of there. I want you to get me out of there before the year is over."

While Justin was with me I did a radio interview for 850 KOA AM. I did it over the telephone. I put the radio in the basement and closed the door so Justin could listen to the live interview.

Justin told me that he wanted to write a book. I kept telling him he was too young to write a book, but he wouldn't take "no" for an answer. So, finally I set him up on the computer and he titled his book Extreme Sports. During one of his writing sessions he asked me how to spell perseverance. Justin had seen me write that word in many of the books that I'd autographed in Cheyenne. He would often sign my books, too, when he was with me.

We had another church softball game on Saturday morning and Justin served as our batboy. We won the game. I didn't hit another home run but I tried.

After the game, we went back up to Cheyenne again, returning that night. Then on Sunday morning we went again for the short go 'round, the finals. Justin was determined to get as many autographs on his cowboy hat as possible. We scurried around before, during and after the rodeo seeking cowboys to sign it for him.

During the rodeo we walked down to the timed event area. Justin had seen a black cowboy compete and he wanted to meet him. While we were there I asked Stran Smith for an autograph. I honestly don't think Stran remembered my name, but he had seen me enough times to know I was one of the guys.

Stran had just competed in the finals of the tie-down roping event when he signed Justin's cowboy hat. Justin asked if he could pet his horse. Stran said, "yes," and then he reached up to the saddlehorn, and handed Justin the rope that he'd just used in the rodeo arena.

That gesture made Justin's whole day. He started jumping around and acting like the rope was a bull rope, and he was riding a bull. I knew Justin would probably keep that rope as one of his most treasured possessions.

I also wrote about that in my monthly column of *Humps N' Horns Bull Riding News* for the October 2006 issue. The story and an accompanying photograph of Justin, Charles Sampson and me were also put on the *Humps N' Horns News* website on the Internet.

I wrote a letter to the *Prorodeo Sports News* in August 2006 thanking all of those cowboys and it was published. At Cheyenne Frontier Days in July 2007 we ran into Stran Smith in the parking lot and he remembered us. In December 2008 Stran became the World Champion tie-down roper in the PRCA.

I hated to send my son back to Charlotte. Justin told me several times that he wanted to live with me. I promised him that I would do everything that I could to make that happen.

We had both experienced an exhausting but very productive visit together. It was sad that the money that I had to spend on those extra airline tickets could've been used for his college education.

On Monday morning when I called his name to wake him up, he took a breath and burst out crying. Justin cried non-stop for about an hour, even as I gave him his shower. Justin didn't want to go back to his mother.

It just tore me up to have to send him back. I could tell that it was very painful for him to leave. If I wasn't concerned about being arrested, I would've kept him. I was a law abiding citizen while Lorena had been far from that. I was more concerned than ever about Lorena's emotional instability and the effect it was having on Justin.

On our way to the airport, I called her and let Justin tell her that I wasn't going to bring him back. She needed to be at the gate to meet him. It was ridiculous and a waste of my time and money to fly to Charlotte, and just turn around and get on another plane back to Denver.

A few weeks later, in August, I was at a rodeo at Castle Rock, Colorado. I ran into a co-worker from TIARRA.

Robert approached me and out of the blue started ranting and raving about Lorena. I didn't initiate the conversation. Robert had also worked on that January business conference with her.

"That ex-wife of yours is something else. That woman is crazy. Man, she needs some help. She is...I can't think of the word."

"Bipolar?" I offered.

"Yes. That's it, bipolar. I don't ever want to have to work with her again!"

Robert, now a manager at TIARRA, had known Lorena since June 1998. They were hired at the same time and had been in the same training class together.

As soon as Justin returned to Charlotte, I contacted my new attorney and told him that I wanted to file for sole legal custody. He convinced me to wait until right after Justin's Christmas visit to New Jersey. He didn't want to ruffle Lorena's feathers, because if we did before that visit, I probably wouldn't get to see Justin the rest of the year.

In mid August, I was invited to do a book signing at the PRCA Hall of Fame in Colorado Springs, Colorado, as part of a two day concert series fundraising event.

In late August, I went to Fort Worth to attend a Cowboys of Color Rodeo and visit my sister Rosalyn and her family. Then one night in September, I received a call from Mom. She said, "Congratulations. You have been selected to be the Salem County New Jersey Sports Hall of Fame." My sister Patricia had campaigned very hard to get me voted in. She had submitted my name and ballots the past two years and I had been turned down twice.

I was elated. It was an honor to be elected to any Hall of Fame. It was especially nice that the hometown committee could see the value of what I had accomplished and to be recognized in that fashion. The induction ceremony would be held on December 28, 2006 at the Salem County Community College.

I had also been invited to participate in the Equality State Book Festival in Casper, Wyoming. I would be in some elite company. The criteria for the invitation was the author had to be from, live in or write about the state of Wyoming. The festival was held October 19-21, 2006.

In Casper, I stayed for two nights in a motel and was on a speaking panel called *Cowboy Myths/Cowboy Realities.* I met Linda Hasselstrom, a well-known author originally from South Dakota. She was a speaker on the same panel. Linda said she had wanted to read my book after she found out we were on the same speaking panel. She was living in Cheyenne. She said that she hadn't read my book yet because it was always checked out of the public library.

Linda also gave me the greatest compliment. "You are very articulate and a very handsome guy. You'll be able to write your own ticket one of these days. You are going to be very successful in this career."

Annie Proulx, the author of *Brokeback Mountain,* was also on our panel. Her story had been turned into the award winning movie. Our panel was by far the most popular. The room was filled to the brim with an overflow of people outside and standing along the walls on both sides of the room.

Afterward, I was told by one of the authors, "Everyone came to see Annie, but you stole the show with your speech."

Right after the panel, I was whisked out the side door and to the front of the building. A table had been set up so I could sign some of my books. I felt like a celebrity being escorted quickly away from the crowd.

The guy who escorted me said, "I want to get you out of here as soon as possible before people have a chance to come up and talk to you. Otherwise, you'd never get away."

I sat right next to Annie Proulx at the table and signed quite a few books. It was a lot of fun. I'd been looking forward to the book festival for months. It was an honor to be invited. It was nice to rub elbows with some famous authors from Wyoming. I was paid nicely and it was a very successful weekend.

On my way home, I stopped at the PRCA rodeo in Fort Collins on Saturday night. It had snowed a little. The road was icy in spots so I slowed down for awhile and took it easy.

The next morning I went to church at New Hope Baptist. That evening my publisher held a special dinner for her authors in the Denver area.

In December of 2006, I went out to Las Vegas for the Wrangler National Finals Rodeo with Gerry Strom. It is always exciting to go to the WNFR. I always see friends that I haven't seen in years.

I signed my books at the PRCA Hall of Fame booth at Cowboy Christmas again. While I was there, I met Obba Babatunde and James Pickens. Obba is a character actor who has played in several movies. James Pickens is on *Grey's Anatomy*. I had someone take a picture of us together. It was fun to meet them.

One night Gerry and I went to the Gold Coast Casino. The go 'round buckle presentations are held there each night. Many rodeo cowboys and fans attended. People who aren't able to get tickets to the rodeo performances can watch a live feed and simulcast on a large screen in a special room.

Somehow Gerry and I got tickets to the last performance on Saturday evening. Early Sunday morning we flew back to Denver. I thought it was going to be very hectic going through security, but it really wasn't that bad.

I had had some special T-shirts made up with my book cover on the front and my book title and website on the back. I purposely wore it on the flight to attract attention. On the way back I sold two books because people asked about my T-shirt. I also decided to give the T-shirts out as Christmas presents to my immediate family.

There was a lottery at work to see who would be able to take their vacation days around the Christmas holidays. I'd usually bypass Thanksgiving requests, hoping it would give me a better chance at Christmas.

In the first company-wide lottery I received the December 22, 23, and 24 for vacation days. They had been previously blocked out. I told Mickey that I definitely needed to go back to New Jersey because Justin was supposed to fly to New Jersey to visit with me. Given all of the problems I had experienced in the past there was no way I was going to jeopardize my visitation. Also my Hall of Fame Induction ceremony was on December 28. Originally, I didn't get December 26 and 27 off.

Mickey tried to convince me not to go home for Christmas, but leave afterward. I told him that there was no way I was going to stay in Colorado by myself, when I could be at home with my family.

Finally, there was another open enrollment and we had to use the computer to apply for those extra days. Mickey made a special trip to my desk to inform me of the time and date. At the exact moment, I applied for the days.

I was granted December 27 but didn't get the day before. Mickey came over to my desk afterward to see how I'd fared in the lottery. I immediately told him I wasn't going to be at work on December 26. Mickey informed me that I couldn't just say that I wasn't going to show up for work. It wasn't fair to the other employees and their families and would be highly frowned upon by the company.

In so many words I told him I wasn't concerned about the company's policies, and I wouldn't be coming in the day after Christmas. I told Mickey if he expected me to catch a flight back to Denver in order to work one day, and then fly back to New Jersey for the rest of my visit with Justin and my induction ceremony, he was crazy.

Later, Mickey was sitting at his desk and looking at the

vacation schedules on his computer. Another employee was with him. The door was open and I walked in his office just in time to hear Mickey say out loud, "That frigging Abe!"

It was obvious that I was giving him fits, especially, since he'd made that statement in the presence of another employee.

On Tuesday, December 19, 2006 the entire Front Range of Colorado was hit with a massive blizzard. It was snowing pretty hard on our way to work that morning and got progressively worse. Our company let some people go home early. I was very vocal because they wouldn't allow the rest of us to go home.

From the nineteenth floor of our building we could see cars slipping and sliding all over the place on the streets below. I kept saying, "Let my people go," using the story of Moses and the Hebrew children in the Land of Egypt. Reluctantly, they finally did.

I took a different bus home because my bus only ran in the early morning and late afternoon. I got as close to my house as I could, and then I had to walk home. I boarded a second bus and there was so much snow that all of the sidewalks were impassable.

I finally made it home in one piece. It was a trying experience. It was cold and snow was blasting me in the face. It snowed nonstop for about thirty-six hours. We got about thirty inches of snow.

The next day, Wednesday, the entire city of Denver was shut down due to the storm. Denver International Airport was also closed and stranded thousands of passengers making connecting flights.

My flight to Philadelphia wasn't until the next day, Thursday, at 11:55 p.m. The airport was closed until noon. DIA was a mess. My next door neighbors told me that I wasn't going to get out that night. I got nervous. I knew if I missed my flight or it was cancelled, then I wasn't going to get home before Christmas. I decided to go to the airport three hours before my flight. I only lived about fifteen miles away.

The neighborhoods were snowed in. My car was blocked in the garage with three feet of snow in the driveway. I started shoveling part of my driveway and just gave up. I knew it didn't really matter until I came back from New Jersey, so I left it alone.

I asked my friend Katie Flynn to give me a ride to the airport. I told her not to drive into my neighborhood. I would meet her with my luggage a couple of blocks away. She got stuck twice. The roads and streets were a mess.

Then, we got stuck in a traffic jam on the way to the airport. There were a lot of people at the airport. I felt sorry for them. Some had been there for two days.

I was amazed at how long the security line was. But I made it okay. I was sitting at my gate an hour before my flight. I had panicked, but I was finally able to relax. It was an ordeal getting to that point.

Although Lorena had had Justin with her for Christmas of 2005, she refused to let me have him for Christmas 2006. Again, this was a direct violation of the court order which stated we were to alternate visitation for the major holidays.

I arrived safely in Philadelphia the next morning. I never was very high on taking a red eye flight, though. I'd hardly slept all night but I was thankful I'd made it home.

My sister Rosalyn and her family drove up from Fort Worth. It was the first time all of the Morris children would spend Christmas together since sometime in the early 1980s.

We had a great time together. Lorena refused to let Justin come to New Jersey until December 27, and said I could only have him for five days. Despite whatever the court order stated she always made up her own rules. I had to pay for his airline tickets as usual. Of course I never got any credit with the courts for the tickets I'd paid for when she had refused to put him on the plane.

I was at least thankful that Justin would be present for my induction ceremony. The day that I went to the Philadelphia airport, Justin missed his flight. Lorena could have called me at my mom's house to notify me. But of course she didn't. Instead, I drove to the airport and then had to wait almost four hours for the next flight to arrive from Charlotte.

Lorena called me at the airport as I was standing in one of

the lines. Of course I would have preferred to wait at Mom's house instead of at the airport, but it was no inconvenience to her so she didn't care. It was another example of her unreasonable behavior. It cost me seventeen dollars for all those hours parking that day.

Justin finally arrived and we spent some time outside throwing the football around. He sure loved to catch the ball. In the past he had been satisfied with just playing catch with the football. Now Justin wanted to run some pass patterns. Justin was already a prototype NFL receiver.

We had taken our athletic activities to another level. He is the most talented little kid I've ever seen in my life. I'm so proud to be his father.

My family members showed up en masse for the induction ceremony. They wore the T-shirts that I had given them for Christmas presents with my book on them.

The committee asked the recipients to arrive early. My brother David took a few pictures. Before the ceremony started Justin asked, "Daddy, how are the people going to know that I'm your son?"

"I'll ask you to stand up. Better still, I'll ask you to come up on stage while I give my acceptance speech."

I thanked a lot of people especially my father, mother, sisters and brothers. I also thanked my cousins Gene, David, Jimmy Lee and Willie Ed Walker for all of the support during my career as a rodeo cowboy and bull rider.

During my speech I told the crowd that Justin was already a great athlete and couldn't help but brag about all the talent in the Morris family.

Justin asked me if he could have the framed picture that I received of the presentation. I told him yes. Then he said, "Daddy I want you to hang it up in my bedroom." He was referring to his bedroom at my house. He knew what would happen if he took it home.

On the way back to my mom's, I asked Justin what he thought of the ceremony. His response was, "Daddy, I'm really proud of you."

I can't explain how much that meant to me.

The next day there was a color picture of Justin and me on the front cover of the daily *Today's Sunbeam* newspaper that was taken during my acceptance speech.

The remainder of our visit went well. We played touch football a couple of times with some kids from the neighborhood. Justin and I were on the same team as usual. Whenever we played he always insisted on being on my team.

We also did a couple of nights of movies. Justin always insisted on sitting on the couch right next to me.

Back in Colorado it was still a snow mess. It had snowed a lot more while I was gone. In fact, we received record breaking accumulations of snow for about seven weeks in a row. But it wasn't only the snow that I had to contend with. It was my future and job at TIARRA.

I took me about a week to finally shovel my driveway. We weren't able to see our neighborhood street for several weeks. It was one lane and it was an ice bowl for quite awhile. It was late February or early March before driving down my street was back to normal.

On Monday, January15, 2007 I was invited by Shaul Turner to be a special guest on a live telecast for FOX 31 News in Denver. It was Martin Luther King's holiday. It was the second year in a row that I was their guest on that holiday.

That morning it was bitter cold. It had snowed a little the night before and the drive was slow going. That night I attended a special performance, the Martin Luther King African-American Heritage rodeo, at the Denver Coliseum. It was during the National Western Stock Show and Rodeo.

On Sunday January 21, 2007 it was the short go 'round or the finals. It had snowed pretty hard and the roads were a little suspect, so I opted to stay home.

I called Justin to talk to him and he was very upset. I could tell that he had been crying. I asked him what was wrong and he said, "Mommy beat me with a belt."

It wasn't until November of 2008 that Justin told me the rest of the story. He was almost asleep that same night when Lorena burst into his bedroom and violently punched him in the side of the head. He said it was extremely painful. Lorena was angry because he had told me that she had beaten him with a belt.

The next day I called and told my attorney. He advised me to call the school that Justin attended and report the incident. On Tuesday morning on my way to the bus stop, I called the school in Charlotte and spoke to the vice principal.

A couple of days later, he told me that Justin had been examined by the school nurse, and because of some other concerns the case had been referred to child protection and social services. He never would elaborate or give me any specifics. He recommended that I also call social services myself and report the incident. So I did.

When I tried to call Justin in the next few weeks his mother was at it again. She refused to answer the phone or let me speak to Justin.

Social services in Charlotte did follow up with me. I informed them that Lorena had been court ordered in New Jersey to undergo a psychiatric evaluation and had never done it.

They set up an appointment with Lorena and called me afterward. They told me that Justin denied that she had beaten him with a belt. I knew Lorena had pressured him into changing his story. Lorena still refused to let me talk to Justin.

I called the school and asked if I could speak to Justin. I told them I didn't want to interrupt his day. I just needed to hear his voice to know that he was okay. I wanted him to hear mine so he didn't think that I had abandoned and given up on him. I suggested that I talk to him at the beginning or end of his recess period.

I told the vice principal that in the divorce decree, Lorena was required to maintain a separate phone line so that I could speak to Justin. Since she refused to allow me to speak to him at home, I wanted to talk to him at school.

The vice principal asked me to fax over the court document and he would read it and get back to me. He never did. I called him four times in a row, and he refused to return my phone calls. When I finally spoke to him, I asked why he never called me back. He gave me some lame excuse. Then he said he would make a decision and get back to me.

What he did was call Lorena at work and asked her how she felt about me talking to Justin on the phone. Lorena told him that she didn't want me to talk to Justin, so when I called the man again, he refused to allow me to speak to Justin. This was solely based on Lorena's wishes and not the court order. Lorena had him and all of the school staff in the palm of her hand.

I lost a lot of sleep worrying about the welfare of my son. I was afraid that Lorena would flip out and injure him. She was crazy enough to do it.

My January story for *Humps N' Horns Bull Riding News* was titled *Reflections*. At the end of each year, I like to look back and reflect on what kind of a year I had experienced. I also try to set my goals and be in a much better position by this time next year.

I wrote about a lot of things that I had endured and looked at how far I had come since my first book was published. I mentioned my summer visit with Justin. I also wrote about my Salem County Sports Hall of Fame induction in New Jersey.

It was cold outside, but the heat was being applied to me at work. I refused to either bend or break. We were experiencing one of the coldest winters in a long time. It was the way winters in Colorado had been in the 1970s.

I refused to consent to move to the Core Unit or another department. At one point my supervisor sent me a few e-mails regarding some phone calls that I had taken.

Because of my situation, I felt as if he was applying a little extra pressure. I asked if he was harassing me. That was all that it took. After that he didn't send any more e-mails.

In late January someone from human resources sent out an e-mail. It was intended for the managers only. Instead of Mickey receiving the so-called "confidential" e-mail, his name was inadvertently left off of the distribution list and it was sent to me, instead.

The e-mail was a list of about eight employees, including me, who were going to be terminated as of March 1, 2007. There were no reasons listed. When Mickey found out I'd gotten the email he came to my desk, but I was headed out the door and standing by the elevator. He asked me if I had five minutes, saying he needed to talk to me.

I said, "No, I have to go and catch my bus." I left.

After that I called an attorney to see if I would have a reason to file a discrimination lawsuit. I bounced around and talked to several other employees and told as many people as I could that I was going to be terminated.

Mickey and the other managers did their best to keep my pending termination as quiet as possible. I did all that I could to stir things up.

I was also trying to stir things up with Lorena because she wouldn't let me speak to Justin. I hadn't spoken to him since Sunday, January 21. It was extremely hard going to bed each night wondering how Justin was doing. But I wasn't just going to lie down and not do anything about it.

I was very upset and in contact with my attorney on a regular basis. I'm sure he got tired of me bothering him. He never would do anything other than listen to my gripes.

My last day at work was on March 1, 2007. I didn't leave quietly. I was presented with a termination severance package. I took it to an attorney who said she didn't think I had a case to file a discrimination lawsuit. Terms of the package said I couldn't ever work at TIARRA again.

After seeing how they operated and treated their

employees, I didn't have any desire to go back to corporate America. I certainly didn't want to ever work for TIARRA again.

In April, I sent Lorena an e-mail letting her know that I was planning to take a weekend trip to Charlotte to visit Justin. I told her that if she wouldn't let me talk to Justin, then I was going to come and visit him.

In violation of the court order, she told me that I couldn't come and see him. That wasn't supposed to be her decision, but as I've said before, she made her own rules.

The court order said that if we had any disputes we were to seek the counsel of a so-called "parent coordinator." This was something that her attorney in New Jersey had come up with. Lorena wanted us to talk to a parent coordinator before she would allow me to see Justin.

Someone suggested that I call the police and ask them to do a welfare check on Justin.

Unbeknownst to me the police treat the call just like a 911 call. They immediately go to the residence. I hadn't been able to talk to Justin for over two and a half months.

On Thursday May 3, I'd had enough. I called the police in Charlotte and asked them to do a welfare check on Justin. The first time they went over there, no one was home. Later on that day, I called again. This time the police called me back and reported that Lorena was home and they found Justin asleep in his bed.

On Tuesday May 8 we had a phone conference with Lorena and the parent coordinator that she had located in Charlotte. It had been nearly four months since I'd talked to Justin. The woman's name was Dr. Michelle Miles and the company was called Healing and Growth Counseling.

Lorena was upset that I had called the police on her a few days before this conference. As far as I was concerned the conference had nothing to do with the police call. If she was gong to continue to refuse to let me talk to Justin, I was going to do it again and again. I'm sure the police would get tired of going over there. The neighbors were going to ask why the police kept showing up at Lorena's house.

Dr. Miles wanted to know if we could totally forget about the past and be able to move forward. I spoke up first and said yes if Lorena were to stop violating the visitation court orders, and allow me to speak to my son on the telephone as she'd been ordered to do.

Lorena agreed with Dr. Miles that she woul let me speak to Justin. I told the woman some of the shenanigans that Lorena had pulled, and never received a consequence from the court system. I also said Lorena was court ordered to undergo a psych evaluation. She still had never compiled with that court order.

At that point Lorena went off and started screaming, "Why don't you just shut up. Why don't you just shut up!"

I told Dr. Miles that Lorena had driven right past my mom's house in November 2006 during the Thanksgiving holiday. She had refused to stop and let Justin see his own grandmom. Justin hadn't seen my mom for over a year and a half. I thought that was such a cruel thing to do to an innocent little child and his grandmother.

At this Lorena said, "If your mom wants to have some kind of a relationship with Justin, then she needs to go and get a court order."

I thought why get a court order? When did a court order mean anything to her?

Halfway through the phone call Dr. Miles stepped in and said, "Let me call you right back." I didn't hear another word from Lorena. I believe it had gotten too hot in the room for her again. She had a habit of getting emotional and jumping up and running out of the room. I think she got up and ran out.

Dr. Miles called me right back. She said she'd call me again in a couple of weeks so we could continue the sessions. I called her a few times and left her voice mails. I reported that although Lorena had agreed to let me speak to Justin, several days later I still hadn't talked to him. Dr. Miles never called again or responded to my messages.

I honestly believe after Dr. Miles saw how unstable and emotional Lorena acted in her office, and decided that she didn't want to get involved with her and deal with this mess. She was a professional (or at least she seemed so to me) and trained to deal with these situations. But at least a professional counselor should return your phone calls. This case must have been far from what she was used to. I'll never know.

On Sunday May 13, 2007 (Mother's Day), I called the police again and asked them to conduct another welfare check on my son Justin. I called Justin several times before I called the police. The officer called and said he had just talked to Justin, so I knew that they were home.

I immediately called Justin's phone line several times after that and Lorena still refused to answer the phone.

During the time that Lorena had moved to Charlotte with Justin she had left various messages on his phone to me. She had forced Justin to leave one message that said, "I will be forced to testify in court and tell the truth about what you said."

Another automated message said, "You cannot leave a message at this number." Then the call would be automatically disconnected.

Another message was Lorena's voice in a very nasty and harsh tone. Lorena would say "Justin" and then an automated message would fill in the rest saying, "cannot receive a message on this phone."

Another automated message would say, "Sorry, this mailbox is full," and then disconnect.

Again these were all violations of court orders, because the order stated that Lorena must maintain a phone line and that if I wasn't able to speak to Justin, then I could leave him a voice message.

I had filed for sole legal custody through my attorney in Charlotte. Lorena was served the papers by a sheriff on Friday May 18. Those legal papers apparently gave her a change of heart and she allowed me to speak to Justin on Sunday May 20.

It had been exactly four months since I had heard my eight year old son's voice. Justin turned eight on May 15, and I couldn't even call and wish him a Happy Birthday. Pretty sad, huh? People don't think things like this can happen in these cases, but it was happening to both Justin and me.

I called his school and asked his vice principal to go to his room and tell him that I'd called to wish him a Happy Birthday. I put some money in a card and mailed it to the elementary school. Otherwise, I knew Justin would never see it. And that time he did receive it.

Originally, I had signed a motion for sole legal custody in January of 2007, before Lorena had quit allowing me to speak to Justin. My attorney said that he never received the copy I sent in the mail. I signed a second form in late January and there were more problems.

Lorena should have been served sometime in March, but who knows what ever happened to that set of the paperwork? At one time I said to my attorney, "Where are the forms that I signed clear back in January? Why hasn't she been served yet?"

I could tell that he didn't appreciate me questioning him about his job, but I didn't really care how he felt. He was also divorced and had young kids, but at least he saw and talked to his children. You would think he would have appreciated my situation.

I had to sign and get the papers notarized three different times before Lorena was finally served. There was no sense of urgency on my attorney's part despite my frustration at not being able to talk to my son.

When Lorena responded to the motion for custody it was full of lies. Her intent was to bash me and try to make the court think of me as some kind of a sexual pervert. It said things like I dressed and undressed in front of Justin and paraded around totally nude in front of him.

I was extremely hurt when I read the stuff that she had written. It knocked me for a big loop. Emotionally, I was down for a couple of days based on those heinous allegations. To say I was mystified, again, would be an understatement.

Although I had a court ordered, two week visit scheduled with Justin in June, Lorena again refused to let me see him. She insisted that the only way I would be allowed to spend time with Justin was if I traveled to New Jersey. And then Lorena said that I could only see him for five days during that time, at her discretion.

She also tried to get my mom involved. Lorena wanted a letter from my mom agreeing to certain stipulations, before she would put Justin on the airplane. I refused to get my mom involved. Lorena violated the court order, and I didn't see Justin in June of 2007.

I had a second court ordered visitation scheduled for July. I knew she was going to violate that one as well, so I had my attorney file for an emergency court hearing on my behalf.

The judge in Charlotte agreed to hear the case on Thursday, July 26. I flew to Charlotte at the last minute and it cost me $1,100 for a round trip ticket. The judge actually listened and within minutes gave me permission to take my son back to Colorado that evening.

The judge said Justin didn't have to return to Charlotte until a couple of days before school started. Lorena protested saying he should at least have a couple of days to get acclimated again. So the judge subtracted a few days. I had to send Justin back on Wednesday August 22, otherwise he could have stayed until Saturday August 26. School started on Monday August 28.

Then I had to buy a one way ticket for Justin for $867.90 because it was at the very last minute and the only seats available on that flight were first class. I was ordered to pay for Justin's airline tickets. I shouldn't even have had to go to Charlotte to get him. Again, there were no consequences issued to Lorena for violating the previous court orders. Why should she change her behavior?

If the judge had scolded or made her pay for the airline

tickets, Lorena would think twice about violating another visitation order. I asked my attorney about the upcoming Christmas visit. He said we'll try to get the judge to make Lorena pay for the airline tickets for Christmas 2007, but he never did anything about it.

In the courtroom, Lorena couldn't stop with her antics. She told the judge that when Justin came to visit me in July 2006 that I never gave him a shower the entire time he was here. Of course I gave him showers, including the morning that he left to go back to Charlotte.

After we left the courtroom my attorney said to me, "I don't understand how the state of New Jersey would allow Lorena to have physical custody of your son with a psychiatric evaluation hanging over her head."

My response to that statement was, "You can thank the judge for that decision."

The judge vacated his original order (of September 2003) requiring Lorena to have a "psych" evaluation in April of 2004. When we were divorced in July 2004 I asked that it be reinstated. It was put back in writing per our divorce agreement. Then we filed a motion in September regarding her failure to make the agreed on payment to me, violation of the July 2004 visitation and other pending issues. The judge ruled at that time that the psych evaluation must be turned into his court by December 15, 2004. It was never done and Lorena was never held accountable.

Now, finally, it seemed Lorena had run into a judge who wasn't going to allow her to do as she pleased and get away with it. At least that's what I thought. My opinion would drastically change in December of 2008.

My biggest regret was that the judge didn't deliver any consequences for Lorena's behavior. I'm sure finally filing for custody served as a wake up call for Lorena and was a signal that I wasn't going to just sit back and let her do as she pleased any longer. I was going to file motions and we were going to end up in court in front of a judge.

In court, I found out that we couldn't get Lorena for contempt of court, because all of the court papers were still basically filed in New Jersey and not North Carolina. Although Lorena had violated the court order saying that she needed to have a psychological evaluation turned into the New Jersey court by December 15, 2004, there was nothing we could do about it.

That paperwork needed to be filed in North Carolina first. My attorney had requested the paperwork, but was told that only a judge could make that request. The judge said that she would request that paperwork so the next time we showed up in court, it would be there.

I thought, how convenient for Lorena. As long as I never followed up on the psychological evaluation, she had no intentions of having it done. The New Jersey judge apparantly had much better things to worry about than the welfare of my son. That's why he never responded to the letter that I sent him in September of 2005.

Justin and I arrived in Denver late on a Thursday night. Justin wanted to go up to Cheyenne to watch the Frontier Days rodeo and the next morning, that's what we did.

The people are always so nice to us and especially receptive to Justin. On Sunday July 22 I had done a television interview with CBS Channel 5 about my rodeo career and the book. The segment hadn't been aired yet, so I asked the station reporter, Ben Rosenberg, if he would interview Justin and include him in my story.

Justin didn't want to miss any of the rodeo action. I finally convinced him to miss a part of the women's barrel racing to do the interview. Justin was interviewed on Friday afternoon, and the story was aired with the Saturday night news.

Justin was a little disappointed because they didn't include any of his answers to the questions. The reason was that he had been too timid and shy on camera. It was his first time and

I didn't expect much more for an eight-year old kid. I just wanted to allow him the opportunity. Justin thought that it was special, though, to be seen on television with his father. There's no doubt in my mind that Justin knows what a special little boy he is.

During the Saturday performance, I was able to take him behind the bucking chutes. He wanted to get up close and personal with the bucking bulls. I know he thought it was a blast and a privilege to get such a ringside seat. Usually we sat up in the Wrangler booth. Even that was nice because we had access to lots of food, cool drinks and snacks.

While Justin was with me in the summer of 2007 we did quite a bit. We played baseball and football and I pitched to him because I wanted him to work on his batting skills.

I could tell that Justin was extremely competitive. He doesn't take losing very well. I told him that I wanted him to be consistent. Justin asked me what that word meant.

A few days later he was proud of himself since he was hitting the ball very well. I noticed that Justin liked to choke up a little on his bat. It reminded me of the way that Barry Bonds held his bat.

When I played wiffle ball and pitched the ball into his strike zone, I learned to step backwards. Justin had smacked me in the face a few times. He was always polite enough to say he was sorry, but boy can that kid hit! Justin had never been taught to catch a pop fly ball. By the time he left, he was very good at it. The kid is a natural. He just needed someone to help him and to teach him how to do some refining and polishing.

Justin was our batboy at our church softball games on Saturday mornings. In the first game, I hit an inside the park home run. Justin ran toward me all excited after I crossed home plate, and I picked him up and gave him a big hug.

Before our games I would warm up with Justin using a baseball because the softball was too big for his little hands. People were truly amazed at the sound of that ball hitting my glove each time Justin threw to me. I was, too. Justin threw extremely hard for his size and age. His velocity was unreal.

A few days after Justin arrived in Colorado, Lorena called to speak to him. In court the judge had given her permission to call Justin on Tuesdays, Thursdays and Saturdays.

Lorena called about three times on a Monday, and then threw a fit because she wasn't able to speak with Justin. She also called my attorney and threatened him. It was amazing. She hadn't talked to Justin for four days and yet she was going berserk. It was okay when I wasn't able to speak to Justin for four straight months, but four days and she was already going out of her mind.

A few days before Justin left, Lorena wanted to speak to me on the telephone. I refused. I wasn't allowed to talk to her on the telephone due to the restraining order she had refused to drop.

I know this irritated her, because I said it in front of Justin.

The next day she called my cell phone and left me another threatening message. This was another blatant violation of the restraining order. When I complained again to my attorney, he acted like it was no big deal.

At the rodeo in Loveland, Colorado Justin had said the word "fart" while we were in the bathroom. I told him not to say that word. Then he said something to the effect of the other F-word.

"What do you know about the F-word, Justin?"

"Sometimes Mommy says it. Sometimes Mommy goes into a rage. When she really gets mad she calls me a "f-ing piece of sh-t." Justin didn't say these words, but I knew exactly what he meant. He kind of ad-libbed them. I was shocked and dumbfounded!

Even Justin knew there was something wrong with his mother. I thought it was absolutely horrible and inexcusable for a mother to refer to her eight-year old child as a "fucking piece of shit."

Justin will never forget the name calling as long as he lives. All Lorena had done was to transfer her anger about me to Justin. When we were together she would call me those same horrible names. Now she was doing it to him. No matter how much or how many times she apologizes, he still won't forget. He is just like me. Justin has an excellent memory.

On the drive home Justin said that he had hoped that someday his mother and I would get back together. I know I broke his heart, but I told him that there was no way that would happen.

One afternoon when we were playing baseball in the park, Justin said, "Daddy, I want either you or Mommy to get married again. I want to have a daddy and a mommy that live in the same house."

Justin was also good on my computer. He mostly played games but a few other times he worked on writing his own book. He kept telling me that he wanted me to work on my next book.

One day we went on a road trip to visit the University of Wyoming. I wanted to show him where I had gone to school. I showed him quite a bit of the campus. We went to Orr Hall where I had lived for a couple of years.

Justin was very disappointed that we couldn't get in. It was because of all of the things that happen in this day and age. Security is a lot tighter than it was when I was a student there.

We also visited the American Heritage Center and Museum. I wanted Justin to see where my rodeo memorabilia and newspaper items were being archived. Lorena had purposely destroyed many things that I would have donated to them.

The American Heritage Center had contacted me after the January 13, 2003 article in the *Denver Post*. They asked me to donate various items from my rodeo career. A couple of times a year, I take new items to Laramie to be put in my permanent files.

Then, Justin and I went over and watched the University of Wyoming football team practice. While we were sitting up in the grandstand, a man who was down on the field walked up to us and asked why we were there.

I told him I was an alumnus, and then showed him the book that I had written. He introduced himself as head coach Joe Glenn. I had no idea that it was him. Then I showed him a postcard of the front cover of my book, and he asked me to sign it on the front. Coach Glenn said he was going to post it in his office on the bulletin board. I thought that was an extremely nice gesture and I could tell it made Justin proud.

Another day Justin and I visited the Pro Rodeo Hall of Fame in Colorado Springs. Justin was mesmerized by all of the things that were on display. I had to drag him out of there because he didn't want to leave.

Justin was very inquisitive. He asked, Daddy, Why aren't you in this Hall of Fame?"

I told him that I had never been nominated. Justin didn't know the meaning of the word nominated, so I explained it.

It really made me feel good when he responded, "You'll be in here someday, Daddy. I know you will." That kid has a lot of confidence in his father.

As we drove away, I told myself that if I was ever inducted, I surely wanted Justin to be present, just as he had been in New Jersey. In a way I also felt deep down inside that his attendance would mean so much to me, that if he wasn't around, it would spoil the event.

Justin and I also went to the pro rodeos in Castle Rock, Colorado and Douglas, Wyoming. At those events you could feel the eyes of some of the spectators checking us out. It was obvious that we were properly dressed in the right attire.

Justin commented, "Daddy why do these people keep staring at me?"

"Justin, just get used to it. It's going to happen a lot."

At Douglas, I let Justin get on a mechanical bucking bull. He had a lot of fun. I know he got the impression that riding a whirling twisting dervish can be quite difficult.

The last couple of days that Justin was with me, I got out my VHS camera and decided to put together a tape. I should have done it a lot sooner.

Justin called the tape "Father & Son." There was a scene where I was tossing pop ups into the air. On one Justin slightly misjudged the ball and it smacked him right in the upper lip.

He went down with a thud and started crying. It scared me. Later, when we watched it on the tape, Justin laughed at himself and wanted to see it again. I was glad he was able to see the humor in his miscue. Justin sure is a great kid.

During the previous summer's visit we were playing catch with a hardball. I threw the ball directly at Justin and it skipped off of the top of his glove and hit him right squarely in the upper lip. Justin already had a loose tooth and it knocked it out. I told him to put it under his pillow. That night I took the tooth and replaced it with some money like a good tooth fairy should.

Justin continually asked me what day he had to go back to his mom. He kept saying that he wished he could stay longer. I hated to have to send him back again, but I was very thankful and grateful for the time we had spent together. I did all I could to fight back the tears. I managed not to cry at all, although I sure felt like it.

After Justin was on the plane the flight attendant said that he was crying, but that he'd be okay. I know he didn't want to go back to Charlotte. After I came back home to my empty house, I didn't want to talk to anyone for days.

Being alone and silent helped me process my emotional pain. After four or five days I was much better. And I didn't bring anyone else down with me.

The first thing I did was catch up on my rest. Justin had worn me out for four solid weeks. I wasn't complaining though. He was so full of energy.

I had planned to go to Fort Worth to visit my sister Roz and take in the Cowboys of Color Rodeo during the Labor Day weekend. Several former football players from the University of Wyoming had planned to come out for the first home game in Laramie on September 1st. I had told the fellows all summer that I would be there, too. When I discovered it was the same weekend, I called and cancelled the Texas trip. The day of the football game I found out it was sold out. I was very disappointed. I had missed out on the Texas trip and wasn't able to go to the game either. Then, all those guys who said they were coming out for a big reunion didn't show up.

I always feel better when I have something to look forward to. The next item on the agenda was the Wyoming Book Festival in Cheyenne on September 14 and 15. I was one of the invited authors for the weekend.

On Friday I did an interview with the University of Wyoming television network. It was to be shown on public television throughout the state. Several other authors were included as part of a series.

The next weekend I went back home to New Jersey for a quick weekend visit. I attended the football game in Woodstown on a Friday night, and then attended Cowtown Rodeo the following evening. I did a book signing at the rodeo.

I found out that Justin wasn't doing so well in his new school, behavior-wise. Without consulting or notifying me, Lorena had enrolled him in a different school. She had, again without notifying me, switched the after school program that Justin was attending. She had enrolled him into Kids R Kids and he no longer went to the Sunshine House.

The only way that I found out was because Justin told me. He was now going to a more accelerated school. Justin was in the third grade but doing fifth grade work.

At his former school Justin wanted to fit in and be accepted by some of his peers. He was acting and dressing like some of the rough kids. Lorena didn't like it and wanted him out of that environment. Some of his roughness carried over to his new school and he was giving his new teacher fits. She had sent e-mails to Lorena concerning his behavior. Of course, I didn't receive any of this correspondence. Lorena had made sure that I wasn't at all affiliated with my son.

Only after Justin got to be too much for her did Lorena want me to become involved. I was supposed to step in and be the disciplinarian after she'd completely kept me out of his life for four straight months in 2003 and then again in 2007.

Lorena had Justin write and mail a letter to me about his behavior. On Sunday, November 4, 2007 Lorena called and asked me to speak to Justin about his behavior at school.

"I want you to talk to Justin so we're on the same page about his behavior at school. He thinks he can come to Colorado to live with you."

"If I talk to him, I'm going to tell him that he can come and live with me."

"I want you to tell Justin that he needs to listen to and have respect for his teacher and his parents."

"You mean his 'parent' don't you? You have done everything that you can think of in order to keep that boy out of my life."

"I didn't call you to discuss that."

With that Lorena hung up the telephone on me. As usual and despite a restraining order that says she wasn't allowed to contact me via the telephone, Lorena felt as if she could call me whenever she saw fit.

Later, I sent her an e-mail to remind her that the reason the restraining orders remained in place was because she refused to drop hers, despite the recommendation from the judge. I also told her that if she wanted to talk to me, then she needed to go to the court and drop the restraining order.

Lorena fired back with another one of her nasty and hateful e-mail responses.

I ignored it.

I sent an e-mail to my attorney to complain about Lorena calling me on the telephone. He sent an e-mail back to me that seemed like one big yawn. He said he didn't think the court would do anything to her for calling me.

No, maybe not but I was sure they would do something to me if I ever called her.

In December, I went to the Wrangler National Finals Rodeo in Las Vegas with Charles Sampson, the 1982 PRCA World Champion Bull Rider. We stayed at the South Point Hotel and Casino. I did a book signing at the PRCA booth as part of Cowboy Christmas at the Las Vegas Convention Center.

I was only home in Colorado for a couple of days before I flew to Philadelphia so I could spend Christmas and New Year's Day with my family. Justin flew up from Charlotte to spend time with us.

The weather was great for that time of the year. I didn't even take my heavy winter coat and was glad that I didn't. I would never have worn it.

I was able to attend the 2007 Salem County Sports Hall of Fame induction ceremony. I hadn't gotten a chance to get a good look at the plaque that was going to be placed on the wall after I was inducted the year before. I wanted to get a good picture of it.

It was a pleasure to be able to sit there and be on the other side. I remembered being on that same stage a year before with my son present for my induction ceremony.

I was glad that Justin would be able to share some quality time with his family. It was very important to me that he spend some time with his cousins Michael, Coley and Tannah Morris.

Justin asked for and wanted to read a copy of my book while he was at my Mom's house. I asked him what happened to the copy that I had given him when he left Colorado in August 2007.

He said, "I don't know what happened to it. It disappeared."

Lorena had thrown it away, of course. In trying to get even with me she was hurting Justin's feelings.

Lorena had been with her fiancé Lucius for over a year when Justin informed me that they were no longer dating. That really didn't surprise me, but I knew this would make Lorena even more miserable and she might focus her attention on me again and how she might be able to make me pay for her problems. She always thought that she was so much better than everyone else. The fact that she couldn't keep a significant other really had to be getting to her emotionally. The fact that I was garnering more and more media attention bothered her, too.

Lorena or her dilemmas weren't my concern. My biggest concern was how her behavior affected the life of my son.

That visit Justin and I took a long walk and had a good heart to heart to talk. I asked him if he still wanted me to get married again.

"Yes, I want her to be nice and I want her to be black. I don't want a white woman for a step mother. She won't be able to relate to issues like the prejudice like we have to deal with. Also I don't want her to only pay attention to you."

I couldn't believe his responses. The boy was far beyond his years.

During my trip home, I also told Justin that he was the most talented young person I had ever seen in my life. He said, "Daddy, my plans are to write an epic novel."

I thought "epic novel?" Where in the world does this kid up with these phrases? I don't think I'd even heard the word "epic" until I was a teenager.

It always takes Justin a while to warm up to me during his visits, no doubt because our separations are so lengthy. This time he really was clingy after about five days. He would come over to me and try to sit in my lap. I didn't complain. I'm sure this is something that he had missed as he was growing up. I also don't think he realizes that he is rather tall for his age, and that he is a big kid now. It didn't matter to him.

During one of the Sunday morning church services he fell asleep. Before he drifted off to sleep in my lap, he reached up and grabbed my arm and placed it around his shoulders. Justin wanted to make sure that I was touching him, so he could feel at ease.

I know he is such a confused little boy. Now that Lorena realizes that I have filed for sole custody, she is doing all she can to try and hold on to him. I'm sure she tells him more lies about me. That's probably one of the biggest reasons that she agreed to let him visit me for Christmas. Lorena knew the judge in Charlotte would frown on her unrelenting and uncompromising behavior.

Justin was with me in New Jersey for about ten days. He once said he wanted to call and talk to his mom, and then later changed his mind. After that Justin never again asked to call and speak to Lorena.

I came back to Colorado on January 2, 2008. After being gone for so long I was ready to get back down to business. I needed to edit, proofread and finish the manuscript for this book.

I was especially thankful to God that my home was intact since I had been gone for almost two solid weeks. It was good to be back. I told myself that I didn't want to be gone that long again. After Justin had flown back to Charlotte I had been pretty much ready to go back to Colorado.

In New Jersey I had taken along a few extra things such as a glove, hardball, wiffle balls and a bat. We played a lot outside as usual. At times Justin begged me to go outside and play something with him. I loved spending quality time with my son and best friend.

While I was in Las Vegas a gentleman named Dr. Joseph Hatch from Salt Lake City purchased a copy of my book. When I returned from New Jersey there was a check in my post office box with an order for four more books.

Dr. Hatch had read my book and really enjoyed it—so much that he wanted to share it with his friends and relatives. In February, after I returned from my trip to Florida, there was another letter in my post office box with a check for two more signed copies of my book.

I attended the big Wrangler party in downtown Denver held at the Marriott on January 12, 2008. I have gone to this party for about the last ten years. It is always a very nice and first class affair.

On Monday, January 21, 2008 I again was invited by

Shaul Turner to the FOX 31 News studio to commemorate Martin Luther King's holiday. We also discussed the African-American rodeo that was going to take place that night at the National Western Stock Show.

On Friday, January 25, 2008 I was invited back to the FOX 31 News studio as a part of a segment called FOX Box where a panel would discuss current hot topics in the news.

After the live segment I met Tommy Chong, who was famous for the hilarious Cheech and Chong pot smoking movies of the 1970s. He asked me some questions about being a black bull rider from the East coast and I told him that all of those answers were in my book.

Tommy Chong was on the air right after our little segment. He was in town to do a couple of weekend shows at the Comedy Club. I ended up signing a copy of my book for him. I told him if he enjoyed it to be sure and mention it on stage during his shows.

On Thursday, January 31, I flew to Florida to be a part of the Zora Neale Hurston Festival in Eatonville where I signed more books.

Then on Saturday, February 23, I flew to Detroit, Michigan. My first cousin Gwen Cannon wanted me to come up for a week in order to promote my book and do a few speeches during Black History Month.

On Monday, January 14, 2008 I received a very long and detailed e-mail from Lorena. In the seven plus years since our separation she had never addressed an e-mail to me by using my name. Prior to this she had acted as if I didn't have a name. She would simply start every e-mail without addressing me.

This was by far the longest e-mail that she had ever sent to me. She was attempting to reach out to me for all of her past transgressions because she knew that our custody trial was looming on the horizon. If only she knew how obvious she was!

I didn't respond though I wanted to. I wanted to say, Lorena you did everything that you could think of to destroy me emotionally and financially. Now, that you see how successful I've become, you're reaching out to me. I would have gladly separated from you and we could have gone our separate ways. You didn't have to throw half of my personal property into the trash. If I were living in an apartment or a trailer court and was down and out or destitute would you be reaching out to me now? Probably not. You told me many, many times. "You have made your bed, so now LIE in it." It was time for her to reap what she'd sown.

On Wednesday, February 27, 2008 while I was in Detroit, I called Justin a few times to talk to him. I always called him on his landline during the middle of the week. Lorena answered the phone. She tried to act so nice and syrupy sweet. Lorena asked if I had called to speak to Justin. I wanted to tell her I sure as heck wasn't calling to talk to her. I refrained because I knew she'd get upset and hang up the phone. Then she asked if I had received the e-mail that she had sent in January. I still hadn't even opened and read it yet. Then she asked if I was going to respond to it and I said, "No."

In her disgust she said, "I'm going to pray for you." As she put down the phone and went to find Justin I thought to myself, *you need to be praying for yourself instead of praying for me.*

When Lorena and I had gotten married on May 23, 1998, our first dance was to *I Finally Found Someone* by Barbra Streisand and Bryan Adams. The song was quite popular when I met Lorena and I heard it a lot. It of course made me think of her. That was the reason I chose it for our first song. It had a lot of significance in my life. Even after we were married, I often heard the song. After our separation I still heard it a few times, and whenever it came on the radio I would immediately switch it to another station.

The weirdest thing was that after awhile I stopped hearing the song at all. I'm sure it was still being played on the air waves. I honestly believe it's God's way of letting me know that I didn't need to think of Lorena much anymore. I haven't heard the song for a few years now.

Other friends have told me that Lorena now realizes that she made a BIG mistake in treating me like she did. They insist that she now wants me back. I say, too bad.

In divorce court in July 2004, Lorena had asked the court permission to resume her maiden name. It was granted. Here it was five years later, and she still hadn't stopped using her married name. I was sure that she hated the last name of Morris, because she claimed so often that she hated me.

I hope to be extremely successful in life and I hope my life is shared with my son Justin and one day with some other very special woman.

My first goal is to get Justin out of that unsafe environment. I know that I'll need someone to help me raise my son. He needs and wants to have a good woman in his life. We both deserve that. Only time will tell.

In the meantime, I will continue to count my blessings for all of the good things that are coming my way because I never gave up.

Our custody hearing in Charlotte, North Carolina was scheduled for Monday, March 31, 2008 My attorney notified me that I needed to be there in person for the date. But there were still a few glitches involved. The New Jersey court files that had been requested in July 2007 had never arrived in Charlotte.

I hesitated to purchase an airline ticket until I was absolutely sure I had to be in court. Finally, at the last minute my attorney informed me that the hearing had been postponed. He also said he would do all he could to keep me from having to make a trip to Charlotte unless it was necessary. He informed me that he would write up a motion and, if agreeable to all parties, we could sign it and forego the custody hearing. I also wanted to get something in writing concerning the upcoming summer visitation. I'd had to jump through hoops for the past four summers and didn't want to have to go through that again.

Despite my pleas to get something done through the court system, my attorney didn't do anything.

I sent Justin a birthday card and called him on his birthday. I was very hesitant to put money in an envelope and send it to Lorena's home. I didn't trust her. Justin told me that he had received the money and so I asked him the amount to make sure his mother had really given it to him. Later Justin said Lorena supposedly used the money to purchase a few games for him online through E-bay, but he said she never gave them to him.

In late May I called my attorney because I still hadn't heard anything from him regarding Justin's summer visit to Colorado. I had already given him my fax number at home both verbally and in writing. He knew I no longer worked at TIARRA. Nonetheless, he'd faxed a form to me at TIARRA from Lorena and her attorney listing the days that she had already signed Justin up for summer camp at the Kids R Kids Daycare Center.

I was furious. This was exactly what I had been attempting to avoid—another fiasco with Lorena over Justin coming to visit me. It was happening again and my attorney had done nothing to avert it.

Lorena wanted Justin to visit me in Colorado in two separate two week blocks of time. And she also insisted that I pay for two sets of round trip airline tickets. I couldn't believe it. Any rational person would've settled for a consecutive four or five week block of time. And as usual, she refused to budge. I was furious. The thought of having to buy two sets of tickets when all I would've needed was one round trip ticket was absolutely ludicrous. But yet again, Lorena was determined to have her way.

And to add to my predicament, my attorney advised me not to buy the tickets until we had obtained something in writing from Lorena and her attorney in Charlotte. He knew the ongoing problems I had encountered with summer visitations and didn't want me to get jammed up again. It would've have made more sense to purchase the tickets in May for the June visit than to wait until the last minute when they were certain to go up.

My attorney also sent me an e-mail saying that he apologized for not getting back to me in a timely fashion. He said that he had been sick and out of the office for a few days.

I immediately shot an e-mail back to him telling him that I had been on him way back in March to try and avoid this very thing from happening again. He hadn't seen the sense of urgency back then. I also said, "To use your health as an excuse to me now is totally unacceptable. There was absolutely nothing wrong with your health back then, so don't use it as an excuse now."

In late May, my family in New Jersey went to a family reunion in Atlanta, Georgia. They drove right through Charlotte and couldn't even stop in order to say hello to Justin. Mom sure had some anguish about being so close to her grandson again and not being able to see him.

I gave my sister Patricia the phone number and they called Justin to at least say hello to him. Later on I asked him if his mom had allowed him to listen to the message and he said, "Yes."

I called my attorney a few times because I was so frustrated with him as well as Lorena. I had gotten to the point that I only called him when it was absolutely necessary.

On Sunday, June 1, I flew to Fort Worth for my nephew Ryan Hairston's high school graduation. I surprised my mom who was already there for the event. She had flown in on Thursday. She didn't know I was coming but Rosalyn and Roy did.

That afternoon I did a live radio interview with a station WPGR 107.5 FM, from Detroit. The interview was with Dr. Jimmy Womack. I discussed my rodeo career and talked about being one of only a handful of African-American contestants on the professional rodeo circuit. I also talked about my book.

While I was in Fort Worth I dropped off an application for induction in the Cowboys of Color Hall of Fame. It would truly be an honor to make it. But I have always told myself that the accolades mean nothing to me unless I will be able to have my son Justin in attendance.

Soon after I returned to Colorado. I sent another e-mail to my attorney concerning the proposed upcoming June visitation. I was getting more upset by the day because he continued to drag his feet. At times I also had to repeat or give him information that I had submitted in the past and that also really irritated me.

I still held onto the notion that I might be able to see Justin for two weeks in June. I knew that if Lorena didn't send him to me, that she would in turn have to pay to put him in a day camp for those two weeks so I thought there was a chance.

In the past she had always gotten her own way. I had stepped up to the plate at the last minute and paid for all those unnecessary and costly airline tickets. So Lorena figured that she had me right where she wanted me. She had taken her aim and had me right in the middle of those crosshairs again.

As badly as I wanted to see my son, I was more determined than ever to show Lorena that I wasn't going to give in this time. I wanted her to know that I'd finally hit the wall. Apparently my attorney didn't believe it either, because at the last minute he asked if I was going to pay for the airline tickets.

I told him, "No." So he made an offer to me to take $600 off of his legal fees to adjust for the extra $600 it was going to cost me for Justin's last minute round trip tickets. I could have saved this amount if I had purchased the tickets back in May. I was furious. I decided not to take him up on his offer.

The second week in June came and went. I was able to talk to Justin on the telephone right before his scheduled trip. He wanted to know if I had bought his airline tickets.

The original schedule per our divorce decree stated two weeks in June and then two weeks in July. That was originally set because Justin was so young then and Lorena didn't want him away from her for more than two weeks. All parties had the understanding that the schedule would be reviewed and altered once Justin was a little older.

I figured Justin was old enough now to be with me for a solid four weeks instead of only in two week blocks as Lorena had insisted.

I didn't buy the ticket because she refused to pay for

splitting the time. My argument was that if she insisted on the two separate blocks of time, she should have to pay for one set of round trip tickets. Naturally, she refused.

After the visit didn't take place Lorena proposed to her attorney that I should have to reimburse her for the money she spent while Justin was in daycare camp because he didn't come to Colorado per the court ordered visitation schedule. I seemed to be the only one who thought that was outrageous.

Yes, it cut my summer time with Justin in half. I would only have him for a total of two weeks in July but I hoped perhaps it had thrown Lorena off course.

On Friday, June 13, both Tim Russert and Charlie Jones suffered heart attacks and passed away. I was really affected by the death of Tim Russert. He was right on top of all of the political news and was a mainstay on Sunday mornings *Meet the Press*.

I watched all of the tributes to Tim Russert and they almost brought tears to my eyes. I had to stop and think about my own vulnerability and the time that I had missed being with my son. It was especially touching because I knew that Sunday was going to be Father's Day and Justin and I weren't going to be together, again. I was very, very sad.

My brother Reuben called me. He told me that one way or another Lorena will surely get exactly what she has coming to her, if not by God's hand, then through the destruction of her relationship with Justin.

The next morning we had a softball game. I pulled my hamstring muscle running in between first and second base. My leg simply just gave out and I crashed down hard to the ground. I tore up my elbow in the process and it was bleeding.

It seemed to take forever for me to walk to my car after the game. Even driving home it was excruciating to use my clutch to shift gears. I had to use my arm to help with my sore left leg.

On Saturday, June 21, I drove out to Akron, Colorado, to announce a young kid's rodeo production. The contestants competed in mutton bustin', calf riding, steer riding, junior bulls and then senior bulls.

It was a lot of fun. It was about ninety-four degrees, but there was a slight breeze so it didn't seem that warm. I thought about just how much Justin would have enjoyed being around all of those little kids and watching the rodeo action. It really made me sad.

I had to drive with my leg in a certain position so it wouldn't cause me pain. When I returned home that night my calf had swelled up. It was really weird. I woke up in the middle of the night and my left knee was killing me. I couldn't believe I was in so much pain when I hadn't done anything to injure my knee. I even got out of bed and walked on it a bit. I couldn't walk up and down the stairs, either. It was one step at a time. Just when I thought I was out of the woods and I figured things would soon return to normal, somehow I had suffered another major setback. It was very depressing. Both my left knee and hamstring hurt like crazy.

Eventually my old hip injury flared up as well. It was the reason I quit riding bulls in the first place. That injury came back to haunt me. It was times like those when I surely appreciated the good days. If a person didn't have a few bad days sprinkled in here and there, then they might not appreciate the good ones.

I tried to focus on Justin coming out to visit with me for Cheyenne Frontier Days. It also marked the first year I would have an official book signing scheduled on the rodeo grounds. I wanted him to be there to sign books. He always got such a kick out of it.

Midweek I received a very scathing e-mail from Lorena. She proved to be in top form whenever it was close to the time for Justin to come and visit. She was always looking for any excuse to not put him on the airplane and then justify it in her own warped mind and to the judge on the rare chance it ever got that far.

I refused to respond to Lorena's e-mail. So she sent me

another one threatening not to put Justin on the airplane unless I responded. I was still too stubborn and refused to respond. I was determined not to take the bait. Lorena always had to feel as if she was in charge.

On Thursday, July 17, I called and asked to speak to Justin and Lorena refused to let me speak to him. She lied telling me that Justin had already gone to bed. It was about 7:00 p.m. on the east coast so I knew she wasn't telling the truth. Then, despite the restraining order she wanted to talk to me. The only reason I talked to her was because I knew if I didn't then she would have an excuse not to put Justin on the airplane.

I answered all of her questions over the telephone but that wasn't good enough for her. I told her because of the restraining order that I really was uncomfortable talking to her. Lorena got verbally abusive and called me a "loser" and a "leech." At that point I disconnected the call.

I immediately called my attorney in Charlotte and let him know what was going on. Later that evening Lorena wanted to speak with me at length. Lorena called me right back and wanted to talk.

I asked her to call me back on my home phone number if she wanted to talk to me. Lorena called me back twice. The first time I was on another line and didn't take the call. The second time she asked me to get off of the other line and talk to her.

Lorena talked to me for over two hours. Most of the time, I listened. Whenever I spoke or responded though, she would constantly interrupt me. She was so apologetic. Lorena asked me numerous times if I hated her. Each time I refused to answer.

Lorena also told me that she really cared for me. I was shocked at some of the things that she tried to convince me of. such as that she had never tried to block any of my visitations with Justin. She also told me that she was really embarrassed by the way she had conducted herself and all of her antics and actions since our separation.

Lorena said Justin had asked her why I took trips to have book signings and promote my book, but had never bothered to come to Charlotte to visit him. I asked her, "Did you tell Justin that in April 2007 I planned a trip to Charlotte, but you told me I couldn't see him?"

In the end I raised my voice at her as she continued with some of her antics. She got all upset and told me I was a sick person. Then Lorena said "Fuck you," and hung up the telephone.

I sent my attorney a couple of e-mails. I tried to sleep and not allow Lorena to get to me, but I wasn't very successful. All I could do was say a prayer and decide that I would have the faith of a mustard seed.

I was at the airport in Denver in plenty of time on Saturday morning, July 19. Justin's flight was scheduled to arrive at 9:33 a.m. I was at the airport by 8:30 a.m. When I checked in at the ticket counter I found out his flight was expected eighteen minutes early. I was sitting at the gate by approximately 9:10 a.m.

Sure enough at about 9:15 a.m. his plane rolled past the window to park at the gate. One by one the passengers stepped through the doorway. I experienced a minor anxiety spell because after awhile no one was getting off of the airplane. Finally another wave came through the door.

A stranger walked up to me and asked if I was waiting for Justin. I said, "Yes."

He said he had sat next to Justin on the flight and that he was a really nice boy. I thanked him. I was sure glad that the man stopped to speak to me because it was still at least another five minutes before Justin walked through that doorway. Or at least it seemed like a very long time to me.

Finally he appeared. By then I'd learned that Justin would be looking out for me as soon as he came through that gate and he ran to me for a big hug.

Justin and I had a blast all week long at Cheyenne. Justin also signed several of the books that I signed. We attended two performances of the PBR during the evenings. We didn't stay in Cheyenne, so all of the driving back and forth really wore me out.

Justin was allowed to get behind the bucking chutes. He prefers to watch the rodeo action from that vantage point. I introduced him to a lot of the PRCA and PBR cowboys. He has a great memory and remembers their names.

After the rodeo someone asked Justin, "How does it feel to hang out with a celebrity? You call him Daddy, but the rest of us call him a celebrity."

The PBR bull riding event was pretty good. Justin was yelling with excitement again. He loves it.

After the Tuesday night PBR bull riding event there was a very nice fireworks display. It capped off a great evening of entertainment. I put my arm around Justin during the show and he reciprocated.

It started raining a little right after the fireworks. It was unbelievable that it had held off until it was over. Justin said he was going to stay awake with me on the drive home. We talked for awhile but he soon fell asleep.

While Justin was here we would still go to the park and play baseball or basketball. I had him bat left handed just to see if he could do it. He hit the ball like he had been batting left handed all of his life. He blasted several shots with ease and skill.

Justin also opened up and told me more and more about his mother and the relationship with her former fiancé. He also told me that Lorena had grilled him after he returned to North Carolina in the summer of 2007. I was learning that the more time Justin spends with me, the more he opens up and tells me things about his mom.

Justin also said Lorena had slapped him in the face several times. When she was investigated by social services she had groomed Justin before the social worker showed up. Lorena told Justin that he better not tell certain things about her.

Justin told me he had run away from home about four times after she slapped him. One time she found him down the street and yelled and slapped him in the face again. Justin said a little kid in the neighborhood saw the whole incident.

Justin sure gave me a big scare one night during dinner.

All of a sudden he jumped up from the table and kind of bent over. I asked if he was choking but he really didn't give me a response. He was scared to death. He had laughed at the television and sucked a piece of pork chop into his throat. I pounded him on the back a few times. Luckily for both of us, I kept my head and properly performed the Heimlich maneuver on him. A couple of pieces of pork came out of his throat and windpipe. It was sure a relief when I realized that he was breathing again. Justin came over and gave me a big hug for saving his life.

Justin and I watched *Glory Road,* the movie about the black basketball players at Texas Western (now known as the University of Texas at El Paso) UTEP. We weren't able to finish watching the movie because the power went out in the entire neighborhood. It was probably due to too much stress with all of air conditioning units running 24/7. After the power went out we sat together in the dark and Justin told me a lot more about the situation and the environment at home with Lorena.

During the week Justin also told me that Lorena said if he were to come and live with me, he would never see her again. He'd told me the exact same thing in the summer of 2006. That is such a cruel thing to hang over the head of a nine year old child.

Justin also brought along a disposable camera. I took a lot of pictures and had them developed. I gave him copies to take back to Charlotte.

I knew Justin's stay would soon be coming to an end. Of course I was very sad to see my son go after such a short visit. Sometimes I had to wish that time would just stand still. I knew in my heart that this would soon pass. I fervently believed that in the end, we'd come out victorious.

The last Saturday that Justin was here, my leg was good enough to play softball again. I tried to get Justin involved as much as possible. We warmed up by throwing a small little league baseball instead of the softball.

I wrapped up my hamstring very tightly. My teammates

were glad to see me back in uniform. I went four for four. I had two doubles and two singles. I could have done a little better but didn't want to try and stretch myself. I didn't want to take any unnecessary risks. It felt great to be back out there and participating again. I was glad that I played well. More importantly I was glad that we won. Justin had asked me to hit a home run over the fence for him again. After the game we played basketball in the park before returning home again.

That night I was upstairs working on my computer. Justin came to me and just broke down crying. He didn't want to go back to Charlotte to be with his mother. It hurt me to see him in such emotional pain. Then he gave me a kiss. That is something he hadn't done for years.

I'm sure Lorena sensed it and was starting to realize that she was fighting a losing battle with me now. Justin wanted me to sit downstairs and watch the end of the movie *Titanic* with him. He wanted to spend as much time around me as possible since it was our last night together.

On Sunday morning, August 3, I got up and prepared to take Justin back to the airport. I'd known this day would come, even as I'd picked him up two weeks earlier. I wasn't looking forward to it at all. I knew it would tear me up.

Justin, surprisingly, didn't cry at all. I was proud of him. I believe the reason he didn't cry was because he was so worn out and tired. Plus, he said he had a headache.

Justin told me as soon as he headed down the jetway that he would cry. He said he didn't want all the people to see him crying as he boarded the airplane. He preferred to board first and then sit in his seat and cry.

I managed okay. Just as soon as he disappeared from my sight I left the gate. I didn't want to sit there all sad, fighting back tears in front of those strangers, either. It angered me to no end, the way that Lorena treats our son. It is totally uncalled for.

A few hours later Justin called to say he had arrived

safely in Charlotte.

There was a custody hearing scheduled in Charlotte. Mid-week I received a barrage of e-mails from my attorney telling me that he had properly notified me of the custody hearing scheduled in Charlotte on Tuesday, August 12.

I was furious. I was always under the impression that he was going to write up a motion in order to keep me from having to purchase a last minute ticket and make an appearance since that's what he'd told me. Then later my attorney sent me a proposal. The amazing thing is he told me he was going to send me a proposal in late March and then never followed through. It really angered me that he had waited so long.

My attorney called on Friday afternoon, August 8, to notify me that I might still be required to be in Charlotte for court on Tuesday. He said Lorena didn't want to make a decision on the proposal yet. She preferred to ponder it over the weekend. Of course she did. This meant I might not even know that I needed to be in Charlotte until Monday afternoon. My attorney wanted me to be there by Tuesday morning. He asked if I could buy a refundable ticket. He knew that I couldn't do that.

As of late afternoon on Friday, the court file from New Jersey still hadn't arrived in Charlotte. This was such a messed up and convoluted case. How could a judge make rational decisions in such a short period of time? The earliest she would even see the file, if it did show up, was Monday afternoon or night. She was sure to have other cases on Monday. My attorney never even notified me that the hearing was scheduled for 2:00 p.m. Tuesday until sometime on Friday afternoon.

This had become an incredibly emotionally draining process. I'd already realized that Justin didn't have a strong parent in his corner but if I were to go down for the count, then Justin would be placed in a very dangerous position with no one to stand up for him. I was determined to hold on and maintain my sanity. In the end I'd be the one who Justin was going to have to rely on and need the most. He wasn't going to be able to count on Lorena, because eventually she was going to break down and buckle under the stress.

Most of the weekend I stayed around the house contemplating what the North Carolina judiciary could possibly do to me for not showing up in court on Tuesday afternoon. Then on Monday afternoon I received an e-mail from my attorney saying that Lorena had decided to give up her primary custodial rights in order to bypass the hearing and would send Justin to Colorado to live with me. I really couldn't believe what I was reading. I called my attorney in Charlotte right away.

This was news to me. I'd only believe it after Justin was really finally here in Colorado and living with me. I was absolutely dumbfounded that after fighting me tooth and nail for all of these years, Lorena would suddenly agree to give up custody without a court battle.

I was really baffled. There had to be some mysterious reason why she would relinquish her custody. I was going to continue to fight her and even turn up the heat a few notches whenever possible. I wasn't going to weaken and believe the struggle was really over because I knew this news was too good to be true. Lorena had something in mind. She had to.

I continued to go through a whole plethora of emotions at the thought that Justin would soon be living here. I was still in shock that Lorena would give in and allow him to come and live with me. I THANKED GOD for bringing me through the fire.

Of course the rollercoaster ride continued. Lorena refused to allow me to speak to Justin although I called him multiple times for two evenings in a row.

Then the thought that she might harm my son popped into my mind. At that stage I wouldn't have put anything past her. I had the feeling that it was going to be a little longer process than it suddenly appeared. That being said, I still knew I'd never give up.

A couple of days later my attorney sent me an e-mail saying Justin would be traveling to Colorado on Saturday, August 23. It was great news but I still wasn't able to speak to Justin on the telephone. I had only spoken to him very briefly and that was right after Lorena picked him up at the airport, when he'd let me know he'd arrived safely.

Lorena contnued to refuse to allow me to speak to Justin.

I also received a proposed change of custody order from my attorney in Charlotte. I reviewed it and wouldn't sign it as it was. There were several points that needed to be clarified. I wasn't going to lose my main focus and that was to get Justin out of that unstable environment.

I called Justin a few more times but to no avail. Exactly two weeks after I'd last spoken to him, he finally called me back on Lorena's cell phone. Justin's said the battery had gone dead on his land line phone and that was the reason why he hadn't answered it. I knew it was a big lie that Lorena had told him to tell me. I also knew Lorena was standing over him while he was speaking to me. He was very uncomfortable the whole time he was talking to me.

Justin told me that he'd called the police on his mom. I didn't get a lot of details from him but I figured I'd talk to him later about it. He said the police showed up. Otherwise I didn't know anything about the incident.

Later on Justin told me, "Mommy slapped me in the face five times and then threw me down on the floor. Then she threatened to beat me with her fists." That's when Justin had picked up the phone and dialed 911, then immediately hung up.

While he was with me Justin had told me so many horror stories about Lorena attacking him that I gave him very, very implicit instructions that if he ever felt threatened to the point that he felt that his life or physical well-being was in danger to call 911.

I told him it might not happen for a couple of months or a couple of years but to do it to protect himself. A few days later I found out that he had called the police on Lorena only three days after he was back in Charlotte. The incident had taken place on

Wednesday, August 6.

Justin told me not to call his landline the rest of the week. I would need to contact him on Lorena's cell phone. I imagined that Lorena probably had gone berserk and jerked the phone out of the wall. I could imagine her telling him he'd never use that phone to call the police again.

Justin asked if I was going to pay for his airline ticket to come out here on Saturday. I told him that he needed to pack his stuff and I would take care of getting him out here. He sounded really bad. I felt so sorry for the poor little guy. I'm sure by then he was afraid of his mother and afraid to believe he was really coming to live with me.

I called Justin's elementary school in Charlotte and informed the secretary that Justin would be moving to Colorado. She put me on hold and then congratulated me. I wondered if there was a hidden message behind her good wishes.

I asked her if she knew Justin and she did. That also meant she probably knew Lorena, too, and how hard she was to deal with.

Even if Justin didn't make it on Saturday, I was more determined than ever to fight for him. The emotional rollercoaster needed to stop for all three of us. I had no control over what Lorena was feeling—and I doubted she did either. But I could give myself and Justin a stable enviroment where we could both be safe and happy.

I was still looking forward to my family members coming out to visit me on Friday afternoon. They had never seen my home and I had lived there for right at four years.

On Thursday of that week—exactly two days before Justin's scheduled arrival—I received an e-mail from my attorney saying that Lorena was on the warpath again. Now she was refusing to put Justin on a flight on Saturday, even though I had already paid for his airline ticket.

I guess Lorena and her attorney had butted heads and he wanted to fire her and she wanted to fire him. He told my attorney that he had yelled at her over the telephone.

There was a court hearing on Friday morning with the same judge. She'd make a decision on whether or not Lorena had to follow through with her decision to send Justin to me. My attorney intended to obtain a court order from the judge to force Lorena to put Justin on a plane on Saturday as she had already agreed to do.

There was nothing I could really do from my end at that point but pray. It was all in God's hands.

My attorney called first thing the next morning and told me that the judge had told Lorena to have Justin on that airplane the next morning. No excuses.

I spent the rest of the morning getting my house in order. I took care of all of the paperwork and got Justin enrolled in school. He was supposed to start on Monday. I had been able to bypass Lorena—who refused to give me access to his birth certificate and immunization records—by calling his school in Charlotte and they were gracious enough to fax over all of the documents. My sister had warned me to expect Lorena to send absolutely no clothes with the boy if he came, so I planned to take him shopping when he arrived, in case that was what happened.

I made two trips to the airport to pick up my family members. Mom, my sister Patricia, my nephew Michael and my sister Rosalyn would be visiting for the next week. Everyone made it in, safe and sound. We watched some of the Summer Olympics and then folks went to bed. I was surprised that they all went to bed so early. I guess they were tired from all of the traveling and still on New Jersey time. The next morning they were going to rent a car so they could see downtown Denver while I went to the airport to pick up Justin.

Justin's plane arrived about forty-five minutes late. He didn't know my family was here and I didn't tell him. I wanted it to be a big surprise. We got home and didn't go into any of the bedrooms or he would have known. Then Patricia called on my cell phone and said they were at WalMart.

We drove over to WalMart. Justin was shocked. He was so excited. He had never expected to see them in Colorado. We did a little shopping and then we all went to Sonic and ate a burger and fries. It was a little get-together for Michael's birthday.

Justin was so excited that we were having company. Michael, Justin and I played baseball in the park for a while. At home we just hung around the house and did family things. We ate popcorn and watched the Olympics.

We all attended New Hope Baptist Church on Sunday morning. One of the members of our church, Mary English, a deacon and Sunday school teacher, had also graduated from Woodstown High School in New Jersey. Her sister lives right next door to my mom. It sure is a small world, after all.

Pastor Ambrose F. Carroll had my family members stand up and be introduced to the congregation.

On Monday I took Justin to school for his first day. He was very nervous. I really didn't blame him. I would've been very nervous, too. I took him to his classroom and then I left. Justin had to wait outside until his teacher came to the door and got him and his other classmates.

The Democratic National Convention was in Denver that week. It turned out to be a great time for my family to visit. Barack Obama, the Democratic party nominee for president of the United States would be at Mile High Stadium later in the week to give his formal acceptance speech.

My sisters wanted to take in some of the activities. We were able to get tickets for an event in Denver in conjunction with the DNC. Patricia, Roz and I went to the Five Points area and saw Danny Glover and Angela Bassett. They gave short speeches to point out the significance of the possibility of an African-American president. There were tons of politicians, movie stars and celebrities in Denver for the occasion. I gave Danny Glover one of my books and took a picture of Roz and Patricia with Angela Bassett.

Then we went downtown to the 16th Street Mall to take in some of the sights of the convention. There was a mass of people and police on the scene to make sure there were no problems for all of the dignitaries that were in town to visit. It was truly a sight to behold.

I picked up Justin from school. His teacher was delighted that he was in her class. Mrs. Sanstead said she wished she had twenty others just like him. I thought it was a wonderful comment. Later she told me, "He's the most talented student that I've ever had."

There is no way to describe the rewards of having my son with me. Justin constantly says, "Daddy I love you." Or else he'll say, "Daddy you are the best daddy in the whole wide world." Whenever we attend church Justin grabs my arm and puts it behind his back during the service. If we stand up and later sit down, he'll grab my arm and put it around himself again.

One day when I was waiting in the park for him after school he ran across the field and leaped into my waiting arms. It sure makes a guy feel so good to get that kind of a response and see his child really happy.

One day Justin came home from school and showed me a paper he had written in school.

It said:

> *My dad is such an encouraging and special parent that his kind face needs to be on a postage stamp. My dad is my hero because he gets money he needs to protect us by working hard, making speeches and writing. He loves me and takes care of me. He encourages me to do my best and when I mess up, to try again. I think he should be on a postage stamp because he is the best father a boy could ever have in the whole world!*

JUSTIN

Justin left me a message on my computer one night that said, "You are the best father in the entire universe Love Justin!!!!!"

Roping Club
INSURANCE

Epilogue

On Saturday, August 23, 2008 Justin Abraham Morris arrived in Denver, Colorado with only one small carry-on bag. His mother had kept most of his clothes. She didn't send any of his long pants, jeans or any of his jackets. Although I was concerned by her lack of consideration for her son, it wasn't surprising. What mattered was that he was with me.

Justin said Lorena told him not to call her because she wouldn't answer the phone. Also not to leave a message because she wouldn't respond to the voicemail, either. He also said when he boarded the airplane that Lorena refused to hug him. When he turned around to wave goodbye, Lorena refused to look at him and was looking at the ground instead.

She refused to speak to him on the telephone for five weeks after he had arrived. She finally sent some of his clothes and toys to him about two months after he had been in Colorado. By then, of course, I already purchased essential items such as underwear, socks, shoes, jeans, sweatshirts and sweat pants.

WYOMING

In the beginning I tried to give Justin a sense of security by spending a lot of time with him. He was understandably hurt by his mother's apparent lack of interest in him. He even got to the point where he hated to be left alone, even for a short period of time, so we spent countless hours in the park playing football, baseball and basketball. Justin wanted to play organized football, but the season was well underway by the time he arrived in late August.

Justin was very reserved for a few weeks after he arrived. We both went through a period of really getting to know each other on a different level that both of us knew was no longer temporary. There was a testing period on his part to learn the boundaries. He needed to know what he could get away with, and also what I wouldn't put up with. And I could sense he was grateful that those boundaries were reasonable and dependable and not to be changed on a whim.

I confess I had to spank him one time with my open hand for misbehaving. Justin had slammed the front door and later locked me out of the house. I think it was a test and he was surprised at my reaction. He cried for a long time. I suspect that he was more disappointed in himself than he was angry at me. I haven't had any reason to discipline him in that way since that day.

Justin and I went to Laramie to watch a couple of University of Wyoming college football games. We had a blast. He thanked me several times for taking him to those games. On the way back home we stopped and watched a bull riding event in Fort Collins.

Justin also persuaded me to let him get on a steer. There was absolutely no coaxing on my part at all. He came to me with the idea. I judged a kid's miniature bull riding event in Deer Trail, Colorado on Labor Day. Afterward there was a steer riding contest, and so I entered Justin.

He did very well. He rode for about four jumps. He was a

little nervous to get on, but that's considered normal. Steers are larger than calves. It's farther to the ground when you either dismount or buck off. They're tall and lanky though not the size of a full grown bull.

In the evenings, just before bedtime, as Justin got more comfortable around me, he started to divulge things to me saying, "Mommy told me not to ever tell anyone..." Previously, he had been very careful about saying anything negative to me about his mother. He also told me she often stopped at the liquor store to purchase exotic alcoholic drinks. That bothered him.

Some of the other things he told me, which came out at bedtime and in no particular order, seemed to me to be triggered by a need to tell someone who would listen.

He told me that Lorena had punched him numerous times with her fists. She had kneed him in the groin on a couple of occasions and sent him crashing to the floor. He had sprawled out on the floor writhing in pain.

His mother had picked him up over her head a few times and violently slammed him to the floor. One time he had been knocked unconscious. He said when they still lived in New Jersey that she had pushed him down, and he split his forehead on a door handle. It bled quite a bit.

He also said that another time Lorena had grabbed him around the head while he was sitting down at the table, and rammed him head-first into a wall. Another time Lorena had pushed him down the front steps of their home. He still had a scar on his knee and his elbow as a result of that attack.

Lorena in a fit of rage, had thrown a set of car keys at him and hit him in the chest so hard that they left a scar. I saw the scar and thought it was from a place Justin had scratched himself. At first he didn't want to tell me where that scar came from.

Justin also said she cursed a lot and called him names, using the "F" word frequently. She had even told him that he had big lips and a big penis just like his daddy. I thought it was such a shame to say such things to your child.

As a result of being traumatized, Justin said he had run away from home on four different occasions. One time he left at about 4:30 a.m. and didn't return until after 5:30 a.m. He had packed a small backpack with some snacks. Lorena never even found out that he was gone. He left the garage door open and re-entered the same way that he'd left. Justin said his water bottle had leaked in the backpack, but Lorena never found out.

I notified my attorney in Charlotte about these horrifying incidents, and he told me I would need to take Justin to a licensed counselor/therapist. Justin would have to open up to the counselor, and then the counselor would have to write a letter to the presiding judge.

Lorena sent me e-mails asking for a Christmas visit and I ignored them. I was determined not to allow Justin to go back to Charlotte to visit her unless it was supervised.

So as instructed by my attorney, I took Justin to a licensed counselor. He really opened up and told her that he was terrified of what his mother would do to him, since he had divulged her bizarre behavior. Even after reading the assessment letter, the judge in Charlotte ordered Justin to visit Lorena for an eight day visit to include Christmas in late December.

Lorena, as usual, took it upon herself to make up her own schedule, despite what was written in the court order. She purchased airline tickets to stretch the visitation to ten days instead of the eight prescribed by the court. Then, already knowing that I'd be in New Jersey visiting my family over Christmas, she purposely purchased a round trip ticket for Justin from Denver to Charlotte and then Charlotte back to Denver.

She was trying to force me to either return to Denver before New Year's Day, which would keep Justin from seeing my family in New Jersey, or she was going to try and force me to purchase an unnecessary one way ticket from Charlotte to Philadelphia. It was Lorena's same old song and dance.

A few days before his trip, Justin threw a temper tantrum. He was crying uncontrollably, yelling and screaming, "She's going to kill me. She's going to kill me. In a few days I'll be dead and look at you. You're sitting there at the computer and doing nothing about it."

Emotionally, it really tore me up. I was a nervous wreck but Justin was truly terrified at the thought of having to spend ten days with his mother.

I was going to secretly record this outburst. The only reason I didn't was because if I never saw him again, I knew listening to the tape would absolutely destroy me. He was giving me a serious warning about Lorena's instability.

I did everything I could, contacting various attorneys here in Colorado, hoping that now that Justin was here, he would be in Colorado's jurisdiction. One attorney told me that if I didn't comply with the court order, that I was going to be arrested and go to jail. Then he said Justin would be sent to North Carolina at my expense and that I could forget about ever having custody of him.

I broke down in tears and told Justin all of this. He didn't want to see me go to jail, so we got down on our knees and prayed to God to please protect him the entire time that he was in Charlotte. Although we were both extremely terrified, we were still determined to have faith.

The morning I was to take Justin to the Denver Airport, Lorena called my cell phone and left a laugh on my voice mail sounding exactly like the Wicked Witch of the West in the movie *The Wizard of Oz*. She never uttered a single word, she just cackled. It was unbelivably peculiar, even coming from her. Lorena just laughed into the phone and then hung up. Needless to say, I was very frightened at the prospect of putting my son on that airplane. I honestly felt there was a chance that I might never ever see him again.

The court order signed by the judge in Charlotte said

Lorena wasn't to put her hands on Justin. Absolutely no corporeal punishment—as if whatever a judge said meant anything to Lorena. So Justin and I set up a secret password that if he said it to me over the telephone, it meant Lorena had hit him. My attorney had told me prior to the visit, "If Lorena so much as lays a finger on Justin, then you are to call the police on her."

I called the police on Lorena on Christmas Eve. Justin had given me the code word and I wasn't about to take any chances after the things he'd told me.

Justin and I both believed that if something occurred that warrented me making the call, he would be removed from the home at that time. Because there was no evidence of physical abuse, the police left him with his mother. On Sunday, December 28, Justin was supposed to fly to Philadelphia. Lorena had forced me to buy another unnecessary one-way ticket after all, but I had to get Justin away from her.

Lorena called my cell phone voice mail that afternoon and went into a long tirade saying that she wasn't going to put Justin on a plane. Furthermore, she said she was going to go to the courthouse and obtain a court order to keep me from having any communication with him. I went to the Philadelphia airport anyway, but Justin wasn't on the US Airways flight.

I had previously sent an e-mail to my attorney complaining that Lorena was allowed to continue to do as she pleased because neither he nor her attorney would step up to the plate and stop her. He responded by telling me that if I thought he was afraid of my ex-wife, then maybe I should find a different attorney to represent me.

I spent the next few days in constant communication with my attorney to find out where Justin was and when Lorena would comply with the court order. The judge told her, through her attorney, to return the child to his father. Lorena blatantly ignored both and went to work for three consecutive days. She dropped Justin off at the Kids R Kids daycare center during the day.

My attorney was in his office all day on Wednesday December 31, 2008 just because of Lorena. He was livid. He finally wrote out a motion for contempt of court. Her attorney countered with a request to the judge not to find Lorena in contempt.

It really didn't matter. After three straight days of defiance, the judge wasn't going to do anything to Lorena anyway. Obviously, Lorena knew nothing was going to happen to her for disobeying the judge and her court order. It was the same scenario that had happened with the New Jersey court system and was repeated over and over again.

I really don't know why Lorena finally complied with the judge's directives. I suspect that in desperation her attorney may have called her up and told her that if Justin spent another night in Charlotte that the sheriff would come and arrest her the following day. I think her attorney was sick and tired of her defiance and knew the threat of being arrested again would scare her to death.

I honestly still don't believe anything would have happened to her for at least another few days. The presiding judge had left town that afternoon to celebrate New Year's Day. My attorney couldn't find any judges in the building to sign the contempt of court motion. There would have been no court sessions for a couple of days.

I give my attorney a lot of credit and accolades for his work on this extremely emotional day for himself, Justin and me.

Finally, Lorena took Justin to the airport. She had previously purchased a ticket for an AirTran flight going to Atlanta and then connecting on to Philadelphia which would make Justin arrive in Philly at 11:45 p.m. She had probably chosen that flight in an effort to keep me on the road as late as possible. At the last minute she was told that an unaccompanied minor couldn't be placed on the last connecting flight from one city to another. If Justin was late getting to Atlanta, then he might be stuck there overnight alone, which the airlines wouldn't allow, of course.

Lorena knew about this rule but was trying to ignore it. I'm sure she was also trying to save money. It cost her about $250 less to book Justin on that Air Tran connecting flight instead of a non-stop flight on US Airways. Maybe she was getting a first hand taste of what I had been going through for so many years.

She tried to use the "last flight" problem as another excuse not to send Justin that night. Her attorney apparently disssuaded her and she had to buy another ticket on an earlier flight, the one she should have put him on in the first place. Another taste for her of what she had done to me so many times.

Before Justin boarded the flight, his mother told him she wasn't going to call me to tell me what flight he was on. Undaunted by his mother's behavior, Justin took charge and borrowed a cell phone from the passenger sitting next to him, and called to notify me that he was on a plane headed to Philadelphia and I was immediately on my way to get him. Lorena finally called, but it was long after the flight was in the air and after it might have been too late for me to make it to the airport on time.

It was bitter, bitter cold in Philadelphia that night. Lorena was so vindictive that she sent Justin out in the dead of the winter without a coat. She had paid for his winter coat that he was wearing when he left Colorado and therefore she told Justin it was hers. Yet she claimed to be deeply concerned with the health, safety and well being of her child.

Justin called me again right after they landed in Philadelphia. I told him I was in the airport and that I'd be at the gate by the time they were ready to get off the plane. When he saw me he ran to me and squeezed the life out of me for about a minute and a half. I thanked God that he had brought my only son safely back to me.

Justin spent less than forty-eight hours visiting my family in New Jersey due to Lorena having tried to keep him. We even had problems on our return flight to Denver. We were held up at the ticket counter and had to run to the gate. I blamed Lorena. The ticket agent threatened to not to allow us to board the plane because they knew it involved a custody case.

They knew that because I had to rearrange my entire

schedule after the judge court ordered Justin to go to Charlotte. I had purchased our tickets in September for Christmas. The only way I could get a refund and cancel Justin's tickets from Denver to Philadelphia was to provide the airline with proof that the change was due to a court order. The airlines had a ton of notes in their computer system after I spent an hour on the telephone with various agents on Friday December 19, 2008 trying to straighten the mess out.

I had called United Airlines the day before we arrived at the airport in Philadelphia to make sure everything was in order for us to go back to Colorado. The agent I spoke to assured me that we were okay. I told him I didn't want anymore glitches since this entire trip had been a nightmare. He again assured me that we were good to go. Then we arrived at the airport and ran into another barrage of challenges.

Justin was back with me but things still weren't settled. He continued to tell me more horror stories of how Lorena had treated him during the visit. She had scheduled an appointment with a therapist in order to get Justin to recant all of the statements he'd made to the therapist in Denver. Justin had bravely refused, so Lorena had cancelled the appointment.

Justin later told me that when the police rang the doorbell, (after he'd given me the code word and I'd called them) Lorena grabbed him and jerked him away from the door saying, "You better not tell them anything!"

I also learned she had already enrolled Justin in a new school and had driven him there to see it. She had also told him that he wouldn't see his father again for at least two years.

On Monday January 12, my attorney called me in Colorado. He informed me that he had just forwarded an e-mail that contained a court order signed by the judge that said I was to return Justin to his mother in Charlotte immediately. The court order also stated that I was to pay for the one-way airline ticket.

Lorena had signed an affidavit that was full of lies and the judge just accepted it as truth. My attorney was never notified of the motion requesting that Justin be returned to Charlotte. For the second time in less than two weeks he was livid.

I told Justin as soon as he got home from school. He sensed that something was terribly wrong again. He jumped into the air and landed on the floor screaming, "I'm not going, I'm not going. There's no way I'm getting on that airplane!"

This was the straw that broke the camel's back. It destroyed me emotionally. The next couple of days I didn't even want to get out of bed. I was spent. How could this be happening again? Justin was so torn up that he couldn't even go to school the next day.

Considering the shenanigans that Lorena had blatantly pulled off right in the face of this judge just two weeks before about putting Justin back on the plane to me, I was flabbergasted. I had to take Justin to see a therapist because he had been traumatized by Lorena during the visit.

Justin made some statement to the therapist at the Children's Hospital—I was never told what it was—and she, in turn, called Arapahoe County Social Services here in Colorado to report Lorena for child abuse. On Tuesday, January 13, a social worker came over to our home to interview Justin and then me. He launched an investigation that day and said Justin wasn't leaving the state of Colorado until his investigation was completed.

It was a small ray of hope. I jumped up from the table and burst into tears and ran over and hugged Justin saying, "You're not going, you're not going."

Then I called my attorney in Charlotte, while the social worker was still there, to tell him of the news. When Lorena's side heard this, they put up a fight, wanting to know when Justin was going to arrive, and questioning who had jurisdiction over this case, the state of Colorado or the state of North Carolina.

On Thursday, January 15, the judge finally met with our attorneys in her chambers. She reversed her court order and apologized to my attorney for ever signing it in the first place. She must have had time to remember the chaos Lorena had put her through over New Year's.

It was only then that I found out that even though Lorena had agreed to give up her primary custodial rights on Monday, August 11, 2008, it was only considered verbal because she'd refused to sign the official paperwork afterward. So as a result, even though the custody hearing didn't take place and was removed from the court docket, Lorena still legally retained custody according to the old paperwork filed in New Jersey.

I was under the assumption that I had been granted primary custody in August 2008. My attorney informed me in January 2009 that I was only granted temporary custody. He also told me that there would be no visitations to Charlotte by Justin until social services had completed their investigation. Another custody hearing would be scheduled in Charlotte in the summer of 2009 with the hope that all this could be straightened out.

The New Jersey court files that were requested by the judge in Charlotte in July 2007 have never been transferred. There have been multiple follow up requests since then, and the state of New Jersey still hasn't complied and sent those documents.

Lorena hasn't spoken to Justin on the telephone since we returned. She refuses to return his calls, even though he has called her several times and left voice messages. I have not discouraged him from calling her and sometimes ask if he wants to call, but he is adjusting to his mother behaving as if she cares nothing about him.

Despite all of the overpayments of child support to Lorena over the years, she has refused to give me one penny for Justin's support. Though she carries Justin on her health insurance, she refuses to let the insurance pay anything toward his care.

Justin called his mother on Easter Sunday to wish her a Happy Easter and asked her to return his phone call. There was no response. Justin called his mother again on May 10, 2009 to wish her a Happy Mother's Day. He also signed and mailed her a Mother's Day card. Again there was no response.

On May 15, 2009 he celebrated his tenth birthday by spending a few hours at the Boondocks Fun and Entertainment Center. I also gave him several presents for his birthday. Justin received cards and presents from his grandmother, Katie Flynn, and a few other relatives, but his own mother didn't bother to mail him a card or a gift and didn't even call in order to wish her only child a Happy Birthday. Even my friend Stephanie Wolf, who was working on a government contract and assignment half way around the world in Kuwait sent him two presents.

Justin took the rejection well, though these types of actions will surely have an affect on his emotional well-being.

He's playing a lot of little league baseball and that helps him to focus and take his mind off of the negative things going on with his mother. Justin is by far the fastest runner. He is also a great hitter and a pitcher. The coach says he is the best athlete on the entire team and I love watching him play.

It's probably just a matter of time before Lorena will approach her attorney and try to convince the judge in a courtroom that she should be entitled to custody. I can't help but wonder what she thinks her current behavior says about her conern for him.

I can only hope that when we have that hearing, Justin and I will finally be vindicated, but I confess that I fear the justice system will again fail to listen and to take an unbiased look at the facts of our case.

Pray for us.

July 2009

www.ingramcontent.com/pod-product-compliance
Lightning Source LLC
Chambersburg PA
CBHW060252100426
42742CB00011B/1720